W9-BDE-106

Modern and Postmodern Social Theorizing

There is a growing conflict between modern and postmodern social theorists. The latter reject modern approaches as economistic, essentialist and often leading to authoritarian policies. Modernists criticize postmodern approaches for their rejection of holistic conceptual frameworks which facilitate an overall picture of how social wholes (organizations, communities, nation-states, etc.) are constituted, reproduced and transformed. They believe the rejection of holistic methodologies leads to social myopia – a refusal to explore critically the type of broad problems that classical sociology deals with. This book attempts to bridge the divide between these two conflicting perspectives and proposes a novel holistic framework which is neither reductionist/economistic nor essentialist. *Modern and Postmodern Social Theorizing* will appeal to scholars and students of social theory and of social sciences in general.

NICOS P. MOUZELIS is Emeritus Professor of Sociology at the London School of Economics and Political Science.

Modern and Postmodern Social Theorizing

Bridging the Divide

NICOS P. MOUZELIS

CAMBRIDGE
UNIVERSITY PRESS

CAMBRIDGE UNIVERSITY PRESS
Cambridge, New York, Melbourne, Madrid, Cape Town, Singapore, São Paulo, Delhi

Cambridge University Press
The Edinburgh Building, Cambridge CB2 8RU, UK

Published in the United States of America by Cambridge University Press, New York

www.cambridge.org
Information on this title: www.cambridge.org/9780521731539

First published 2008

Printed in the United Kingdom at the University Press, Cambridge

A catalogue record for this publication is available from the British Library

Library of Congress Cataloguing in Publication data
Mouzelis, Nicos P.
Modern and postmodern theorising : bridging the divide / Nicos P. Mouzelis.
   p.   cm.
Includes bibliographical references.
ISBN 978-0-521-51585-6
1. Postmodernism – Social aspects.   2. Sociology – Methodology.   3. Sociology –
Philosophy.   4. Social sciences – Philosophy.   I. Title.
HM449.M62   2008
301.01–dc22

2008030239

ISBN 978-0-521-51585-6 hardback
ISBN 978-0-521-73153-9 paperback

To the memory of Ellen Sutton

Contents

List of figures   *page* xii

Acknowledgements   xiii

   Introduction   1

   **Part I   The theoretical background: the development
of the agency–structure problematic**   7

1 From Parsons' to Giddens' synthesis   9
   Introduction   9
   1 Parsonian functionalism: the emphasis
      on system/structure   12
   2 Interpretative micro-sociologies: the emphasis
      on agency   15
   3 The rational-choice paradigm   17
   4 Decentring the subject I: hidden codes   21
   5 Decentring the subject II: subjectless practices 24
   6 Decentring the subject III: texts   27
   7 Transcending the subjectivist–objectivist divide:
      attempts at a post-Parsonian synthesis   34
   8 The overall abolition of boundaries   38
   Conclusion   39

   Part II   Parsonian and post-Parsonian developments   41

2 Parsons and the development of individual rights   43
   1 T.H. Marshall: civil, political and social rights 43
   2 T. Parsons: rights and revolutions   45
   3 Differentiation and the mechanisms of change   49
   4 Integration: balanced and unbalanced forms   51
   Conclusion   54

3   Evolution and democracy: Parsons and the collapse
    of communism   57
    1   Evolutionary universals   57
    2   The limits of modernization from above   61
    3   Some critical remarks   62

4   Post-Parsonian theory I: neo-functionalism
    and beyond   65
    Introduction   65
    1   The theory of action   67
    2   The theory of culture   68
    3   Action and culture: a critical assessment   70
    4   The theory of civil society   73
    5   The basic dilemma in the conceptualization
        of civil society   74
    Conclusion   77
    Postscript: Alexander's cultural sociology   78
    Introduction   78
    1   On the conceptualization of culture   79
    2   The environments of action   81
    3   Cultural narratives as second-order discourses   84
    Conclusion   85

5   Post-Parsonian theory II: beyond the normative
    and the utilitarian   86
    Introduction   86
    1   Three problematic presuppositions   87
    2   Constitutive theories of action and systemic theories
        of differentiation   89
    3   Some critical remarks   90
    Conclusion   94

    **Part III   Agency and structure: reworking some basic
                 conceptual tools**   95

6   Social and system integration: Lockwood, Habermas
    and Giddens   97
    1   Lockwood   97
    2   Habermas   101
    3   Giddens   104
    Conclusion   105

7　The subjectivist–objectivist divide: against
　　transcendence　107
　　1　On the concept of social structure　108
　　2　The impasse of transcendence strategies　115
　　3　A concrete example: the reproduction of the LSE
　　　　as a social system　121
　　4　Concluding remarks: bridging rather than
　　　　transcending the divide　127

8　Habitus and reflexivity: restructuring Bourdieu's theory
　　of practice　131
　　Introduction　131
　　1　Dispositions, positions and interactions　132
　　2　Reflexivity　133
　　3　Bourdieu's conception of the subject　136
　　4　Restructuring the SDP scheme　139

**Part IV　Bridges between modern and late/
　　　　postmodern theorizing**　143

9　Modernity: a non-Eurocentric conceptualization　145
　　Introduction　145
　　1　Modernity: mobilization/incorporation
　　　　into the centre　147
　　2　Modernity: institutional differentiation　148
　　3　Modernity: a non-Eurocentric conceptualization　154
　　4　Modernity and the West　156
　　5　Variants of modernity　156
　　6　Late modernity and globalization　159
　　Conclusion　161

10　Ethical relativism: between scientism and cultural
　　relativism　164
　　1　The golden rule perspective　164
　　2　On the self-evidence of the golden rule　166
　　3　Basic assumptions and difficulties of the
　　　　relativist position　167
　　4　Stepping stones towards growing socio-cultural
　　　　interpenetration　169
　　5　Eurocentrism　171
　　Conclusion　173

11   Cognitive relativism: between positivistic and relativistic
     thinking in the social sciences   175
     1   Objectivity and the issue of mediation   175
     2   The postmodern critique of representation
         and empirical evidence   178
     3   The 'internality' of a discipline's subject matter   183
     Conclusion   188

12   Social causation: between social constructionism
     and critical realism   191
     Introduction   191
     1   The Harré thesis   192
     2   Giddens' conflationist strategy   197
     3   Archer's anti-conflationist strategy   199
     4   Articulation of agentic and structural properties   206
     Conclusion   211

     Part V   Towards a non-essentialist holism   215

13   Grand narratives: contextless and context-sensitive
     theories   217
     1   'Grand narratives': context-sensitive and insensitive   217
     2   Holistic conceptual frameworks: open and closed   221
     3   Non-essentialist holism: three types of openness   224

14   The actor–structure dimension: anti-conflationist holism   225
     Introduction   225
     1   Structures and actors   226
     2   On the linkages between the causal powers of actors
         and of structures   232

15   The micro–macro dimension: anti-essentialist holism   237
     Introduction   237
     1   Strong and weak types of essentialism   237
     2   Interpretative sociologies: obstacles to micro–macro bridges 249
     3   Three guidelines for bridging micro and macro approaches   253

16   The inter-institutional dimension: beyond economism
     and culturalism   261
     1   Economism   261
     2   Culturalism and the priority of the lifeworld: from
         Marx to Parsons and Habermas   266
     3   Beyond economism and systemic culturalism   270

Instead of Conclusion: Twelve rules for the construction
of an open-ended holistic paradigm 274
  The actor–structure dimension:
  anti-conflationist holism 274
  The micro–macro dimension:
  anti-essentialist holism 275
  The inter-institutional dimension:
  anti-economistic holism 276

Appendix. In defence of 'grand' historical sociology 279
  1 The conflation of history and sociology 279
  2 The comparison with Spencer 280
  3 On the tenuous linkages between evidence and interpretation 281
  4 On the arbitrary character of grand historical
     sociology's interpretations 283
References 285
Index 299

Figures

7.1 A fourfold typology of social structure   *page* 111
7.2 Variations in the relationship between actors and
     their environments of action   127
8.1 Restructuring the SDP scheme   140
14.1 Actor–structure linkages   233

Acknowledgements

I want to thank Sally Sutton for her excellent editing.

I also want to express my love and gratitude to Thalia Dragona for her intellectual, practical and moral support – support which made this book possible.

Introduction

There have been fundamental changes in the past three decades, both on the level of social theory, and on the level of the social realities that this theory tries to describe and explain. Concerning the former we have witnessed a post-positivist/anti-foundationalist as well as a linguistic/cultural turn. With regard to the latter, the abrupt opening of world markets (particularly financial ones) in combination with the new information technologies has led to a type of neoliberal globalization within which nation-states have had to change profoundly both their internal structures and their external strategies in their attempts to thrive or even just survive in a new, highly competitive world order.

For some social theorists the above changes have been so radical that the term 'modern' should be replaced by the term 'postmodern' – both on the level of second-order theoretical discourses, and on the more practical one of first-order laypersons' discursive and non-discursive practices. Hence the talk about postmodern theory and postmodern society: a social order within which the belief systems and the collective certainties of early modernity have evaporated – this state of affairs leading to constant references to the 'death of the subject', the 'end of history', the 'dissolution of metaphysics', the 'implosion of the social', the 'eclipse of the political', etc.[1]

Against this hyperbolic tendency to exaggerate partial trends to the point of showing them as totally dominant, other theorists (including myself) consider that the term *late*-modern rather than postmodern is a more appropriate characterization of present-day society and theory.[2] Since there are strong continuities between the old and the new, the logic

---

[1] For a critique of the postmodern declarations on the various 'deaths' (of the subject, history, metaphysics), see Benhabib, 1992.

[2] For a position which stresses the continuity between the modern and the late modern, see Giddens 1990, 1991. For structural similarities between the transitions from pre-modernity to modernity and from modernity to late modernity, see McLennan, 2003.

of modernity has not been interrupted or transcended, it has merely been accelerated. Moreover, certain theoretical themes (like relativism, anti-essentialism, anti-foundationalism), or cultural (pessimism, nostalgia, irony) or socio-structural ones (e.g. the notion of flows, networks, simulacra) – all these elements are to be found both in the old and in the new social order, albeit in different combinations and with different weights given to the specific elements. This being so, the central issue is less one of how the new replaces the vanishing old, and more how the new *articulates* with the persisting old.[3]

As regards sociological theory – the main concern of this book – I believe that there is a strong need not to turn our backs on classical theory or on the type of conceptual tools that Talcott Parsons (the father of modern sociological theory) bequeathed to us during the early post-war period. There is also a need to avoid not only discontinuity but also the type of compartmentalization of the numerous theoretical paradigms that developed partly in reaction to the Parsonian synthesis, and partly in response to the new global social developments. (In the text, when reference is made to societies I use the term late- rather than postmodern. On the other hand, when reference is made to theories, given the standard usage and in order to avoid confusion, I use either the rather awkward term late/postmodern or simply postmodern.)[4]

The essays contained in the present volume are tentative attempts to build bridges between modern and late-modern/postmodern theoretical developments, with the aim not of reversing the growing theoretical division of labour or the growing differentiation between various approaches to the social, but of combating compartmentalization and enhancing inter-paradigmatic communication. This entails a twofold task:

— *negatively*, eliminating obstacles that prevent the move from agency to structure/system, from micro to macro, from economic/political to socio-cultural analysis and vice versa;

---

[3] For theories emphasizing the need to replace the old with new conceptual tools more useful for the study of postmodernity, see Urry, 2000a, 2000b; Bauman, 1987, 1992.

[4] 'Post-structuralist' is a term which is often used interchangeably with 'postmodern'. In what follows it will only be used for the characterization of theories which reject the surface-depth distinction underlying various structuralist approaches.

— more *positively*, reconstructing already existing conceptual tools in an effort to move from theoretical compartmentalization and/or mere *juxtaposition* to the effective *articulation* of different perspectives, modern and late-modern/postmodern.

The volume is divided into five parts.

Part I ('The theoretical background: the development of the agency–structure problematic') gives a bird's-eye view of those postwar theoretical developments that are relevant to the issues examined in the rest of the book. In dealing with Parsons' theoretical synthesis and the numerous reactions to it, the focus is on the way agency and structure/system are conceptualized. Starting from a critique of Parsons' systemic overemphasis in his middle and late work, I very briefly examine the reaffirmation by interpretative sociologies of the agentic qualities of laypersons, as well as the linguistically and culturally informed attempts to decentre the subject via a focus on hidden codes, subjectless practices and texts/narratives. I also refer critically to two major attempts at a post-Parsonian synthesis, those by Giddens and Bourdieu. These two theorists have tried to transcend the subjectivist–objectivist, actor–structure divide in the social sciences, a divide which has pitted interpretatively orientated sociologies (like those of symbolic interactionism, phenomenological sociology and ethnomethodology) against more objective approaches (structural functionalism, structuralism and post-structuralism).

Part II ('Parsonian and post-Parsonian developments') tries to show the continuing utility as well as the serious limitations of some basic conceptual tools Parsons has offered us by looking at the way in which he has described and explained the spread of individual rights in Western societies (chapter 2), as well as how he has used the notion of evolutionary universals in an attempt to assess the chances of democratization in the pre-1989 East-European communist regimes (chapter 3). Part II also reviews the work of two authors (Alexander's in chapter 4, and Joas' in chapter 5) who, while taking Parsons' work seriously, have tried to reformulate it in ways which acknowledge the theoretical developments that became important after the American theorist's death.

Part III ('Agency and structure: reworking some basic conceptual tools') starts by examining the way in which the key distinction between social and system integration has been conceptualized by Lockwood, Habermas and Giddens. I argue that Lockwood's conceptualization, if partially reformulated, is the most useful one for the task of bridging actor- and system-orientated approaches in the social sciences (chapter 6). Part III continues with an essay which argues against the abolition or the transcendence of the subjectivist–objectivist divide in the social sciences (chapter 7). Finally, this part examines Bourdieu's notion of habitus and its connection with that of reflexivity, in a tentative attempt to restructure his theory of practice in such a way that teleological functionalism is avoided (chapter 8).

Part IV ('Bridges between modern and late/postmodern theorizing') tries to bring the modern and late-modern perspectives closer together by:

— elaborating the notion of modernity in such a way as to meet the postmodern objection about its Eurocentric character (chapter 9);
— exploring the issue of ethical relativism, taking a middle position between attempts to establish the transhistorical/universal validity of certain values, and those rejecting principles related to human rights as Eurocentric and as instances of cultural imperialism (chapter 10);
— considering the issue of cognitive relativism, again taking a middle position between positivistic and relativistic, postmodern modes of social analysis (chapter 11);
— developing an intermediate position between social constructionism and critical realism (chapter 12).

The bridging exercise continues in part V ('Towards a non-essentialist holism'). Here an effort is made to bring closer together the late/postmodern anti-essentialist orientation with the type of holistic conceptual frameworks which underlie conventional political economy and macrosociology – frameworks useful to those interested in the examination of how social wholes (formal organizations, communities, nation-states, global social formations) are constituted, reproduced and transformed (chapters 13 to 16).

The volume ends with an appendix ('In defence of "grand" historical sociology'). In this I defend the comparative macro-analyses of historically oriented sociologists such as Moore, Mann and Skocpol against a rather positivistically oriented, empiricist rejection of their writings.

It is important to stress here that the volume is not a textbook. Although part I deals with the development of postwar social theory, its main focus is on a single issue – that of the agency–structure problematic. Neither is the text a set of disconnected articles. It consists of a number of interrelated essays all of which, directly or indirectly, focus on ongoing debates between modern and postmodern theories – they also focus on ways to bridge the gap between them. More specifically, all chapters either examine issues crucial for the above debates, such as Eurocentrism, ethical relativism, cognitive relativism, etc.; or, on a more abstract level, explore the agency–structure problematic and its relevance for bringing closer together modern/holistic and postmodern anti-holistic, anti-essentialist approaches. This is a rather urgent task.

At a time when social scientists, by focusing on culture, discourses and the construction of identities, have turned their backs to the type of macro-transformations that have radically changed the face of the globe; at a time when holistic approaches (in the political economy and historical macro-sociology tradition) are rejected as essentialist and/or as having authoritarian connotations, it is vital to show that one can use holistic conceptual tools while avoiding essentialism as well as authoritarianism.

In a more general way this book is the end result of a continuous attempt, during the four decades of my career as a sociologist, to resolve theoretical puzzles and to construct or reformulate concepts which can help social researchers to avoid empiricism and to explore, in a theoretically relevant and empirically sound manner, the way in which social wholes work and the way in which they change. It is a synthesis of my previous endeavours in social theorizing (*Post-Marxist Alternatives, Back to Sociological Theory, Sociological Theory: What Went Wrong?*); it is also an attempt, against present, fashionable, postmodern trends, to show that some of the conceptual tools that classical sociology, as well as the Parsonian tradition of modern social theory, have given us are still useful for understanding the world in which we live.

Finally, I wish to make some brief remarks about the book's overall organization.

Part I (the very long chapter 1), which provides the general background, and the concluding part V (chapters 13 to 16), which tries to link together the various threads of the 'bridging' argument, have not been published before. In parts II–IV some of the essays have already been published, as mentioned in the initial footnote to the appropriate chapters. I have, however, modified them in order to show how each chapter is linked to other chapters and to the book's overall theme.

Concerning the mode of exposition, I have tried to strike a balance between two antithetical requirements: avoiding excessive repetition on the one hand and maintaining the self-contained character of each essay on the other. So in some chapters I have eliminated arguments already extensively discussed earlier, but mention where they can be found. In other cases, I have not eliminated, but shortened, points already discussed, so that the main argument can be grasped without the reader having to refer to previous chapters.

Finally, I have tried to make the major points of the book as clear as possible by providing concrete and straightforward examples to illustrate abstract arguments, and by putting more technical points in footnotes.

PART I

The theoretical background: the development of the agency–structure problematic

1 | *From Parsons' to Giddens' synthesis*

Introduction

The development of the social sciences in general and of sociology in particular is inextricably linked with the emergence and consolidation of the nation-state in nineteenth-century Europe. The nation-state and the more general modern social organization it entails have two basic dimensions that distinguish it from all pre-modern social formations:

(i) the decline of segmental localism and the massive mobilization/ inclusion of the population in the national centre.[1] This 'bringing in' process entails the concentration of the means of not only economic but also political, social and cultural production at the top; as well as the shifting of attachments and orientations from the traditional, non-differentiated community to what Anderson (1991) has called the 'imaginary community' of the nation-state;

(ii) the top to bottom differentiation of the societal whole into distinct institutional spheres, each portraying its own logic, values and historical dynamic. This differentiation, unlike that of complex, pre-modern social formations, is not confined to the top but reaches the social base or periphery as well.[2]

Classical sociologists have tried to understand the social realities resulting from the British Industrial Revolution and the French Revolution by focusing holistically on the above two major features of modernity. Spencer (1972) and Durkheim (1964), for instance,

---

[1] On the decline of segmental localism and its linkages with the emergence of the nation-state and nationalism, see Gellner, 1969: 147–78; 1996. For the process of mobilization/inclusion into the national centre, see Bendix, 1969.

[2] For the concept of differentiation and its linkage to modernity, see Parsons, 1966, 1977; Eisenstadt, 1990a, 1990b. For the segmental character of the social base in pre-modern, complex social formations, see Marx, 1859/1964; Hindess and Hirst, 1975.

explored differentiation as a major feature of the evolutionary process leading to the emergence of modern societies. Marx (1859/1970) and Weber (1925/1978), without neglecting differentiation, emphasized more how the centralizing, bureaucratizing aspects of the bringing-in process led to an unprecedented concentration of the means of production and domination at the top.

Marxist political economy is the discipline's holistic framework *par excellence*. More than any other paradigm it raises questions about the constitution, reproduction and transformation of whole social formations, particularly capitalist ones. One of its major features is striking a balance between a systemic/'externalist' and an actor/'internalist' perspective.[3] As Lockwood (1964) puts it, in Marx's overall work we see a combination of *system-integration* and *social-integration* views of how societies persist and change. Questions are asked about the logical compatibilities and incompatibilities of institutional complexes (e.g. contradictions between technology and the institution of private property), as well as about how actors react or fail to react to such incompatibilities. It is true of course that, as Althusser (1969) has pointed out, Marx's early work puts more emphasis on actors and their struggles, whereas in his late work the focus is more on systemic contradictions and the tendential 'laws of motion' of a mode of production. But, as I will argue more extensively in chapter 16, looking at his *oeuvre* as a whole, there is no doubt that its conceptual framework helps us view the social both in systemic and in actor terms – without conflating the two approaches and without reducing the one to the other.

This is not to deny that there are serious drawbacks in the Marxist holistic framework. It is based on an economistic view of social differentiation that leads, in aprioristic fashion, to the systematic underemphasis of non-economic institutional spheres and their specific logics. It also leads to the underemphasis of actors' struggles over the non-economic means of social construction (political, cultural).

Of course, humanist and voluntaristic versions of Marxism have tried to overcome economism by stressing the relative autonomy of the political or the ideological. But in so far as they continue to conceptualize and analyse the non-economic levels by the use of economic categories (such as class, reproductive requirements of capital, etc.), they have not succeeded in overcoming economic reductionism (Mouzelis, 1990).

---

[3] For the internalist/externalist distinction, see Habermas, 1987.

If the balance between an action and a systemic perspective is marred by economism, critics have also pointed out difficulties in terms of macro–micro linkages. Marxism, focusing on such macro-phenomena as class struggles, mass movements, revolutions, etc., has neglected to show how these relate to the actions and interactions of concrete individuals in the context of their everyday existence; it has failed, in other words, to provide micro-foundations of societal stability and change.[4] This failure is responsible, say the critics, for essentialism, for the reification of social structures, for a view of society as a mystical entity pulling all the strings behind the actors' backs. Moreover, essentialism is reinforced by Marx's philosophical materialism – both leading to a constant reference by Marxists to material structures, material conditions, material struggles. This accent on the material goes strongly against the linguistic and cultural trend in the social sciences today, against the growing realization that all aspects of social life, from ideologies to stock markets, are symbolically constructed (see chapter 12).

The decline of the Marxist macro-holistic framework is not, of course, exclusively due to its theoretical weaknesses. A full explanation must link intra- with extra-theoretical developments, such as the collapse of the Soviet Union, the generalized crisis of the Left, the neoliberal character of present-day globalization, etc. But the *internal* logic and dynamic of the debates of how societal wholes are constituted, reproduced and transformed is also important to the understanding of not only the decline of Marxism but, more to the point, the theoretical failure to replace it with a less economistic and less essentialist holism – a holism useful for raising in a theoretically coherent manner questions about the functioning and transformation of nation-states in today's globalized, late modernity.

If, as I believe, it is true that globalization does not lead to the decline or disappearance of the nation-state but to a radical change in its functions, it is also true that at present we lack the conceptual tools for systematically studying either this transformation or the global system within which nation-states are embedded. This is to say that even in late modernity, the need persists for an investigation of nation-states and their development within the global system. The present 'anti-foundationalist' postmodern trend in the social sciences, however,

---

[4] For the concept of micro-foundations and its linkage to the micro–macro distinction, see Collins, 1981a, 1981b; Mouzelis, 1991b: 80–8.

tends to reject any attempt at constructing conceptual tools for such a holistic investigation on the grounds that any type of holism leads to essentialism and eventually to political authoritarianism (Lyotard, 1974). This state of affairs may suit the defenders of the global, neoliberal status quo, but it definitely undermines the efforts of both those who want to understand better the present character of the globalization process, and those who want to change it in an emancipatory direction.

In this introductory chapter the aim is not to cover in any systematic and/or exhaustive manner the numerous theoretical paradigms in post-war social theory. Instead, I give a brief overview of those developments in theory which focus on features (such as the action/structure and macro/micro distinctions) which are related to the major concern of this volume: the building of bridges between modern and late-modern approaches to the study of social phenomena.

1 Parsonian functionalism: the emphasis on system/structure

Talcott Parsons is rightly considered the father of modern sociological theory. It was his work that established sociological theory as a sub-discipline within sociology, specializing in the systematic production, not of substantive theories (not Generalities III, to use Althusser's useful terminology) but of conceptual tools (Generalities II) which prepare the ground for the empirical investigation of the social world (Althusser, 1969: 183–91). They do so by helping us to overcome empiricism and to ask *sociological* rather then merely *social* questions about the social world.

In terms of the thesis of this book, Parsons' holistic paradigm should be assessed along two basic axes: the micro–macro and the action–system dimensions. In contrast to Marx, in Parsons the methodological balance of social and system integration is upset in favour of the latter. Particularly in the middle and late phases of his work, as he moved from the analysis of the unit act to the theorization of the social system, the voluntaristic dimension of his theory becomes peripheralized or disappears altogether. As many critics have noted, in phases II and III of Parsons' work[5] the direction of influence is always from the system and

---

[5] If phase I of Parsons' work is marked by the publication of *The Structure of Social Action* (1937), in phase II we have his classical work *The Social System* (1951) and in phase III *Societies: Evolutionary and Comparative Perspectives* (1966).

its functional requirements to the actors and their roles, rather than the other way around. Actors (particularly collective actors) are either portrayed as passive products of systemic determinations, or they disappear completely from the social scene.

More specifically, consider the three-level relationship of the cultural, the social and the personality systems. Parsons always starts with the core values of the cultural system, which are then institutionalized into roles/normative requirements at the social-system level, and finally internalized in the form of needs/dispositions at the level of the personality system. The direction is invariably from core values to normative expectations and need dispositions – never the other way round. We are never encouraged to ask how core values are constructed or transformed, how actors creatively handle their roles while playing interactive games, or how actors, through constant reflexive accounting, set about making sense of the games in which they are involved.

If in the above instance actors are portrayed as mere puppets, they disappear altogether in the Parsonian subdivision of the social system into the four famous subsystems (adaptation/economic, goal-achievement/ political, integration/social and latency/value-commitment – AGIL for short).They vanish, because each subsystem is further divided into four sub-subsystems following the same systemic, institutional logic. This results in an onion-like (system within system) view of society where broad systems contain less encompassing subsystems. Within this framework the theoretical space for actors, particularly collective actors, is obliterated. If collective actors do make an appearance in Parsons' more empirical work, it is *despite*, not because of, the AGIL scheme (Mouzelis, 1991a: 55ff).

It is important to stress, however, that, contra Parsons' early critics (Dahrendorf, 1959; Mills, 1959), this passivity does not entail norm conformity. The American theorist repeatedly states that whether or not actors comply with their roles' normative requirements is a matter of empirical investigation. Sometimes they do; at other times they do not.[6] The passivity has rather more to do with the fact that Parsons fails to

---

[6] A similar point can be made about early criticisms of Parsons for overemphasizing social harmony, equilibrium and stability and neglecting disharmony, disequilibrium and instability. In fact, the Parsonian framework can cope with instability and disequilibrium, even with systemic breakdowns. But all these disruptive developments are viewed from a system rather than a social-integration or disintegration point of view; they are seen in terms of role 'strains' or

show how role players, *conforming to normative requirements or not*, handle such requirements in actual interactive contexts. It is the difference between knowing or 'orienting oneself' to game rules, and actually applying such rules in a syntagmatically unfolding game. As it has rightly been pointed out, Parsons' actors are constantly rehearsing their roles but the actual play never starts; the theatre curtain never rises. There is more orientation to than 'instatiation' of rules. The analysis always moves on the paradigmatic or institutional level, rarely on the syntagmatic, interactive one.

Another point to be made here is that, as far as the construction of a holistic paradigm is concerned, one can find useful elements in the Parsonian synthesis. First of all, Parsons rejects economism. In dealing with the differentiation of institutional spheres in modern societies, he clearly refuses any privileging of the economic. Following Weber, he argues that the problem of sphere dominance is an empirical question, and that therefore the construction of conceptual tools should not lead to the a priori favouring of one sphere over the others. It is true, of course, that Parsons' late work moves from the Weberian position on the issue of institutional dominance to the a priori privileging of the cultural sphere via his cybernetic hierarchy scheme (Parsons, 1966: 11–14; chapter 16, sections 2 and 3 below). But this does not undermine Parsons' previous efforts to conceptualize the differentiation of modern societies into spheres with their own specific logic and values, spheres whose relationships are amenable to an open-ended empirical investigation.

Another positive contribution by Parsons towards the construction of a holistic paradigm is that, unlike Marx, he does provide conceptual bridges (albeit inadequate ones) for linking the macro with the micro

---

'incompatibilities' between institutional subsystems rather than in terms of conflicts and struggles between such collective actors as interest groups or classes.
 It is because of this systemic one-sidedness, because of the unidirectional *system→actor* instead of *actor→system* perspective, that society becomes hypostasized and explanations of social development tend to be partial and/or misleading. They are partial because there is no prompting to link systemic incompatibilities or contradictions with the conflictual or non-conflictual relations between actors; and they tend to be misleading, or downright wrong, because, in the absence of relatively autonomous actors reacting or failing to react to systemic contradictions, there is a great temptation to transform functional requirements into causes. This type of strategy misdirects us from legitimate functional or institutional analysis to teleological functionalism (see, on these points, chapter 15, section 1a).

level of analysis. His conceptualization of social systems and subsystems is so constructed that it can be applied to the empirical study not only of societal systems but of all types of social whole – macro, meso and micro. In fact, Parsons' numerous disciples have used the functional-structural paradigm for the empirical investigation of social systems ranging from empires and nation-states to formal organizations and small groups.[7] Now one might argue that the micro–macro bridges that Parsons offers do not overcome the systemic bias of his overall scheme, and that in this sense, as his critics have emphasized, his categories tend to lead to essentialist views of the social (see chapter 15). However, it is better to have system-privileging bridges than no bridges at all.

2 Interpretative micro-sociologies: the emphasis on agency

The development of interpretative micro-sociological paradigms in the 1960s and 1970s can be seen as a reaction (or rather over-reaction) to the non-voluntaristic, oversystemic aspects of the Parsonian synthesis. With symbolic interactionism and ethnomethodology, actors are seen (contra Parsons) as producers rather than passive products of their social world. With interaction/intersubjectivity and reflexive intra-action put at the centre of the analysis, the concern is less with how roles influence actors' behaviour or the extent to which actors do or do not conform to normative expectations, and more with how actors creatively use their roles in their attempts to interact with others and to participate actively in complex social games. In doing so their concern with meaning goes beyond Weber's emphasis on *verstehen*. They are less interested in meaning as an end-product and more in the ongoing construction of meanings in interactive contexts. This leads them to explain social order less in terms of common values and norms (as Parsons does) than in terms of social skills, of emergent situational meanings (Mead, 1934; Blumer, 1969) – and, in the case of ethnomethodology, of taken-for-granted cognitive assumptions about the reality of the social world and the commonality of perspectives (Garfinkel, 1967; Cicourel, 1976).

There is no doubt that both symbolic interactionism and ethno-methodology do bring into the analysis the voluntaristic aspects that

---

[7] See, for instance, the empirically oriented works of Bellah, 1957; Allport, 1962; Smelser, 1962; Stouffer, 1962; Eisenstadt, 1963; Barber, 1985.

Parsons' 'voluntaristic' theory has neglected; in that sense their provision of micro-foundations does combat the essentialism of both the Marxist and the Parsonian holistic schemes (see chapter 15). However, micro-sociologists' excessive fear of reification makes them reject all macro-concepts (such as social structure, societal differentiation, class struggles, etc.) as referring to imaginary essences clouding the obvious truth that all social phenomena are symbolically constructed. This has created obstacles in the way of developing micro–macro linkages. It has led to the rejection of all conventional macro-sociologies, and/or to the reductive and empiricist idea that one should first understand and empirically investigate the micro-worlds of day-to-day interaction before moving on to tackle issues referring to macro-phenomena.[8]

Although this micro-imperialistic tendency is somewhat mitigated in later developments,[9] there is no doubt that interpretative micro-sociologists' suspicion of macro-concepts has created serious obstacles to the construction of a holistic paradigm capable of integrating, of creating effective bridges between micro and macro approaches to the study of social phenomena (see chapter 15). This has caused micro-sociologists to turn their backs on the types of issue (e.g. about the emergence, reproduction and long-term development of nation-states) that were so central to the writings of classical sociologists from Marx to Durkheim and Weber. That type of social myopia was further exacerbated by the erroneous tendency to link face-to-face interactions with the micro-level of analysis, and institutional structures with the macro. This is quite wrong. Face-to-face interaction involving powerful actors, such as heads of state for instance, have consequences which, to use Giddens' terminology, stretch very widely in time and space. Moreover, as Parsons has convincingly shown, institutional structures can be both macro and micro; they can refer to whole societies, formal organizations, communities or small groups.[10]

Interpretative micro-sociologies suffer from yet another limitation. Their adherents' fear of reification results in a rejection of not only all macro-concepts, but also all systemic concepts – whether macro or

---

[8] For a critique of this approach and a defence of macro-sociological concepts, see chapter 15.

[9] For an attempt to use interactionist concepts on the macro-level of analysis, see Maines, 2001.

[10] For a debate on this issue, see Rawls, 1987, 1988; Fuchs, 1988, 1989; Mouzelis, 1991b. See also chapter 15.

micro. So, for instance, the idea of a system's functional requirements or needs for survival/reproduction are considered an illegitimate use of biological concepts in a field which should focus not on organisms but on interacting agents and their symbolic constructions. In this view of the social world as an interactive accomplishment, all social-science concepts must *directly* refer to actors and their meanings, interpretations and strategies. It is argued that any attempt to complement or combine an action with a systemic orientation would unavoidably lead to the essentialist construction by sociologists of mysterious, imaginary entities misleadingly shown as pulling all the strings behind the actors' backs. The fact that an exclusive focus on action concepts often results in 'empirical findings' that the actual participants in the games being investigated find obvious or trivial does not deter interpretative micro-sociologists from their refusal to combine social- with system-integration perspectives.

In conclusion, interpretative micro-sociologists have provided us with micro-foundations of value for overcoming the essentialism found in the holistic paradigms of both Marx and Parsons. On the other hand their over-reaction to holism, their tendency to reject macro as well as systemic concepts (micro and macro) seriously obstructs any attempt at creating a new holistic paradigm that aims, in both the micro–macro and the actor–system perspectives, at replacing walls with bridges.

3 The rational-choice paradigm

a. The ideal-typical nature of rational-choice theory

Rational-choice theory, in both its Marxist[11] and non-Marxist [12] variants, constitutes another important attempt to overcome, via the provision of micro-foundations, the essentialism of conventional holistic paradigms. Following the neoclassical, *homo economicus* tradition, it is based on the idea of actors making choices on the basis of optimization or maximization criteria. To the often repeated criticism of empirically oriented social psychologists and micro-sociologists that *homo rationalis* is a fiction, that human beings do not behave in the perfectly rational way the model implies, rational-choice theorists reply that

[11] See, for instance, Cohen, 1978; Elster, 1985, 1986, 1989; Roemer, 1986, 1988.
[12] See Olson, 1965; Popkin, 1979; Boudon, 1987; Coleman, 1990.

despite or because of its ideal-typical exaggeration the model provides useful tools for illuminating a number of phenomena on both the micro- and the macro-level of analysis.

Consider, for instance, the case of an entrepreneur having to decide whether or not to go ahead with a specific investment strategy. Industrial sociologists will point out that if we abandon armchair modelling and investigate real actors taking actual decisions in specific settings, we shall find serious discrepancies between the empirical findings and the rational-choice model. Rational-choice theorists accept that such discrepancies are inevitable, but argue that, following Weber, their constructions are not substantive theories but ideal types whose exaggerated, 'unrealistic' character does not negate their heuristic utility. Let us take as an example the rational-choice-based statement that a rise in interest rates will, other things being equal, lead to a drop in the rate of investment. A critic may well object that in actual life other things are never equal; that, for instance, a rise in interest rates might, contra the model's prediction, be related to a rise in investment if the state intervenes and provides other incentives to interested entrepreneurs, such as tax reductions.[13]

The rational-choice reply to the above objection is that the model's logico-deductive character helps one to formulate certain tendencies (e.g. that of the investment rate to fall when interest rates rise) – tendencies that can, of course, be neutralized or reversed by countertendencies. Therefore it is a question of articulating the rational-choice, logico-deductive approach with a historico-genetic one:[14] an approach focusing more on specific historical and institutional contexts – an approach, in other words, capable of showing in which conditions the tendencies derived from the logico-deductive model will materialize and in which conditions they will not.

However, rational-choice theorists cannot show us how to articulate the logico-deductive with the historico-genetic, institutional approach. Neither, as I argue below, can they tell us how to safeguard the elegance and rigour of the rational-choice theory once the historical, institutional dimension is seriously taken into account. If, for instance, both goals and means of achieving them are historically and culturally specific, what exactly is the use of a theoretical paradigm based on transcultural,

---

[13] Przeworski (1986: ch. 4) advances this argument.

[14] For a discussion of the logico-deductive and historico-genetic approaches in Marx's writings, see Mouzelis, 1995b: 28–40.

transhistorical orientations? Could it be that such orientations lead to quasi-universal generalizations which, like all such constructions in the social sciences, are either trivial or actually wrong (wrong in the sense that they are valid only under certain conditions not specified in the theory)?

b. Rational-choice institutionalism

It is important to note, however, that there have been attempts to introduce considerations of institutional context into the rational-choice model. In the so-called 'rational-choice institutionalism' actors' preferences and utility maximization assumptions are still taken for granted – but institutions are brought in as mechanisms which can resolve collective action dilemmas: in so far as actors are often inhibited in following the most rational strategy because they are unable to predict other actors' behaviour, institutions provide the rational decision-maker with useful information about the likely reactions of others. Institutions therefore stabilize, render more predictable the decision-maker's social environment (Hall and Taylor, 1994, 1996, 1998; Hollingsworth *et al.*, 2002).

Another element which rational-choice institutionalists introduce is the idea that strategic interaction, a notion which occupies centre stage in their approach, is partly structured by institutions. Actors still have fixed preferences, but the strategic calculations which are necessary for achieving their preferred goals are not given in advance; rather, they are shaped by the institutional context within which they interact.[15]

---

[15] For Hall and Taylor (1994), in rational-choice institutionalism actors' identity and their preference function are exogenous to the institutional analysis:

> What then do institutions do? Institutions affect behaviour by providing the actors with greater or lesser degrees of certainty about the present and future behaviour of other actors. This formulation captures the central role that strategic interaction plays in most such analyses. In more specific terms, institutions may provide information relevant to the behaviour of others, enforcement mechanisms for agreements, penalties for defection and the like: but the key point is that they will affect individual action by altering the expectations an actor may have about the actions that others will take in response to or simultaneously with his own action. (1994: 14)

Hall and Taylor in the same text (1994: 14–17) compare, or rather contrast, the rational-choice 'strategic calculation' with the 'cultural' approach. The former is

Rational-choice institutionalism, by considering preferences as pre-constituted but calculations as internal to its model, occupies a position midway between conventional, or 'pure', rational-choice theory (where both factors are external) and an approach called 'historical institutionalism' which seriously takes into account context, time- and space-wise; and which therefore considers both preferences and modes of calculation as internal.[16] In the latter approach, interests and identities are shaped, reproduced and transformed by actors who interact within historically evolving institutional contexts. Needless to say, historical institutionalism, which developed as a reaction to rational-choice theory's neglect of institutional context, does not differ much from historical sociology, or, for that matter, from sociological analysis *tout court*. Another way of putting this is to argue that the more rational-choice institutionalists come close to historical institutionalism – let's say by considering information or modes of calculation as not given in advance – the more their generalizations lose their deductive rigour; and the more they portray the 'messy', context-sensitive character of conventional sociological generalizations.

All in all, attempts to date to bring closer together the rational-choice, logico-deductive and the conventional historico-genetic approaches have not been very successful. For in the rational-choice institutionalist

based on strategic calculation which aims at utility maximization, whereas the latter is based on 'interpretative and reflexive' behaviour – a behaviour which merely aims at achieving *satisfactory* rather than maximum outcomes. Moreover, in the former model, institutions merely reduce uncertainty related to others' reactions, whereas in the latter they shape identities, preferences and interests. If we view the two approaches as ideal types, there is no doubt that in actual situations an actor's conduct is influenced by a mix of both 'calculative/strategic' and 'interpretative/reflexive' elements; in which case the issue is to specify under which conditions the former and under which the latter is dominant.

    An alternative way of bringing the rational-choice perspective and that of conventional sociological analysis closer together is to link the calculative/strategic and the interpretative/reflexive orientations of actors with social norms embodied in specific roles/institutions and internalized as dispositions (habitus). For instance, in a market context, actors, as consumers, by following their taken-for-granted dispositions as well as their role requirements, will tend to adopt predominantly instrumental/calculative orientations; whereas in a friends' reunion context, internalized dispositions as well as normative requirements will stress expressive/affective orientations and behaviour. For the distinction between instrumental and expressive orientations see Parsons, 1951: 99ff.

[16] For an exposition of historical institutionalism, see Thelen and Steinmo, 1992. For a debate between critics and defenders of the approach, see Hall and Taylor, 1998; Hay and Wincott, 1998.

model there is a fundamental tension between external- and internal-to-the-model dimensions. More concretely, if institutions simply help rational actor A (who has pre-constituted preferences and modes of calculation) to predict the behaviour of actors B_1, B_2, B_3 etc. – then there is a fundamental, unaccounted difference between A and B_1, B_2, B_3. The behaviour of the former is not influenced by the institutional context, whereas that of the latter is. And one has similar problems if one considers those rational-choice institutionalists who focus on the dimension of 'strategic interaction'. When actors interact, since both preferences and modes of calculation are affected by the interactive process, why consider the former as external and the latter, internal? This type of logical incongruity can only be eliminated if rational institutionalists abandon the 'middle course' and move either towards the more conventional rational-choice perspective or towards historical institutionalism.

In closing this section it is important to stress that the difficulties discussed above do not mean that rational-choice approaches are useless. They can be useful if one takes into account that they have a different logical structure and therefore raise different questions from those approaches which take institutional context seriously. More precisely, the rational-choice model tends to raise *counterfactual* questions such as 'If we assume that actors have pre-constituted, fixed characteristics (such as interests or identities), how will they react to various changes (e.g. price fluctuations) in their environment?' The historico-genetic approach, on the other hand, adopting an anti-essentialist orientation, raises questions about the mode of construction of actors' interests or identities and about how these interests/identities are in a constant flux within an ongoing interactive game.[17]

4 Decentring the subject I: hidden codes

If in the rational-choice model, in contrast to interpretative micro-sociologies, actors' identities are taken for granted, in Lévi-Straussian structuralism there is an attempt to go beyond the analysis of actors'

[17] For Roy Bhaskar, rational-choice theory entails praxiology rather than sociology: 'It is a normative theory of efficient action generating a set of techniques for achieving given ends, rather than an explanatory theory capable of casting light on actual empirical episodes' (1989: 72). On this point, see also Wendt, 1999: 314ff.

features (given or constructed); as well as beyond the question of whether the subject is passive or active. The focus here shifts from the surface meanings, identities, interpretations, strategies of actors and their embeddedness in specific institutional contexts to the hidden codes they follow without any theoretical knowledge/consciousness of them.[18]

a. Anthropological and Marxist structuralism

Following Saussure's (1915) linguistic structuralism, Lévi-Strauss has set out to see to what extent it is possible to find 'hidden grammars' not only in language but also in such institutional fields as kinship, myth-making, cooking, etc. When structuralist anthropologists concentrate on the internal logic of a specific whole, they try to grasp it by breaking up this whole into elementary parts and then seeking to uncover the logical linkages between these parts that are 'hidden' from the actors (Lévi-Strauss, 1968, 1973).

In terms of Marxist rather than anthropological structuralism, Althusser attempted (less successfully, I think) to pursue a similar methodology in his modes-of-production analysis: breaking up a mode of production into elementary parts (e.g. raw materials, means, end-products, relations of ownership, relations of control) and then bringing the hidden connections between these parts to the surface (Althusser, 1968: 216ff).[19]

There is no doubt that structuralist methodology, particularly in its non-Marxist versions, has yielded interesting results that, unlike ethno-methodology's taken-for-granted 'deep' rules, are surprising even to those who themselves unknowingly follow these rules in a variety of fields. When it comes to explaining how such codes are constituted, however, or how they are transformed, structuralism has very little to offer. Either it resorts to extremely crude reductive explanations (e.g. with constant references to the structure of the human mind), or it tries to explain the historical transition from one type of code to another by

---

[18] For the distinction between practical and theoretical consciousness of actors, see Giddens, 1984: 41–5.

[19] For a critique of Althusserian Marxism, see Benton, 1984; Elliott, 1987. In certain ways Althusser's work is much nearer to Parsons' functionalism than to Lévi-Straussian structuralism. See Mouzelis, 1995b: 81–100.

constructing supercodes or transitional codes[20] – theoretical practices which obscure rather than illuminate the mechanisms of change.

Structuralism, in its more moderate, less imperialistic versions, recognizes that hidden codes, whether in myth-making, cooking or novel-writing, provide only a very partial explanation, and one that needs to be complemented by the more conventional accounts that entail reference to actors and 'surface' institutional structures. Lévi-Strauss himself concedes that hidden codes, whether in myths or in cooking, only provide a very partial illumination or explanation that needs to be fleshed out by accounts of actors' strategies, etc. For instance, the French anthropologist accepts that a structuralist analysis of some specific type of myth – especially if one wants to go beyond unearthing hidden logical connections between '*mythèmes*' and account for its transformation in time – requires historical and sociological explanation as well. What Lévi-Strauss fails to do, however, is to show how structuralist analysis can be articulated with the more conventional approaches.

b. Decentring and recentring the subject

A possible bridge between structural and structuralist sociologies is Barthes' distinction between code *elucidation* and code *creation*. In the former case, specialists/experts (e.g. linguists, sociologists, anthropologists), by following the structuralist methodology, try to elucidate, to reveal the hidden (to laypersons) codes underlying a set of practices in a specific institutional sphere (e.g. kinship, cooking, etc.). In the latter case, experts, rather than revealing already existing codes, create new ones. Writing about the garment industry the French scholar argues that 'the language of fashion does not emanate from the "speaking mass" but from a group which makes the decisions and deliberately elaborates the code' (Barthes, 1999: 55).

So, in the case of elucidation, the decentring of the subject is a necessary methodological procedure that *theoretically orientated* specialists use in order to discover 'hidden' (i.e. unknown to both specialists and laypersons) rules; in the case of code creation, *practically oriented* experts are considered by Barthes as 'centred subjects'. To put it

[20] For a Marxist structuralist example of transitional codes, see Althusser and Balibar, 1973: 278ff.

differently, code elucidation requires the examination of the practices of decentred subjects (i.e. laypersons), whereas code creation requires the examination of the relationship between two types of subjects: those who create codes (centred subjects) and those who more or less unconsciously adopt or follow them (decentred subjects).

One can *move a step up the reflexivity ladder* by raising structuralist questions about the hidden rules underlying the code creators' practices. More concretely, those who create and ~~surreptitiously~~ impose fashion grammars on potential customers, also operate in an institutional field whose underlying syntagmatic and paradigmatic rules might be unknown to them – but known to a sociologist of fashion who uses structuralist methodology to study the garment industry. If one accepts the above, then the dialectic between subject decentring and recentring can be a useful way of bringing structural and structuralist sociologies closer together.

5 Decentring the subject II: subjectless practices

With Foucault's middle and late work (1978, 1980, 1984, 1986), and leaving structuralism for post-structuralism, the decentring of the subject takes a different form. The quest for hidden codes is abandoned, and so is the surface/depth distinction. Given the 'fragile, chaotic, discontinuous and contingent character of the social', post-structuralists think that the search for hidden regularities is simply a waste of time. Hidden codes are out, therefore, but the structuralists' hostility to the portrayal of actors as relatively autonomous creators of their social world continues. The decentring of the subject now takes the form of either material, 'docile' bodies[21] being shaped by discursive and non-discursive practices, or that of subjectivities as constructions without consciously oriented constructors. Foucault holds that whether we examine such subjectivities as the lunatic, the pervert or the saint, each is the outcome of 'subjectless' discursive and non-discursive practices[22] emanating from a variety of fields or disciplines – from medicine and jurisprudence to religion and lay education. With the advent of modernity we see the spread of micro-technologies of power

---

[21] For a critique of Foucault and for an approach which views the body as less passive, see Burkitt, 1999.

[22] For a discussion of the connection between the discursive and the non-discursive in Foucault's archaeological and genealogical phase, see chapter 11, section 3.

from incarcerating, total institutions (prisons, military academies, boarding schools) to society as a whole. In other words, we see a shift from conventional forms of exploitation and domination (where the cleavage between exploiter and exploited, dominators and dominated is obvious), to a type of subjugation where the subjugated cannot identify their subjugators. We move, therefore, to a situation of generalized, impersonal, unintended subjugation.

Foucault is not concerned with the Marxist or Weberian discourses on power, discourses which enquire into who has and who does not have power, who controls and who does not control the macro-technologies of production and domination. As does Parsons, Foucault sets aside the issue of how power is distributed. But unlike Parsons (1951: 121–7), he does not conceive of power as a social system's capacity for mobilizing resources for the achievement of its goals. The focus is rather on power/knowledge, on a type of power that creates not only a 'scientific' understanding of a subject matter but also, at least partially, creates the subject matter itself. For example, power/knowledge not only creates medical, legal and psychiatric discourses about the insane; these discourses, together with others originating from a variety of fields, also create insanity itself. This means that the subject matter to be studied by the social sciences is not external but internal to these disciplines (see chapter 11, section 3). It is in the above sense that power takes a *capillary* form, its disciplinary micro-technologies penetrating all areas of social life, creating a generalized regime of subjugation – something like an elastic, stretchable cage from which escape is almost impossible.

If the structuralist focus on hidden codes makes it difficult to *explain* the constitution and transformation of social codes, so does the Foucauldian conceptualization of subjectless discursive practices that constitute the social. Even accepting that subjectivities are the passive constructs of a variety of discursive and non-discursive practices, there is still the question of their *hierarchization* in terms of their constructive capacity. Are certain discourses more effective than others, and, if so, how is this differential efficacy to be explained? Why, for instance, in the construction of the modern consumer subjectivity are discourses emanating from the mass media more potent than those emanating from the Church or the family? And what about antagonistic/antithetical discourses which require subjects to make painful choices? How are the micro-technologies of subjugation that Foucault explores linked with the macro-technologies of domination and violence that Weber, for instance, has examined?

فوکو جواب این که در به هرحال این قدرت های discoursive به سری بیشتر از دیگران بردگُبیر کنند .
می باعث میشه ین برنده بشه ؟ آکه نوع اع subject رو دارد کنیم نیست . re-center بر ل .
کسم شلا بگم علا ان قدرت فلا ان اثر به ریا نقر داشت ۶ برنده شد .

Foucault cannot answer such crucial questions. To do so would require 'recentring' the subject, bringing back into the picture powerful actors and the complex games they play in their attempt to control (locally, nationally, globally) not only the means of production but also the means of domination as well as the cultural means of identity production. When this actor-centred dimension is set aside, there may be incisive descriptions but no effective explanations. Without systemic reference to the complex struggles of those who control economic, political, social and cultural technologies it is not possible to satisfactorily explain the type of macro-transformations (like the transition from one regime of punishment to another) that are so central to the French philosopher's work.[23] It is not therefore surprising that, despite his explicit rejection of functionalism, Foucault frequently resorts to functionalist explanations – both teleological and non-teleological.[24]

---

[23] For similar critiques of Foucault's work, see Dreyfus and Rabinow, 1982; Dews, 1987; Norris, 1993; McNay, 1994; Elliott, 2001.

[24] Concerning non-teleological explanations, Foucault's constant efforts to explore the conditions of existence of certain types of knowledge entails functionalist, quasi-Parsonian connotations. 'Conditions of existence' more often than not operate as 'functional requirements'. Both notions point to necessary but not by themselves sufficient preconditions, i.e. to factors without which the social phenomena studied could not exist or would break down. In neither case does the mere identification of the conditions of existence constitute an adequate explanation of the phenomena under consideration.

To argue, for example, as Foucault does, that the establishment of medical archives in hospitals was one of the conditions of existence of medical knowledge today, tells us nothing about the precise mechanisms that brought this new knowledge about. In a similar fashion, Parsons' reference to the four functional requirements (i.e. conditions of existence) that a given social system has to solve in order to survive tells us nothing about the actual processes that constituted, reproduced and have transformed the system.

This is to say that by their very logic, neither conditions of existence nor functional requirements can provide causal explanations. The only difference between the two terms is that the former is preferred by those (like Foucault or Giddens) who use functionalist logic while denying that they are doing so.

Concerning teleological explanations which are not only incomplete but also erroneous, the French philosopher, in an indirect manner, often turns needs or functional requirements/conditions into causes. For instance, in trying to explain the spread of the micro-technologies of power from carceral institutions to society as a whole, he resorts more or less directly to a type of teleological thinking: he stresses the fact that neither collective actors nor powerful individuals planned or consciously imposed the modern regime of subjugation; it came about because there was a 'need' for it (see Gordon, 1980: 114); see also chapter 15, section 1a and note 1.

It should be mentioned of course that in Foucault's late-late work (1978, 1984, 1986) the structuralist/post-structuralist subject decentring ceases to be as dominant as before. In his *History of Sexuality* (1978), for instance, he refers not only to practices of subjugation but also to those of freedom. He also talks about the care of the self, about the possibility of aesthetic self projects, etc. But this change of orientation did not lead to a systematic reworking of his view of modern societies as prison-like. Moreover, Foucault's self-reflexive subject has a quasi-monadic character – in the sense that the emphasis on intraaction does not lead to an exploration of the interactive dimension of social life (see, on this, Elliott, 2001: 55).

6 Decentring the subject III: texts

a. Textualism

If Lévi-Strauss thought that institutions other than language operate also as languages, some post-structuralists went a step further and completely conflated language and society. By this theoretical move, society is conceptualized as a chain of signs, signifiers or texts – 'intertextuality' becoming a central tool for analysing social phenomena. From this perspective the structuralist attempt to find underlying grammars hidden from the subject is not abandoned, but the explanation of such grammars or codes is not to be found, as Lévi-Strauss thought, in the structure of the mind but in extra-mental, extra-corporeal texts and their interconnections. There is therefore a move from 'internal' *mentalism* to 'external' *textualism* (Reckwitz, 2002: 246–50).

Moreover, this type of structuralism is often combined with a hermeneutic approach aimed at reconstructing, via 'thick description', the symbolic structures of the social world. For if in conventional sociology,

> Finally it is worth mentioning in this context that another form of subject decentring which resembles that of Foucault – particularly in its functionalist connotations – is Luhmann's rejection of the 'obsolete' notion of the subject. Despite his emphasis on meaning, this notion is exclusively seen from a systemic perspective. The subject is not the source of meaning – rather it is constituted by a pre-existing system of meanings. Therefore if in Foucault's case we have subjectless discourses, in Luhmann's we have *subjectless meanings*. The fact that subjects, particularly in interactive settings, are not only the products but also the producers of meanings is ignored (see Luhmann, 1982: 324–5; 1998).

social structures refer to relations between roles (institutional structures) and/or relations between actors (figurational structures), symbolic structures refer to relationships between signs or symbols. The logic of the symbolic thus prevails over the normative logic of role requirements or the practical logic of dispositions and interactions (Alexander, 2003).

Considering agency, there is little *emphasis* on the texts' authors. Agents and their interactions, if they do not disappear, are seen as the 'effects' of language. In Lacanian fashion, it is language and the symbolic that 'talk to subjects', rather than the other way around. Subjects become 'ways of speaking' within a specific discourse.[25] Or, to put it differently, we are shown how 'subject positions' lead to practices, rather than how agents' practices shape, reproduce or transform subject positions.[26]

b. The conflation of the discursive and the non-discursive

The above comes close to Foucault's conceptualization of subjectivities as the passive products or effects of subjectless practices. But in textualism Foucault's distinction between discursive and non-discursive practices is abandoned, as are his references to the inscription of practices on the human body. The bodily/material as well as the practical/non-discursive become aspects of discourse. In fact, everything becomes discourse, given that it is language that constitutes the social and given that discourse is equated with the symbolic. In this way bodies, artefacts and material objects, by acquiring meaning via discourses or texts, always have a symbolic dimension. The same is true of 'silent' practices, since all human practices involve symbolization. Once one collapses the discursive, the non-discursive and the material, then the conflation of language and society makes sense – both language and society consisting of systems of signs or symbols.[27]

However, the non-differentiation between the discursive and the non-discursive, and the rather arbitrary labelling of both as discourse[28]

---

[25] For a critique of Lacan's psychoanalytic decentring of the subject, see Castoriadis, 1999: 54ff; Kristeva, 1999: 67–80; Elliott, 2001: 81–94.

[26] See, on this aspect of discourse theory, various articles in Howarth *et al.* 2000.

[27] For a critique of Foucault's distinction between the discursive and the non-discursive, see Laclau and Mouffe, 1985: 108.

[28] For Laclau and Mouffe the conceptualization of discourse as an all-inclusive concept encompassing all social reality is a 'creative misapplication'. It is justified on heuristic grounds. See Howarth, 2000: 106.

hinders the exploration of the interesting discrepancy between the 'said' and the 'done', between what people say they do and what they actually do. It also hinders the study of structures which, although symbolically constructed, are at the same time 'hidden', in the sense of not entering the subjects' (or some subjects') consciousness.

Moreover, Derrida's idea that there is a strict equivalence between texts and social relations often leads to a crude linguistic reductionism which tends to ignore relationships that have a hierarchical character. I cannot, for instance, see any equivalents in language of social hierarchies in the field of distribution (of income, of life chances, etc.), or in relations (between exploiters and exploited, rulers and ruled, etc.). Of course, one can show how social hierarchies are depicted in texts (if we use the notion of text in its conventional, narrow sense); but there is a fundamental difference between hierarchized social space as portrayed in texts (as second-order historical, literary, philosophical narratives) and hierarchical relations, as these are produced by laypersons' first-order discursive and non-discursive practices. Conflating first- and second-order discourses,[29] or trying to derive first-order symbolic constructs by exclusive reference to second-order ones can be highly misleading. It is one thing to show how relations of political domination, for instance, are depicted in Brazilian novels or films, and quite another to explore such relations as they unfold in historical time and hierarchized space via the study of first-order discursive and non-discursive practices of rulers and ruled. In other words, social space in modern and late-modern social formations portrays hierarchical features (bureaucratic and non-bureaucratic) that have no equivalent in language.[30] Language may in part constitute the social but it does not exhaust it.[31] Once the text is defined in such a broad fashion that the extra-textual disappears – then it becomes impossible to examine how different speech genres are chosen according to context, how actors create or use texts in dialogic relationships or why certain texts have greater effectivity than other texts (Burkitt, 1999: 96ff).

---

[29] For the distinction between first- and second-order discourses and their utility in avoiding essentialism, see chapter 15.

[30] For a theorization of the concept of hierarchies and its utility in bridging micro and macro approaches to the social, see Mouzelis, 1991a: 67–116. See also chapter 15.

[31] For a critique of Derridean deconstruction along similar lines, see Said, 1978: 703; Foucault, 1979; Burkitt, 1999: 99ff.

The difficulties of textualism become more apparent when one leaves the analysis of cultural products for the analysis of such social wholes as communities, nation-states or political systems. For example, in Laclau's linguistically oriented work, discourse entails two basic notions: *moments*, referring to differential subject positions as these are articulated within a discourse; and *elements*, referring to differences that are not 'discursively articulated'. During periods of social stability, moments prevail – in the sense that subject positions generate subjectivities in an overall context where the conservative notion of differences (the notion that the social world is organized in complementary, non-contradictory, non-antagonistic ways) displaces the more radical notion of equivalences. In periods of crisis, on the other hand, moments become unfixed – they are transformed into 'floating signifiers' or floating elements amenable to rearticulation. It is during such periods of dislocation that political subjectivities are forced to act. This tends to result not so much in conflict between actors with different economic interests, but in *antagonisms* related to the change and defence of identities (Howarth and Stavrakakis, 2000: 1–24).

According to Laclau, the notion of economic interests, because it implies pre-constituted positions, leads to essentialism, whereas that of social identities does not. For instance, referring to Wolf's classical study of peasant revolutions (1971), Laclau and Mouffe (1985: 125ff) disagree that the development of capitalism and the radical mobilization of certain sections of the peasantry was due to their economic interests being threatened (an essentialist position), arguing that it had more to do with the threat to their peasant identities (a non-essentialist approach). But replacing the notion of economic interests by that of social identities is less a question of essentialism and more one of the cultural imperialism that textualism often generates. While the concept of economic interest can be used in an essentialist manner (i.e. as a given, pre-constituted objective reality), it can also be used in a non-essentialist manner (Swedberg, 2003): as symbolically constructed by both the first-order discourses of those directly involved in specific economic settings (peasants, landlords, merchants, state officials); and by the second-order discourse of ideologues, militants, intellectuals, priests, etc. Why is the notion of social identity more of a symbolic construct than the notion of economic interests? Both concepts can have the same status as far as essentialism or non-essentialism are concerned.

Furthermore, the tendency to replace interests by identities is not only theoretically arbitrary, it is also misleading. It diverts attention from the crucial issue of how symbolically constructed interests (economic, political, social) are linked with equally symbolically constructed identities. It precludes the possibility of strategies that threaten identities more than economic interests or vice versa.

So, for instance, certain forms of exploitation may lead to the extraction of greater resources from the direct producers without affecting their identities, whereas other forms may threaten both their economic interests and their identities (e.g. the reduction of free smallholders to serfs). To exclude the dimension of interest and to replace it with that of identity simply shows up the distortions required to be made to the discourse/textualist vocabulary in order to investigate social realities that require a less linguistically reductive form of analysis.

Laclau argues that his method of discourse analysis merely attempts to shift the focus from the more conventional

research categories which address the group, its constitutive rules and its functional determinations to the underlying logics that makes these categories possible. It is in this sense that we have spoken of the underlying logics of equivalence and difference, of empty and floating signifiers and of myths and imaginaries. (Howarth *et al.*, 2000: xi)

But the problem with the above position is that we are never convincingly shown how the 'underlying logics' link up with more conventional categories of groups operating within specific institutional contexts (economic, political, social, cultural) – groups which, in their attempts to defend or promote their symbolically constructed interests, interact with other groups, initiate strategies that constantly reappraise their adversaries' counter-strategies, etc. Wolf does exactly this, and his analysis is illuminating, notwithstanding unavoidable empirical and theoretical shortcomings. Laclau, on the other hand, dismisses the conventional distinction between collective actors and the institutional contexts that create both enablements and limitations, and replaces it with 'articulatory practices' that constantly construct and deconstruct self-identities, subject positions, 'nodal' points, moments, etc. But the conditions of existence of such practices, the way articulatory practices are linked to specific actors who are sustained by the more permanent institutional and relational structures, are never spelled out. This results in either a highly abstract analysis disconnected from the strategic and structural realities of the case under investigation, or in a dual type of theory where the inadequacy of the textualist vocabulary is supplemented in *ad hoc* fashion by more conventional concepts such as exploitation, domination, commodification, civil society, labour process, etc.[32]

c. Cultural sociology

A less imperialistic approach to textualism is to be found in the recent work of Alexander (2003). The American theorist attempts a 'strong program' not for the sociology of culture, but for a *cultural* sociology. Whereas the former focuses on how social structures impact on such cultural phenomena as art, religion and knowledge, the latter focuses on *symbolic structures* that are analytically distinct from institutional structures and social networks. Once the analytical autonomy of symbolic structures is established, the task of cultural sociology is to explore them using a combination of structuralist analysis and 'radical hermeneutics'. The first methodology explores the underlying codes, binary oppositions, and rules of syntagmatic succession and paradigmatic substitution, etc.; the second provides a 'thick' description of narratives or symbolic wholes in the Geertzian, anthropological tradition (Geertz, 1973).

Unlike Laclau, Alexander, in his strong programme of cultural sociology, does not reject the actor/social-structure distinction. The author of *The Meanings of Social Life* (2003) does not consider it sufficient to explore symbolic structures in structuralist and hermeneutic fashion, but thinks that they should also be linked with actors and social structures – the latter conceptualized as institutions and social networks. In this way Alexander tries to continue and also go beyond the Parsonian view of culture.

For Parsons, as already mentioned, the cultural system consists of core values institutionalized in the form of the normative requirements of roles and internalized as needs/dispositions on the level of the personality system. Alexander continues in the Parsonian tradition in that he sets out to link the cultural with the social and the personality systems. On the other hand, he tries to go beyond Parsons' functionalist view of culture (core values geared to the social system's functional requirements)

---

[32] For a more extended critique of Laclau's approach along these lines, see Mouzelis, 1990: 25ff.

by an analysis that is hermeneutically richer and methodologically (by using structuralist tools) more rigorous. Chapter 4 provides a more systematic exposition and critique of certain aspects of Alexander's early and late work. At this point I simply want to retain his emphasis on the necessity of relinking the analysis of the symbolic with a framework that focuses on concrete actors whose strategies and interactions are both limited and activated by social structures. I take this to entail the necessity of combining subject decentring (as it operates in structuralism and discourse analysis) with *subject recentring*. In fact, it is a major thesis of this book that – whether one's interest is in the constitution of hidden codes, in the hierarchization and differential effectivity of subjectless practices or in the transformation of symbolic structures – it is not possible to move from description (however deep or thick) to explanation without going beyond the decentring of the subject.

This does not mean of course that methodologies based on subject-decentring procedures are not useful. It is useful to conceptualize actors as following hidden codes (Lévi-Strauss, 1973), as being addressed by language and the symbolic (Lacan, 1977), as interpellated by ideologies (Althusser, 1973) or as constituted by discourses (Foucault, 1980). In other terms, the various subject decentrings which have developed as a reaction to the enlightened, Eurocentric notion of *homo rationalis*[33] are important as methods exploring the symbolic, the textual/discursive and, more generally, the social operating as *langue/parole*. But recentring the subject is equally important. It is crucial because both stability and change (of codes, discourses and texts) can only be explained via the interaction of relatively autonomous agents being constrained and empowered by social structures.[34] The interactive as well as the intra-active dimension is indeed crucial: if, as postmodern theorists argue, identities are not stable or pre-constituted, they are constantly reproduced and transformed via complex processes of intra- and interaction.[35]

Finally, linking decentring with recentring the subject is also important for building bridges between the multiplicity of theoretical paradigms in the social sciences. Building bridges does not necessarily imply

[33] For the view of decentring as a postmodern reaction to the Eurocentric conception of the 'rational subject', see Elliott, 2001: 10–12.

[34] For an early theory stressing the importance of social actors in the explanation of social phenomena, see McIver, 1942.

[35] For the crucial role that the concepts of reflexivity (intra-action) and interaction play in the production of social practices, see chapters 8 and 12, section 4.

the construction of an overall framework which will reduce the relative autonomy of such 'localized' theoretical traditions as those of symbolic interactionism, ethnomethodology, structuralism, post-structuralism, etc. It can simply entail a set of conceptual tools with the help of which impregnable walls can be transformed into two-way passages between theoretical traditions which could and should retain their specific logic while being open to external influences within and outside the social sciences. To speak more metaphorically: the aim is less a monolithic theoretical edifice, than a highly decentralized 'confederal' structure providing effective means of communication and translation from one theoretical region to another.

7 Transcending the subjectivist–objectivist divide: attempts at a post-Parsonian synthesis

Since the demise of Parsons' grand synthesis, as shown above, there has been a proliferation of theoretical paradigms trying to conceptualize social structure and actors in a variety of often contradictory ways. If in Parsonian theory actors are portrayed as passive, symbolic interactionism and ethnomethodology reverse this quiescent status of micro-actors to an active one; and in the structuralist and post-structuralist approaches subjects are decentred while hidden codes, subjectless practices or texts replace strategies and intersubjective understandings. The proliferation of theoretical paradigms has led to a state of acute fragmentation as well as to the so-called 'war of paradigms': interpretative micro-sociologists reject all structural-functionalist work as an exercise in reification, whereas macro-sociologists point to the trivial and/or socially myopic character of all micro-sociologies. Meanwhile the structuralists viewed all conventional sociologies (macro and micro) as incapable of grasping the hidden regularities of institutionalized, 'surface' conduct. As to the post-structuralists, they turn their backs on all other approaches in their exclusive concern with discursive practices and their contribution to the formation of subjectivities/identities.

By way of reaction to the above, there have been several attempts at overcoming the lack of constructive interchanges and the growing fragmentation and compartmentalization of the early post-Parsonian period (1960s and 1970s). Two theoretical attempts at overcoming the compartmentalization and creating a new synthesis bridging 'objectivist' and 'subjectivist' sociologies stand out: Giddens' structuration theory and Bourdieu's theory of practice.

a. Giddens' transcendence strategy

Giddens' aim is to bring closer together the three types of sociology discussed above: structural functionalism, structuralism/post-structuralism (emphasizing the 'objectivist' side of the divide), and interpretative micro-sociologies (focusing on the 'subjectivist' side). His key concept for transcending the divide and drawing the three sociologies closer together is the *duality-of-structure* scheme (Giddens, 1984: 25–9, 297–304).

Giddens starts by rejecting the actor/social-structure *dualism* found in the conventional social sciences, the idea of actors being constrained by social structures external to them, structures which set limits in the way that walls limit the movements of those within them. For Giddens, structure entails rules and resources that are both *means* and *outcome*, and in that sense they refer to both the subjective and the objective. They are subjective means in that they enable subjects to relate to other subjects in their social environment; they are objective outcomes in that every time rules and resources are used as means, every time they are actualized and so reproduced, they become more strongly institutionalized. Structures as rules and resources, therefore, relate to actors in terms of *duality* rather than *dualism*. There is no externality, no distance between actors and structures – the two are inextricably linked in the process of structuration. Social systems, from small groups and formal organizations to nation-states and global formations, are produced and reproduced via the duality-of-structure mechanism. When actors, in a taken-for-granted, routine manner, use rules and resources, they reproduce them – and in doing so they reproduce social wholes (Giddens, 1984: 1–40, 227–80).

As I argue more extensively in chapter 7, the displacement of the actor/social-structure dualism by that of duality generates serious problems. It neglects a fundamental dimension of action/interaction. The duality-of-structure scheme does not and cannot take into account situations where actors do not take rules and resources for granted but rather distance themselves from them for theoretical and/or strategic reasons.

Consider the institution of marriage for instance. Its continued reproduction is only partially explained by the duality mode, i.e. by the fact that millions use the relevant rules and resources in a routine, taken-for-granted manner. An adequate explanation of the reproduction of marriage rules must also include cases where powerful actors (such as legislators, religious elites, feminist leaders, patriarchally oriented politicians, etc.) distance themselves from rules and resources, with the intention of either changing or maintaining the status quo. In such cases we have not duality but actor–structure *dualism* on the paradigmatic level. Therefore, for a full explanation of the reproduction and/or transformation of marriage rules one has to take into account both duality and dualism (Mouzelis, 1991a: 25–47).

b. Bourdieu's transcendence strategy

Like Giddens, Bourdieu has sought to transcend the divide between the objectivist, structuralist paradigm on the one hand, and the subjectivist, phenomenological tradition on the other. Here it is via the famous *habitus* concept that the subject–object dualism is transcended, where habitus refers to the generative schemata (cognitive, perceptive and evaluative) that actors acquire in the course of their socializations. These generative schemata or dispositions enable actors to relate skilfully to others in varied social contexts. Bourdieu sees the habitus as entailing an objective dimension, given that it is based on the internalization of historically evolved and evolving objective social structures; it also entails a subjective dimension since (like Giddens' rules and resources) it is the means of relating to others, of participating in the games of everyday life (1990).

More precisely, in order to understand a certain type of social practice one must take into account the *positions* of the relevant *field* as well as the *dispositions* that actors carry with them and bring to the power games played in that field. Schematically, therefore, we have

Field/positions + dispositions = social practices

What this formula does not consider, however, is the interactive logic of a social situation or game (see chapters 7 and 8).

Although Bourdieu talks constantly about actors' strategies, he uses the strategy concept very idiosyncratically. For him, actors' strategies are more or less the automatic outcome of their dispositions/habitus. They do not entail the rational calculations, voluntaristic targeting and reflexive strategizing that interactive situations or games often show.[36] Yet the peripheralization of this type of voluntaristic element, the emphasis on strategies' quasi-automatic, quasi-unconscious nature is necessary if the subjectivist–objectivist divide is to be transcended. In other words, Bourdieu's attempt to overcome subject–object dualism conflates two dimensions of social games that should be kept analytically apart: the dispositional and the interactive. For, in order to fully understand a social game (regardless of whether it is in the field of religion, science, art, education, etc.), one has to pay attention not only to positions (roles) and dispositions (habitus), but also to its interactive dimension – which often entails calculations, reactions to the other players' strategies and reflexive accounting,[37] and the constant cognitive monitoring of the ongoing game. Bourdieu's attempt to accommodate all of the above within the habitus notion reduces its utility as a conceptual tool which helps the researcher to examine empirically the strategic games played in specific fields.[38] To put the above in Giddensian terminology, Bourdieu (like Giddens), in explaining social practices, brackets subject–object dualism (which entails the subject taking strategic and/or theoretical distance from rules and resources) and focuses on subject–object duality.[39]

---

[36] Bourdieu argues that 'the most profitable strategies are usually those produced without any calculation ... These strategies *without strategic calculation* produce an important secondary advantage for those who can scarcely be called their authors: the social approval accruing to apparent disinterestedness' (Bourdieu, 1990: 292, emphasis added).

[37] For the problematic connections between reflexivity and habitus in Bourdieu's theory, see chapter 8.

[38] It is precisely because of the underemphasis of the interactive element that Bourdieu's theory of practice has been criticized (rightly, I believe) as functionalist (Jenkins, 1991: 81ff). It is for the same reason that Bourdieu's very important empirical work on how various traits (economic, social, cultural) are distributed among specific groups or individuals has a static, social-stratificational character. His underemphasis of the strategic (in the conventional sense of the term) dimension of social games renders him unable to explain the constitution or transformation of the distributions he is studying. For such an explanation, systematic reference is required to the interactive games of macro-actors, to the historical struggles over the control of economic, political and cultural technologies – the outcome of which explains the specific form taken by the distributions of social traits. In a nutshell: Bourdieu's focus is more on the distributional than the interactive structures of social wholes (on this, see Mouzelis, 1995b: 114–16).

[39] In chapter 8, in examining how Bourdieu links the notion of habitus with that of reflexivity, I argue that the French sociologist underemphasizes not only interaction but also intra-action.

To sum up: both Giddens' and Bourdieu's attempts at transcending the subjectivist–objectivist divide fail. In both cases the procedure involves a subject–object conflation that leaves out of the analysis fundamental aspects of actors' strategizing. It is not surprising, therefore, that they inevitably bring in the subject–object, actor/institutional-structure distinction by the back door, so to speak. Giddens distinguishes between institutional analysis (system-integration analysis in Lockwood's terms) and analysis in terms of strategic conduct (Lockwood's social-integration perspective). Bourdieu too brings back the subjectivist–objectivist distinction when he talks about positions (or, in more conventional terms, roles) and *stance* (i.e. an actor's relation or reaction to his/her role or position). In chapter 7, I critically examine Giddens' and Bourdieu's transcendence strategies in greater detail.

8 The overall abolition of boundaries

If Giddens and Bourdieu have tried to cope with theoretical compartmentalization by transcending the boundary between objectivist and subjectivist theoretical traditions, postmodern theorists like Lyotard (1974) and Baudrillard (1979, 1983) have abolished boundaries altogether – not only between different sociological paradigms, but also between social sciences and the humanities. Respect for the autonomous logic of various disciplines or sub-disciplines is delegitimized, on the grounds that social-science fragmentation and compartmentalization are based less on cognitive reasons and more on administrative convenience or bureaucratic power games between academic elites. This facile solution of the compartmentalization issue results in an 'anything goes' situation. It leaves the social researcher free to pick and choose concepts from a variety of fields (psychoanalysis, linguistics, semiotics, literary criticism, cultural studies, etc.) without requiring him/her to translate or rework such concepts in order to integrate them in a theoretically coherent manner into a specific discipline.

This strategy of theoretical dedifferentiation or 'postdisciplinarity'[40] often leads to extremely crude, reductive forms of explanation as

---

[40] For an exposition and critique of postdisciplinarity, see McLennan, 2003. One can argue that Marxism, like postmodernism, is also against the boundaries existing among social-science disciplines. But Marxism replaces the theoretical division of labour among economics, politics and sociology, with a theoretically

complex institutional structures, multilevel social games, and macro-historical developments are all too easily explained by reference to signs, texts, the unconscious, desire, etc. The end result is the displacement of serious analysis by an obsessive search for the paradoxical, the obscure and enigmatic, the playful, and so on. Unfortunately, this ironic, highly imaginative, 'clever' but cognitively impotent theoretical posturing is tending to take a central role at a time when the means of economic, political and cultural production are more than ever concentrated in the hands of a few (mostly unaccountable) global actors, and when the majority of the earth's population is marginalized and excluded from the tremendous wealth that is generated by today's technologies.

It is in this context that social theory is turning its back on any attempt to offer conceptual tools for a macro-holistic understanding of how late-modern nation-states and the global networks within which they are embedded are constituted, reproduced and transformed. In the present self-indulgent, navel-gazing mood, serious attempts at the construction of a new holistic framework useful for the empirical study of national and global systems of institutions and actors are dismissed as 'grand narratives' conducive to foundationalism and/or authoritarianism.

Conclusion

While Parsonian functionalism overemphasizes system integration and tends to portray actors as passive, the interpretative micro-sociologies, by over-reacting to Parsons' too systemic, 'essentialist' tendencies, put exclusive emphasis on the actors' voluntaristic, agentic qualities with the result that both micro–macro and action–structure linkages are discouraged. As to the structuralists' decentring of the subject, it fails to show how the constitution and transformation of the 'hidden' codes they seek relate to the more 'surface' phenomena of actors' strategic orientations and the institutional contexts within which they are embedded. Post-structuralists, meanwhile, have abandoned the search for hidden grammars, but continue the decentring of the subject by focusing on 'subjectless' discursive practices or texts. However, this disconnection between subject and discourse prevents the raising of

congruent (albeit economistic) political economy. Postmodern theories abolish boundaries but put nothing in their place.

questions about the differential effectiveness of discourses, as well as about the mechanisms leading from the dominance of one type of discursive regime to that of another. Finally, more recent attempts at transcending the subjective–objective or the actor–structure divide in the social sciences tend to conflate the internalist/actor and the externalist/system perspective in such a way as to leave out of systematic investigation the 'strategizing' dimension of social games.

In several of the chapters that follow (particularly chapters 2 to 8 and 12 to 15), various aspects of the action–structure and the micro–macro problems are explored. The general underlying thesis is that these two fundamental divides in the social sciences should neither be abolished nor transcended; instead, one should create concepts which eliminate obstacles and enhance communication between micro and macro, as well as between action- and system-oriented approaches.

PART II

Parsonian and post-Parsonian developments

2 | Parsons and the development of individual rights

In dealing with the issues of rights and citizenship in modern societies, Parsons was very much influenced by T.H. Marshall's account of the successive development of civil, political and social rights in the United Kingdom. Given this, it is appropriate briefly to examine Marshall's contribution – before considering how Parsons integrated it into his broader, more theoretical framework.

1 T.H. Marshall: civil, political and social rights

With his elegant prose, which systematically eschewed sociological-theoretical jargon, Marshall (1964) based his analysis of citizenship on a rather non-deterministic theory of social differentiation. According to him, citizenship, as a movement for the spread of rights 'downwards', began in the seventeenth century together with the development of capitalism and the marked emergence of national consciousness.

But in the seventeenth century 'rights were blended because institutions were amalgamated' (1964: 72). It is in the eighteenth century that institutions became less 'amalgamated' (in evolutionist terminology, more differentiated), and a process of 'unblending' of rights can be discerned, with each category of rights (civil, political, social) beginning to acquire its own logic and dynamic trajectory. The civil aspects of citizenship developed first. Civil rights related to property, free speech, free association and other 'individual freedoms' gradually destroyed the feudal principles of social stratification, and durably established the principle of equality under the law. It was therefore in the legal sphere and, more specifically, in the institutional arena of the courts of justice, that we see the first thrust from 'subjects' to 'citizens', from a situation where different laws and juridical principles applied to different classes, to a situation where all were equal before the major legal codes of the national community.

The second step towards a 'defeudalized' community of citizens occurred in the nineteenth century with the gradual elimination of property qualifications and other restrictions to the right to vote and to be elected to Parliament. During this second phase, the focus shifted from the juridical to the legislative sphere as political participation increased, and the citizenship community became unitary not only in its legal but also in its political aspects.

Finally, according to Marshall, the third major advance in the construction of a unified civic community occurred in the twentieth century with the development of social rights – the right of everyone to a decent education, to health care and to provisions for old age. During this phase the institutional focus shifted again, this time from the political to the social sphere, as reflected in the massive development of schools, hospitals, health care and community centres, etc. The introduction of social rights is a move, however hesitant, from formal to substantive equality, from class inequalities to relative citizenship equality. Because, while class differences easily undermine both equality under the law and the one-person, one-vote principle, the spread of social rights gives greater substance and meaning to citizens' civil and political rights. It ensures that people's legal and political participation in the citizenship community is no mere formality.

This does not, of course, mean that the development of the social aspects of citizenship eliminates class inequalities. What it does mean is that there is a better, more solid balance between the principle of equality/solidarity, as expressed by the notion of citizenship, and the class principle of inequality/competition (1964: 84). In other words, under capitalist conditions, citizenship rights can never eliminate class inequalities, but they can certainly mitigate their worst excesses.

In so far as Marshall's account *describes* the broad macro-stages in the construction of the UK citizenship community, what are the basic mechanisms that *explain* such a transformation? Here Marshall's texts are less informative. Clearly, his overall aim was to provide a detailed description rather than explanation of the transformation. But in so far as he briefly refers to transformative mechanisms, these are seen from the point of view of agency rather than the social system. To use Lockwood's well-known distinction (Lockwood, 1964; Mouzelis, 1974), Marshall sees the development of rights from a social- rather than system-integration perspective. The spread of rights has more to do with collective actors and their struggles, and less with systemic requirements leading to differentiation and greater adaptive capacity.[1] Marshall points out, for instance, that the social aspects of citizenship would not have been possible without the prior acquisition of political rights that enabled the working classes to organize themselves politically. Moreover, it was only when the individual civil liberties of free speech and the right to form associations were exercised collectively (via the creation of trade unions) that the welfare state became a possibility (1964: 111).

2 T. Parsons: rights and revolutions

When Parsons appropriated Marshall's insights for his theory of citizenship, he placed them within a broader evolutionary and comparative perspective (Parsons, 1971). As noted already, in Marshall's analysis the theory of social differentiation is neither explicit, nor does it have any strong explanatory function. In Parsons' analysis, on the other hand, the neo-evolutionist framework of social differentiation takes centre stage. This framework allows him both to describe in a theoretically more sophisticated manner the long-term development of citizenship in modern societies in general, and to explain this trend from a systemic, functionalist (but non-teleological) perspective.

a. Economic and political differentiation

For Parsons, the first major breakthrough in the transition from early (less differentiated) to late (more differentiated) modernity came with the British Industrial Revolution. This great upheaval led to the constitution of an economic subsystem, which is clearly separate from the three other major societal subsystems (the goal-achievement/political, the integration/social-community and the latency/value-commitment subsystems). The great industrial transformation, by dramatically freeing land, capital and labour from ascriptive controls – by allowing these three 'factors of production' to follow a strictly economic/market logic – very quickly established an economic space with a logic quite distinct from that of the other three subsystems.

It is in this differentiated space that the American theorist locates Marshall's idea about the development of civil rights. It is civil rights

UK اسلاب: نقش , 6

differensia
+ion

econ
sub sys
رو ایجاد کرد

---

[1] For the concept of a social system's adaptive capacity, see Parsons, 1966: 22ff.

related to property, to contractual relations between labour and capital, to the freedom of all to sell their labour power as a commodity to the highest bidder; it is all the rights establishing everyone's equality not only under the law but also in the market-place, which sharply differentiate the adaptation/economic subsystem from the integration/social-community one (Parsons, 1971: 36ff).

The second major breakthrough in the long-term process of differentiation came with the French Revolution. This brought the distinct emergence of a national societal community (integration subsystem) that included all members, no longer on a particularistic basis but rather on a universalistic one. In this new context, therefore, the emphasis was less on economic freedom and more on political equality as this found expression in the French Declaration of the Rights of Man. It is here that citizenship becomes the central concept: 'the claim of the whole population on inclusion' (1971: 80) on the basis of one-man, one-vote. Moreover, the members of the societal community were to be considered not only free and equal, but 'also bound together in a national autonomous community' (1971: 83–4).

It is with this type of democratic revolution that the particularistic solidarity of the pre-modern communities (based as they were on ethnicity, language, religion, etc.) gave way to a universalistically defined solidarity leading to a non-fragmented, nationally unitary modern community. In this way, Marshall's idea of the development of political rights in the United Kingdom is generalized, and placed by Parsons in a conceptual framework that focuses on the differentiation of early modern societies into the integration and goal achievement subsystems.

Finally, if the first differentiation breakthrough came in Britain and the second in France, the third occurred on the other side of the Atlantic. In the United States, the development of civil and political rights was complemented, however rudimentarily, by the social right to education. It is in that country that a third revolution took place: the educational one which, in its consequences, was to be as crucial as its industrial and democratic predecessors.

Prior to the educational revolution, access to education in the United States was limited to a small elite. The mass of the population remained illiterate:

> To attempt to educate the *whole* population was a radical departure … This movement has thus meant an immense extension of equality of opportunity …

The relatively stable situation of late nineteenth-century Europe accorded higher education to a small elite group, never more than five percent of the age group. The United States has broken decisively with this limitation; the proportion of youth receiving some higher education is around 40 percent and is steadily edging upward. (1971: 95)

b. Educational differentiation

The educational revolution brought with it a radical differentiation between the societal community and the latency or pattern-maintenance subsystem. As is well known, Parsons' latency subsystem is concerned both with the institutionalization and maintenance of society's core values and with the strengthening of people's motivational commitments to such values. The educational revolution, by contributing significantly to both of these functional requirements, enabled the latency subsystem to become relatively autonomous from the societal community.

The above makes sense when one considers that in the United States the separation between church and state and the ensuing extreme religious pluralism has not led to the destruction of society's moral and value consensus (1971: 99). This was possible because of the process of *value generalization*: the generation of more abstract, general secular values that could provide a common denominator, an 'integrative' framework, subsuming the myriad differences in religious beliefs and world-views that the numerous religious denominations were putting forward.

In this context, the educational revolution played a crucial role. The extensive spread of university education and research related to 'intellectual disciplines' (including that of the social sciences) and to the 'arts' was then able to play the integrative role that established churches had been playing in previous, less differentiated contexts. In other words, the educational revolution introduced the broad institutionalization of a secular culture, the more generalized values of which could create moral consensus in a society marked by extreme religious pluralism and fragmentation.

Moreover, mass education has taken from the kinship unit some of its socializing functions, particularly those related to the work and occupational sphere:

Increasingly socialization with respect to achievement in non-familial roles is left to institutions, which are differentiated from the family. It is the educational system and not the family that increasingly serves as the direct source of labour for the economy. Similarly it is the educational system, and not kinship, that increasingly determines the distribution of individuals within the stratification system. (1971: 101)

This leads to a differentiated situation where, on the one hand, the latency subsystem (education) becomes more autonomous, while at the same time the societal community (integration subsystem) is organized more on meritocratic-universalistic lines and less on aristocratic-particularistic-ascriptive ones. If, therefore, the Industrial Revolution was the catalyst for a differentiation of the 'system of modern societies' along economic lines, and the French Revolution for doing so along political lines, the educational revolution accelerated the differentiation process along cultural lines. And, since the educational revolution first occurred in the United States, it is not surprising that the United States, portraying as it does an advanced combination of the three types of differentiation (economic, political and cultural), is placed at the top of modernity's evolutionary ladder.

This does not mean, of course, that all strains and incompatibilities between and within the differentiated subsystems have disappeared in that first fully developed modern society. According to Parsons' view of the US stratification system, although the criteria of classification have shifted from ascription to achievement, there is an inbuilt tension between the 'egalitarian' principle of citizenship, on the one hand, and the 'functional' principle of productivity and performance, on the other. The egalitarian principle stresses the inclusion of all community members as equal participants in a society based on the universalistic notion of citizenship; whereas the functional principle legitimized inequalities in terms of dissimilar capacities, dissimilar achievements and dissimilar contributions of members to the successful functioning of the whole. The tension between these two principles produces inequalities which, when combined with the persisting racial discrimination against the black population, creates enclaves or ghettoes that undermine social rights and the principle of the inclusion of all in a universalistically organized societal community.

While Parsons does consider these problems to be both real and serious, in the long run he thinks that such difficulties cannot reverse the trend towards increasing differentiation of the various subsystems and their balanced reintegration at a higher level of complexity and adaptive capacity. Indeed, at the time he was writing, Parsons thought that inequalities were less acute than they had been during the early stages of industrialization. Moreover, the persistence of particularistic mechanisms of exclusion based on race was for him a transitory phenomenon that was bound to weaken and disappear as socio-structural differentiation advanced further (1971: 111ff).

Summing up, Parsons both broadens and rearticulates in a more theoretical manner Marshall's account of the development of civil, political and social rights in the United Kingdom. He argues that the broad trend that Marshall traced in the UK can be seen in all modern or modernizing societies. He also believes that this trend can be better understood if looked at from the perspective of the three modern revolutions (the British industrial, the French democratic and the US educational). Via diffusion and/or other mechanisms, these revolutionary transformations have brought about the differentiation of modern societies along economic, political and cultural lines. From such a broader theoretical perspective the successive spread of civil, political and social rights to the population as a whole can be seen as the differentiation/autonomization from the societal community of the economic (adaptation), political (goal achievement), and value/pattern-maintenance subsystems respectively. The successive spread of rights also indicates the transition from a societal community organized on the basis of particularistic-exclusionary principles, to a citizenship community based on universalistic-inclusionary ones.

3 Differentiation and the mechanisms of change

How does Parsons' analysis of the spread of civil, political and social rights fit with his more abstract theory of social differentiation? Which are for him the underlying mechanisms that can explain (rather than merely describe) the transition from a particularistic-exclusionary to a universalistic-inclusionary societal community in modernity? In order to answer this question we shall have to focus more closely on Parsons' general scheme of evolutionary change (1966, 1977).

For Parsons, evolutionary change has four analytically distinct aspects:

(i) Differentiation: a unit or subsystem 'having a single, relatively well defined place in the society divides into units or subsystems (usually two) which differ in both structure and functional significance from the wider system' (1966: 22). They differ in functional significance in the sense that the new units, because they are regulated by more role-specific, distinctive norms, operate more effectively than the less differentiated units they are replacing.

(ii) The proliferation of new units increases complexity, and creates the key problem of *integrating* the more differentiated parts into the wider system.

(iii) Effective integration requires *value generalization*. It requires a shift from particularistic-ascriptive to more universalistic values. When we view the differentiated units in terms of roles, it is quite obvious that the replacement of more diffuse by more specialized roles creates problems of integration and co-ordination. These can be solved only by the emergence of more abstract, general, and hence more flexible, less situation-specific values that are able to subsume under their umbrella the more specific normative logic of the differentiated roles or role complexes.

When, on the other hand, we view differentiated parts in terms of collectivities or groups,[2] there is the problem of including newly created groups, or groups previously excluded, in the more complex, universalistically regulated social whole. 'Differentiation and upgrading processes may require the inclusion in a status of full membership in the relevant general community system of previously excluded groups which have developed legitimate capacities to "contribute" to the system's functional requirements' (1966: 22).

Therefore, whether one looks at differentiation in terms of roles or in terms of groups, in both cases mechanisms are needed for reintegrating the differentiated units along more universalistic lines. That is to say, the more generalized values must be capable of effectively integrating differentiated or specialized roles; they must also be capable of including formally excluded or newly created groups in the more universalistically organized community.

(iv) If and when integration of roles and inclusion of groups is successful, a process of *adaptive upgrading* is set in motion: the differentiated units are efficient because 'a wider range of resources is made available to

---

[2] In this context Parsons does consider groups and collectivities; but as I have argued in chapter 1, section 1, when collective actors do not disappear altogether, they are portrayed as passive products of systemic/structural determinations.

social units, so that their functioning can be freed from some of the restrictions of its (less differentiated) predecessors' (1971: 27).

How does the above evolutionist scheme explain the development of rights in modern societies? For Parsons, if it was the three major revolutions that provided the initial push towards differentiation, it was the successive spread of civil, political and social rights that facilitated and consolidated the post-revolutionary situation both by enhancing the autonomous logic of each differentiated subsystem and by providing some of the mechanisms for integrating them into a more complex societal whole.

To start with the Industrial Revolution: new technologies, in conjunction with other factors, resulted in the growth of the factory system and so in the greater differentiation between family and occupational roles.[3] In this context, it was civil rights (mainly related to contracts and property) that 'freed' the factors of production (labour, capital, land) from ascriptive ties – enabling them to follow more rigorously and legitimately the logic of the economic/adaptation subsystem. Simultaneously, the same rights, by creating (via the adaptive upgrading of the whole societal system) more 'free-flowing' resources and facilities (i.e. new resources not tied to ascriptive contexts), made possible the inclusion of new or previously excluded groups in the societal community as full members.

With the French Revolution, on the other hand, the development of political rights and the subsequent trend towards the democratic participation of citizens not only enhanced the autonomy of the polity (the goal achievement subsystem), it also provided political mechanisms for including in the societal community lower-class groups peripheralized or excluded by rapid industrialization. The same process we see again in the subsequent educational revolution, when integrative and inclusionary mechanisms were even more prominent.

4 Integration: balanced and unbalanced forms

If we consider the overall evolutionary process we call modernization, the spread of first civil, then political and finally social rights contributed, for Parsons, both to the enhancement of the differentiated logic of

---

[3] For a detailed analysis of how family and work roles were differentiated during the Industrial Revolution in England, see Smelser, 1962.

each of the four subsystems, and to their effective integration (via value generalization and inclusionary processes) into an adaptively upgraded societal whole. For the American theorist the successful integration of the differentiated parts into a more complex whole is not inevitable. Unlike nineteenth-century unilinear evolutionists, Parsons and his followers repeatedly stress the possibility of *integrative failures* and of *evolutionary regression*. What he fails to stress, however, is that integration, if and when it occurs, can take both *balanced* and *unbalanced* forms.[4] With regard more specifically to roles or institutional subsystems, the integration of the differentiated parts or units may take place in such a way that the logic of one institutional subsystem (e.g. the market logic of the adaptation subsystem) may dominate that of another or other subsystems. In that case, 'value generalization' has become 'value colonization' to use Habermas' (1987) terminology, with the specific values of one subsystem displacing or undermining the values of another or others.

To express the above in terms of groups/collectivities rather than roles/institutions, the inclusion of new or previously excluded groups can take both *autonomous* and *heteronomous* forms. In the first case, the *only* case that Parsons considers, the integrated groups become full members of the societal community. In the second case, there is inclusion without 'full membership': inclusion does not eliminate the distinction between first- and second-class members.

Let us take an obvious example: poor peasants may be included in the central mechanisms of the nation-state via universal army conscription, but this type of 'bringing-in', unless accompanied by the acquisition or granting of political and social rights, is a highly authoritarian form of inclusion. It does bring 'outsiders' into the political centre, but in a very heteronomous manner. The same is true when inclusion (as in Bismarck's Germany or Perón's Argentina) entails the paternalistic granting of social benefits while at the same time withholding the granting of political or trade union rights.[5]

Parsons can argue, of course, that sooner or later inclusion in one sphere will lead to inclusion in other spheres as well – at least when there

---

[4] For a critique of Parsons' differentiation theory along similar lines, see Alexander, 1998a. See also chapter 4.
[5] For a development of the concepts of autonomous and heteronomous inclusion, see chapter 9.

is no evolutionary regression and the process of adaptive upgrading continues to be consolidated. But this argument is fallacious, because stable integration and impressive adaptive upgrading can be perfectly compatible with highly heteronomous forms of inclusion. This is the case, for instance, of the Asian type of capitalist modernization that portrays various degrees of authoritarianism, from the Japanese partial suppression of trade union autonomy, to the Chinese quasi-totalitarian forms of rule. Despite the 'Asian crisis' some time ago, there is no doubt that the export-orientated, so-called 'developmental' states of the Asian Pacific are more capable of achieving Parsons' adaptive upgrading in the increasingly global economy than are the profoundly anti-developmental states to be found in the capitalist periphery or semi-periphery – whether they are democratic or not (Haggard, 1990; Wade and Veneroso, 1998). In Asian countries, the people are certainly 'included', being drawn into the modernizing centre (both in the sense that they have much closer ties with the central state and in the sense of sharing some of the wealth produced); yet at the same time this inclusion is heteronomous/unbalanced rather than autonomous/balanced as far as the granting of civil and political rights is concerned.

To give a rather different example: in Western developed societies modes of adaptive upgrading can be identified that entail value colonization rather than value generalization on the level of roles/institutions; and heteronomous rather than autonomous inclusion on the level of groups/collectivities. In fact, since the 1974 worldwide economic crisis and the subsequent accentuation of neoliberal globalization, many societies have shown a marked trend towards growing unemployment as well as growing inequalities, which has led to the economic and social peripheralization of large sections of their populations. These processes have taken place in an institutional context where the market logic of productivity and competition colonizes the logic of solidarity in the social one. In such cases, therefore, there is *unbalanced* integration and *heteronomous* inclusion *with* adaptive upgrading: the economy keeps growing, resources and facilities increase, but without 'value generalization' or 'full-membership' inclusion.

To put this differently: Parsons' four dimensions of evolutionary change do not always vary in the same direction. There can be differentiation and adaptive upgrading with forms of integration that are unbalanced-authoritarian rather than balanced-democratic. There can also be forms of inclusion that by no means guarantee 'full membership' to previously excluded groups. There can be, that is to say, *post-traditional*, highly differentiated and even stable societal systems based on particularistic rather than universalistic forms of solidarity.

This kind of situation can by no means be considered as transitional. If one refuses to reify the societal system, it is obvious that there are no automatic, systemic mechanisms for leading modern societies from unbalanced to balanced forms of integration, or from particularistic to universalistic modes of inclusion. Such a shift is indeed possible – but it will never be realized because of 'systemic needs' for equilibrium and balance. There is no 'systemic' reason in modernity favouring balance rather than imbalance, value generalization rather than value coloniza- tion, a decrease rather than increase in economic and political inequal- ities. Both modes of integration are, to use evolutionary language, non-regressive – they are both compatible with the growing differentia- tion and complexity of late-modern social structures.

Whether the present highly unbalanced forms of integration will persist or not depends on collective struggles and their outcome. For the moment, the decline of trade unionism, the prevailing 'casino capit- alism' of the world economic system, and the market fundamentalism that characterizes the World Bank, the IMF and similar organizations, obstruct the shift from unbalanced to balanced modes of integration. Given, however, that the current neoliberal type of globalization may in the future change in the direction of more global regulation (via, for instance, the political unification of social democratic Europe), the possibility of less callous forms of modernity cannot be ruled out (Mouzelis, 1995a).

Conclusion

Looking, with the benefit of hindsight, at the elements that Marshall's and Parsons' view of the development of rights have in common, we may say that both social theorists have given us a rather linear, over- optimistic view of the spread of rights and the development of citizen- ship in the twentieth century. Writing at a time (i.e. before the world economic crisis of the 1970s) when capitalist growth seemed to be compatible with low unemployment and conventional, social demo- cratic forms of welfare, the acquisition of rights by the underprivileged was viewed as a cumulative, quasi-irreversible process.

The continued economic crisis, the abrupt liberalization of financial markets and the rise of neoliberal ideologies have created a post-Cold War context within which the balance between capital and labour has been upset in favour of the former, class parties and ideologies are on the decline and the threat of communism no longer operates as an incentive to improve the lot of marginalized populations in the third and/or first worlds. In a certain way, the situation at present reminds one, as far as labour–capital relations are concerned, of the period of early industrialization where the weak organization of the newly emerging working class and the non-interventionist character of the state led to extreme forms of exploitation (see Thompson, 1963). One sees a similar capital–labour imbalance today on the global level. The extreme mobility of multinational capital, the difficulty of labour in organizing globally and the absence of a socially oriented global governance is leading to new forms of overexploitation both on the level of the nation-state and on that of the globalized economy and society.[6] In this new situation, which neither Marshall nor Parsons foresaw,[7] the civil, political and social rights that seemed so irreversibly established have been seriously undermined.

To be fair, neither Marshall's nor Parsons' account of the development of rights is, strictly speaking, deterministic. But on this point there is a fundamental difference between the two theorists. Marshall's very hesitant evolutionism led him to view the mechanisms leading to the

---

[6] The Scandinavian countries are an exception to the above trends. Countries like Sweden, for instance, managed to contain growing inequalities and to achieve relatively high rates of growth and low unemployment despite the neoliberal global context. The United States, on the other hand, has achieved, in recent years, reasonable growth and low unemployment at the expense of inclusionary forms of integration (deterioration of work conditions, growing inequalities, peripheralization of large sections of the population); see Sapir, 2005. On the other hand, it must be mentioned here that despite growing inequalities (within and between nation-states), neoliberal globalization has led to a situation where the percentage of the planet's population that lives under conditions of absolute poverty has decreased.

[7] If Parsons did not foresee the economic crisis of the 1970s, he was more successful in predicting the collapse of communism. By theorizing democracy as an evolutionary universal, he argued that in late modernity the Soviet Union would either have to open up and become more democratic (as the only way of moving to higher levels of differentiation and adaptive capacity), or, if it failed to do so, would be peripheralized (Parsons, 1964a). See also chapter 3.

development of rights from a social-integration, agency perspective. For him it was mainly the working class acquiring the right to vote that explained not only the processes of growing democratization, but also the spread of social rights downwards. Marshall, therefore, would have no difficulty in accepting, without any radical restructuring of his conceptual framework, the present-day challenge to the spread of social rights and the possibility of a reversal of the 'progressive' movement towards full citizenship.

For Parsons the situation is different. In his case the optimistic scenario is built into the very conceptual scheme that he uses. What is happening today not only was not envisaged by him, but also challenges his oversystemic, functionalist framework. By locating the development of rights within his theory of differentiated adaptive upgrading, Parsons has made it possible to compare the spread-of-rights process in different developed societies and to link it with broader macro-historical developments. On the other hand, his functionalist schema is so constructed that it is unable to allow for the fact that differentiation and adaptive upgrading can, in conditions of late modernity, be institutionalized in a variety of ways – some of them encouraging, others discouraging or obstructing, the spread of rights downwards. In other words, Parsons' neo-evolutionist framework prevents the student of modernity from realizing that the integration of differentiated roles can take both balanced and unbalanced forms; or that the inclusion of the lower social strata in the societal community can be both autonomous and heteronomous.

This insensitivity to the possibility of the existence of highly differentiated 'adaptive', stable, and at the same time unjust, unequal, unbalanced, authoritarian social arrangements is directly due to the fact that Parsonian functionalism (as many critics have pointed out) overemphasizes system and underemphasizes social integration.[8] In his middle and late work, Parsons' oversystemic conceptualization led him to put increasing weight on how roles and institutional subsystems shape actors' behaviour, and less on how the latter construct, reproduce and transform institutional structures (Mouzelis, 1995b: 69–81). In other words, he put greater emphasis on social actors as products rather than producers of their social world.

---

[8] See, on this point, Lockwood, 1964.

3 | Evolution and democracy: Parsons and the collapse of communism

In the previous chapter, I argued that Parsons' attempt to link institutional differentiation with exclusively balanced, democratic forms of integration led him to overlook the possibility that unbalanced, authoritarian forms of differentiation/integration can achieve both durability and increased adaptive capacity. In this chapter I examine another way by which Parsons has tried to link differentiation/modernization with the prevalence, in the *longue durée*, of democratic forms of integration/governance.[1]

A standard comment in relation to the democratic revolution in Eastern Europe is that nobody in the social sciences managed to foresee the spectacular collapse of the collectivist regimes in those countries and/or theoretically explain what brought it about. In this respect, Parsons, for years the *bête noire* of radical and Marxist sociology, is the one conspicuous exception. In an article published in the 1960s (Parsons, 1964a), he developed a set of evolutionist notions that throw some light on the cataclysmic changes experienced since 1989 by Eastern European societies.

1 Evolutionary universals

In his late work, Parsons tried to inject his structural-functionalist approach with some dynamism by integrating it with a neo-evolutionist perspective (Parsons, 1964a, 1966). Central to this perspective are the notions of *structural-functional differentiation* (as this has been developed by classical sociology and anthropology) and of a society's *adaptive capacity*. As societies move from lower to higher levels of complexity, multifunctional social units (such as extended kinship groups) become less self-contained, their functions being taken

---

[1] An earlier version of this chapter appeared in *Theory, Culture and Society*, vol. 10 (1993).

over by more specialized institutions. This process of differentiation –
provided it is accompanied by an effective integration of the differentiated parts – makes possible a more effective mobilization of available
resources, and therefore a more successful adaptation to the changing
environment.

Within this perspective Parsons uses what he calls *evolutionary universals* in an attempt to define some of the mechanisms that allow
societies to increase dramatically their adaptive capacities. Evolutionary
universals are institutional innovations or breakthroughs which make
possible a given society's move to higher levels of differentiation and
adaptive capacity:

Evolutionary universals are innovations endowing societies with a very substantial increase in generalized adaptive capacity – so substantial that societies
lacking them are relatively disadvantaged. And that not so much from the
point of view of survival, but rather from the point of view of the opportunity
to institute further major developments. (Parsons, 1964a: 240)

Starting from the primitive stage, Parsons identifies four structural
features common to all human societies. These are kinship, religion,
language and technology. Thereafter, along the road from primitive to
more advanced developmental stages, he postulates six key evolutionary breakthroughs: those of social stratification, cultural legitimation,
money and markets, bureaucracy, a universalistic legal system and
'democratic association'.

The full institutionalization of the last two universals marks the
stage of modernity. Concerning particularly 'democratic association',
although one sees elements of it in the ancient Greek *polis*, in the
municipia of the Roman Empire, and the late-medieval Italian and
North European city-states, it is only in eighteenth-century Western
Europe that democracy put down strong roots and led to the eventual
adoption of universal suffrage and of the other major features of parliamentary democracy (freely elected leadership, secret ballot, account-
ability for decisions to a total electorate, etc.).

For Parsons, the above features, as they have been developed and
strongly institutionalized in Western capitalist societies,[2] are not simply

---

[2] Parsons has written extensively on the democratic features of the American
political system. Against both left-wing critics (such as C. W. Mills) and right-wing
ones (such as followers of McCarthy), he argued that democratic pluralism in the

transitory aspects of development, nor peculiar to Western European culture. Moreover, he does not think, as certain Marxists tend to, that political pluralism and the alternation of political parties in government are merely epiphenomenal expressions of underlying class divisions. Instead, he sees them as universally necessary preconditions if large-scale industrial societies are to move to higher levels of complexity and adaptive capacity. The more complex the society, the more it needs effective political organization; and this in turn requires that it is based on the broad societal consensus that only widespread democratization can achieve.

In consequence, Parsons considers industrial societies that have failed to achieve parliamentary democracy (independently or derivatively) as not merely different from Western capitalist ones, but also, from an evolutionist point of view, more *archaic*. As they continue to lack participatory and pluralistic political institutions, they will show rigidities and 'dysfunctions' which will eventually peripheralize them in an increasingly interdependent modern world order:

I realize that to take this position I must maintain that communist totalitarian organization will probably not fully match 'democracy' in political and integrative capacity in the long run. *I do indeed predict that it will prove to be unstable and will either make adjustments in the general direction of electoral democracy and a plural party system or 'regress' into generally less*

postwar United States was threatened neither by a communist conspiracy nor by the industrial-military complex (see, on this point, Baxton, 1985: 146–64).

In a paper (1964b) published at approximately the same time as his evolutionary universals article, Parsons develops an argument which comes close to the convergence thesis: capitalist societies, through a more egalitarian distribution of resources, and socialist ones, through a growing division of labour which undermines monolithic political controls, are not such antagonistic or antithetical social systems as they appear on the surface.

However, even here Parsons' emphasis is on the impossibility of communism surviving in the long term:

In the same sense in which strict Calvinism and Jacobinism were short-lived, it seems as certain as such things can be that communism also will prove to be short-lived. The basis of this judgement is the hypothesis, first of all, that the iron dictatorship of a self-appointed elite cannot be legitimized in the long run ... The basic dilemma of the communists is that it is not possible in the long run either to legitimize dictatorship of the Party or to abolish all governmental and legal controls of behaviour, as the 'withering-away' doctrine would have it. Political democracy is the only possible outcome – except for general destruction or breakdown. (Parsons, 1964b: 396–7) *advanced and politically less effective forms of organization, failing to advance as rapidly or as far as otherwise may be expected.* (Parsons, 1964a: 356, emphasis added)

When these arguments first appeared in print in the mid 1960s – a period marked by the ascendancy of Althusserian Marxism and the facile dismissal of Parsonian sociology as vacuous, static and conservative – they were criticized as grossly ethnocentric and naive. To label the 'socialist' societies of the Soviet bloc as developmentally backward, and to put Western democracies at the top of the evolutionary scale, sounded at that time more like Cold War propaganda than serious analysis. In the 1960s, 'serious' sociological analysis of capitalist and collectivist industrial societies was based on the belief that these societies neither could nor should be ranked in terms of evolutionary backwardness or advancement. To do so was condemned as blatantly ideological.

That this was so becomes very clear indeed if Parsons' contribution is seen in the wider context of the protracted discussions of the 1960s on the future course of capitalist and 'socialist' industrial societies. Early on in the decade, this debate revolved around the well-known *convergence thesis* developed by Kerr *et al.* (1962). This posited that there is a marked tendency of the social structures (and particularly the stratification systems) of capitalist and socialist industrial societies to converge, this convergence being due to the similarity of the technological infrastructures underpinning all industrial societies. It was held that, given these similar technologies, occupational structures and the rewards systems linked with them would tend to become more alike as industrialism advanced in both East and West.

Critics of the convergence thesis, meanwhile, were arguing that superficial similarities notwithstanding, capitalist and socialist societies are fundamentally different on the level of economic, political and cultural social organization. Moreover, since technological similarities (to the extent that they matter) do not automatically or necessarily lead to common features on the level of socio-political and cultural institutions, it becomes quite obvious that capitalist and collectivist societies portray qualitatively different, non-convergent developmental trajectories.

In other words, whereas the advocates of the convergence thesis were theorizing a long-term, two-way movement towards decreasing differences, their opponents kept arguing that such a trend was neither discernible at that time nor probable in the future, given the different logic and internal dynamic of the two systems (Goldthorpe, 1967).

Parsons' analysis of the evolutionary universals, although not directly related to the above debate, entails a rejection of both the convergence and the anti-convergence thesis. He did not regard the communist societies as simply qualitatively different from the capitalist ones (as the opponents of the convergence thesis were implying), but above all as *more archaic*: from an evolutionary perspective they were at a lower level of differentiation and adaptive capacity. So if there was going to be a diminution of the differences between capitalist and collectivist societies, this would not be the *two-way* process of the convergence theorists, but a one-way move. He predicted that if the collectivist societies wished to avoid peripheralization, they would be forced to open up and adopt more liberal, democratic forms of organization.

2 The limits of modernization from above

I think that despite the problematic links that Parsons established between differentiation/integration and adaptive capacity (see chapter 2), his analysis provides useful insights for understanding the recent developments in Eastern European societies. It would be a pity if the unpopularity of evolutionist notions with sociologists today were to make one overlook the fact that Parsons predicted the course of events in Eastern Europe both accurately and with theoretical rigour.

Furthermore, Parsons' argument can be extended by applying a similar logic to not only the political but also the socio-economic level of organization. Adopting a long-term developmental perspective, it can be argued that modernization from above – so vigorously pursued by the tsarist government during the second half of the nineteenth century and pushed to its grotesque extreme by Stalin's industrialization drive – did work in the initial stages, when the primary purpose was the creation of a heavy industrial sector. There is no doubt that, despite its enormous human cost, Stalinist industrialization, and the overall planning that went with it, did make Soviet Russia into a world power with a markedly enhanced 'adaptive capacity'.

However, subsequent changes in the international division of labour, and the world shift from heavy industry and the Fordist mass production model of capital accumulation to the post-industrial emphasis on services, flexible specialization and the other well-known trends of the post-Fordist era, proved the Soviet command economy pathetically inadequate for coping with the new realities. In other words, what had partially worked during the take-off period – when, following Gerschenkron (1982), the later one enters the race the more one has to mobilize resources in a highly centralized manner – fell disastrously short at later stages of development. In the end, given the radical expansion of the mass media and the growing interpenetration of nation-states, it became impossible to conceal this inadequacy from the peoples of Eastern Europe. These factors, in combination with the political shortcomings discussed above and with *perestroika* unleashing nationalist sentiments that had been brutally suppressed for so long, do elucidate to a substantial extent the sudden collapse of collectivism in Eastern Europe.

3 Some critical remarks

I believe that Parsons' notion of 'democratic association' as an evolutionary universal considerably clarifies the nature of the recent democratic revolution in Eastern Europe. His view of Western parliamentary democracy, not as a historical peculiarity of Western societies but as a universal and necessary (though not by itself sufficient) precondition for effective adaptation and survival in the modern world, does point to some of the reasons that explain the extraordinary retreat or collapse of authoritarian regimes in a great number of *industrialized* countries all over the globe.

Needless to say, Parsons' insightful analysis of Western democratic institutions and their evolutionary potential in the modern world should not blind us to certain gross misconceptions in his overall scheme. These include its oversystemic character and its conceptualization of societal values as disembodied entities regulating all developments behind actors' backs (see chapter 1, section 1).

Adopting a different conceptual framework, one could argue for instance that Parsons' prediction was right, but for the wrong reasons. In fact, contra Parsons, a society can be highly 'adaptive' in the global order of late modernity without democratizing its polity. This is quite obvious from the impressive development of Asian capitalism. As I pointed out in the previous chapter, whether one looks at the quasi-authoritarian structures of Japanese capitalism, the repressive organization of South Korea and Taiwan or the dictatorial Chinese polity – in all these cases 'adaptive capacity' has been enhanced without democratization, i.e. without balanced or inclusionary forms of social integration.[3] Therefore an attempt at understanding the collapse of communism should focus less on democracy and more on the structure of the Soviet communist state and its relationship to the rapidly changing world order.

Looking at this relationship from a macro-historical, comparative perspective makes it clear that, in the European context at least, *as the inter-state system changes*, single states have to change their internal organization drastically if they are to avoid peripheralization or extinction. This becomes obvious if one adopts a long-term historical perspective.

To start with 'pre-modern' *European absolutism*, the French model of centralized patrimonialism (as shaped by Louis XIV and his successors) rapidly spread to the rest of continental Europe, all major states adopting more centralized forms of tax collecting, army organization, population surveillance, etc. Given this new system of inter-state relations, any state that failed to centralize (e.g. Poland) was condemned to peripheralization, partition or extinction (Anderson, 1974).

Something similar happened when the inter-state system of European absolutism gave way to the system of European *nation-states*. If European absolutism entailed drastic centralization of the means of violence and taxation at the top, the nineteenth-century nation-state entailed further centralization as well as an unprecedented state penetration of the societal periphery. Unlike all pre-industrial states (including the absolutist state), the bureaucratic machinery of the nation-state destroys segmental localism and draws the whole population into the broader economic, political, social and cultural arenas of the national centre (Bendix, 1969; Mann, 1986). Once the inter-state system of nation-states is consolidated, any state failing to 'modernize' (i.e. to make the shift from segmental localism to differentiated national arenas) tends to become peripheral or to break up (e.g. the Ottoman, Romanov, Habsburg imperial states).

---

[3] One can argue, of course, that regimes like the Chinese are bound to 'open up' their polity – since further development will create a mass of middle strata who will press for democratization. This has to some extent happened in South Korea and Taiwan (see Haggard, 1990).

Today we are rapidly moving from a system of nation-states with predominantly military/geopolitical orientations to a system of predominantly economic/developmental ones – a system of nation-states based less on geopolitical and more on market competition. Within this newly emerging inter-state system, any nation-state with an *anti-developmental* character (i.e. any nation-state that systematically sacrifices the logic of economic productivity and competition for that of political domination or religious indoctrination, for instance) is bound to either collapse (the Soviet state) or be relegated to the periphery (North Korea, Cuba).

One can argue therefore that the collapse of Soviet communism has to do less with its democratic and more with its developmental deficit. Within the *neoliberal global order* of economically competing nation-states, an anti-developmental state such as the Soviet one is like a giant with leaden feet – totally disabled from participating in a race where the main competitors must run fast not only to win but in order to keep themselves in the game at all.[4]

To conclude: despite the shortcomings discussed above there is no doubt that, as the recent reassessments of Parsonian sociology have stressed, there is much more to Parsons' *oeuvre* than such early critics as Mills (1959) and Dahrendorf (1959) have implied. There is also no doubt that evolutionism, whatever its present unpopularity, is here to stay. It is simply not possible to entirely eliminate certain basic evolutionist notions (such as structural-functional differentiation, evolutionary breakthroughs, etc.) from any serious attempt to understand how complex societies are constituted, reproduced and transformed.[5]

---

[4] Contrary to conventional wisdom, globalization does not entail the demise of the nation-state – in the short or the long term. But it does entail the weakening of *statism* and the decline or disappearance of profoundly anti-developmental states like the communist ones.

[5] For the way in which the concept of differentiation is essential for understanding the unique features of modernity, see chapter 9 below.

4 | Post-Parsonian theory I: neo-functionalism and beyond

Introduction

In the previous two chapters I critically examined some of the strong and weak points of Parsons' functionalist-evolutionist theory and its relevance in understanding democratizing tendencies in the modern world. In the following two chapters I examine some of the writings of two theorists, Alexander and Joas, who, although taking Parsons' work seriously, try to restructure it in an attempt to resolve some of its more problematic aspects.[1]

If Parsons is the father of sociological theory, Jeffrey Alexander in the United States and Anthony Giddens in Britain are his main heirs presumptive. Like Parsons, they both try to create a set of concepts to help raise interesting sociological questions and investigate the social world in a non-empiricist, theoretically rigorous manner.

Giddens' theorizing is quite as 'grand' as Parsons'. His aim, at least in his more theoretically orientated work (1984), is to provide a fully worked-out post-Parsonian armoury of concepts, with the help of which we can conceptualize sociologically major dimensions of social life (such as power or trust), compare different types of social systems, and establish logically coherent linkages between different levels of analysis and different ways of viewing the social.

Alexander's theorizing, without being any less significant, is less 'grand' in two senses. For one thing, he tries to retain, in more or less restructured form, some major components of the Parsonian edifice, and for another he offers us, on a more modest scale, a set of 'tactical' concepts that attempt to bring Parsonian functionalism and the various theoretical reactions to, or critiques of, Parsons that developed from the 1960s onwards closer together.

---

[1] An earlier version of this chapter (without the postscript) appeared as a review article in *Sociological Forum*, vol. 14 (1999).

Both Alexander's and Giddens' work can be located in what the former has called the 'third wave' of postwar social theorizing. If the first wave was dominated by Parsonian theory, and the second by various paradigms (symbolic interactionism, ethnomethodology, structuralism, neo-Marxism, etc.) which, partly at least, can be seen as reactions to the serious shortcomings of the Parsonian synthesis, the third wave has, again, a synthesizing character. It is marked by works that try to put an end to the 'war of paradigms' of the second wave and to overcome the extreme fragmentation and compartmentalization that these conflicts engendered.

More specifically, in their attempts to overcome the fragmentation brought about in the 1960s and 1970s, Parsons' two major successors have chosen different strategies. Giddens (like Bourdieu) tries to 'transcend' the subjectivist–objectivist divide in the social sciences by constructing a conceptual framework (his structuration theory) that combines in a novel manner elements from structural and structuralist sociologies on the one hand and interpretative sociologies on the other. In contrast to this, Alexander opts less for 'transcendence' and more for 'rapprochement'. As I see it, his rapprochement strategy consists of two basic moves.

His first move is an attempt to reassess the Parsonian *oeuvre*, which had been misinterpreted and rejected in the 1960s and 1970s in a rather crude and/or facile manner. This reassessment entails not only a more accurate and subtle interpretation of Parsons' writings, but also a systematic attempt at restructuring some of its basic components in the light of various criticisms from not only the interpretatively oriented micro-sociologies but also from conflict theory, historically oriented neo-Marxist macro-sociologies, etc. For instance, in the past two decades Alexander and other neo-functionalists have tried to inject the notion of social struggle and class conflict into Parsons' functionalism in general, and into his neo-evolutionist differentiation theory in particular (Alexander, 1985; Alexander and Colomy, 1990).

With this first move, Alexander and his colleagues, together with theorists from other and different theoretical traditions (e.g. Habermas, Luhmann) have rehabilitated Parsons as a classical thinker whose work (like that of Marx, Durkheim and Weber) constitutes a permanent source of inspiration to all social scientists, irrespective of their theoretical orientations and preferences.

Alexander's second move towards 'rapprochement' is clearly reflected in the two books under review here, *Neo-Functionalism and After* (1998a) and *Real Civil Societies* (1998b). Although still retaining some major features of Parsons' original work, it aims at a more radical restructuring that leads from neo-functionalism to 'post-functionalism'. This second move, as Alexander himself makes clear, can mainly be seen in three areas: the theories of action, of culture and of civil society. In all three of these, Alexander proposes a profound restructuring of Parsons' functionalism in the light of the two major theoretical breakthroughs that gained momentum towards the end of Parsons' life, breakthroughs that Parsons himself did not take seriously into account: the culturalist-linguistic turn in the social sciences, and the 'micro-sociological revolution'. Let us now see what Alexander proposes for the above-mentioned three areas.

1 The theory of action

In reconceptualizing action, Alexander starts with the well-known Parsonian analytic distinction between the cultural, the social and the personality system. As already mentioned, on the level of the cultural system, Parsons views values in a highly abstract, 'disembodied' manner. On the level of the social system, however, they become, via institutionalization, the norms or normative expectations embodied in the various social roles that we routinely play. These norms, in turn, become needs/dispositions on the level of the personality system via socialization and internalization. Alexander considers the distinguishing of these three analytical levels a definite advance that should not be discarded. In fact, it should be consolidated and improved by viewing the cultural, social and personality systems as three 'environments' of action. Two of these (the cultural and the personality, or psychological) are *internal* to the actor, whereas the social environment is *external*. In his *Neo-Functionalism and After*, action is coded by the cultural environment and motivated by 'personalities' (Alexander, 1998a: 215). More specifically, cultural and motivational patterns that help to shape action are, ontologically speaking, not external but internal to the actor. The social environment, by contrast, in so far as it consists of social networks formed by persons through their interactions in time and space, is external to a situated actor.[2]

---

[2] Perhaps a more satisfactory way of expressing the qualitative difference between cultural and psychological environment on the one hand, and social environment on the other, is to replace internal/external with the linguistically

However, neither cultural codes nor motivational patterns or social networks can, in themselves, explain the concrete activities of human beings. In order to understand how the three environments articulate with each other and lead to specific action, one has to take *agency* into account. As a major dimension of a person's subjectivity, agency entails the processes of *typification*, *invention* and *'strategization'*. Alexander contends that it is via these 'free will' agentic processes – as they articulate with each other and with the cultural, social and psychological environments – that the actor (as a person who acts and interacts with other persons in time and space) is constituted (1998a: 210–16).

For Alexander, therefore, action must never be conflated with agency. It is agency as an *analytic dimension of action* which entails the creativity, spontaneity and unpredictability described by interpretative sociologists. In this sense it is misleading to characterize the social actor in general as knowledgeable, self-reflective, rational, creative, etc. For whether the agentic qualities of actors will lead to knowledgeable, rational or creative ways of acting will depend on how the external and internal environments of action articulate with agency. Given certain types of cultural codes and motivational patterns, or given certain types of social network, action can perfectly well be ignorant rather than knowledgeable, irrational/non-rational rather than rational, and mechanistic rather than creative (Alexander, 1998a: 218).

2 The theory of culture

In the problem area of culture, Alexander concedes that Parsons' schema of the cultural, social and personality systems does respect the relative autonomy of the cultural field, in so far as it allows us to avoid conflating the cultural and the social levels of analysis. However, Parsons, being more interested in the internal differentiation and integration of the social than the cultural system, did not seriously investigate the symbolic structure of the cultural sphere *per se*. Instead, his functionalism led him to view cultural narratives and symbols as *values* whose institutionalization is related to the basic needs or functional requirements of the social system. Therefore, while Parsons did not

derived virtual/actual or paradigmatic/syntagmatic distinction. For the use of this distinction in a critique of Giddens' structuration theory, see chapter 7.

actually reduce the cultural to the social, he certainly neglected to investigate the cultural as such. He never seriously considered culture as *'langue'* (in the Saussurian sense), as a symbolic universe whose internal logic and hidden grammar should be studied or understood independently of 'external' contexts (such as the functional requirements of the social system; see the postscript to this chapter).

The same culturalistic critique can be addressed, according to Alexander, to those who view values less in terms of systemic needs and more as 'material' interests. Gramsci, for instance, exactly like Parsons, allows for the autonomy of the cultural-ideological sphere but does not take this autonomy into proper account. He is less interested in the internal logic or structure of the symbolic sphere than in the way in which symbolic constructions are shaped by economic interests. Therefore both Parsonian functionalism and Gramscian Marxism, despite assertions to the contrary, underplay the cultural-symbolic dimension and overplay the social one.

However, while the semiotic approach to culture has succeeded in establishing the importance of analysing culture as a relatively self-contained symbolic whole, it often tends to go to the other extreme: failing to show how the autonomous cultural logic, how narratives and/ or cultural codes, articulate with 'external' contexts, with political struggles, economic interests or systemic exigencies.

For Alexander, the 'dramaturgical' approach to culture seems to strike a better balance between ultra-culturalism and the underemphasis of the autonomous symbolic logic of culture that we find in the work of Parsons or Gramsci. Dramaturgically orientated theorists like Goffman (1959, 1961) or Geertz (1964, 1973), for instance, link the cultural-symbolic with its external contexts via what Alexander calls 'aesthetic performance'. For instance, Geertz, in his famous account of Balinese cock-fighting, manages to describe the phenomenon itself in depth, but without neglecting the various social contexts (e.g. status differences of the players) within which it takes place.

Cockfighting is neither a functional reinforcement of status distinctions – a view Geertz attributes to functionalism – nor an automatic deduction from texts. It is an active, aesthetic achievement, an art form that renders ordinary experience comprehensible by casting it into an exaggerated dramatic form. Geertz insists that it is the actors and the event that create this structure, not the structure that creates the event. (Alexander and Seidman, 1990: 15)

3 Action and culture: a critical assessment

Alexander's radical restructuring of Parsons' three-system model is a significant step forward. It combines the useful Parsonian emphasis on the analytic dimensions of action with the interpretive micro-sociologists' less analytic but equally valuable focus on the actor as producer rather than product of the social world. What is even more significant is that this synthetic endeavour, this rapprochement between functionalism and subjectivist approaches, is not haphazard but firmly based on a set of new concepts that manage to retain valuable elements of both the Parsonian and the interpretatively orientated micro-sociological traditions. So the former's useful three-system analytical schema (cultural, social and personality systems) is retained, but in such a way as to avoid Parsons' misleading unidirectional portrayal of concrete action as the passive result of cultural values having become institutionalized into norms and internalized into needs/dispositions. Parsons' puppet-like portrayal of social actors has been repeatedly and rightly criticized as one-sided (see chapter 1, section 1). While it shows how values, norms and needs/dispositions influence actors, it badly neglects the other side of the coin. It does not show how the actors – whether or not they follow the normative expectations inherent in their roles – strategically put values, norms and their dispositions to use in concrete interactive situations. Although it is true that Parsons has allowed for actors not following normative expectations, and although, as Alexander points out, the difference between Parsons' early and late work may not be as radical as is currently thought (Alexander, 1998a: 92–103), there can be no doubt whatsoever that Parsonian sociology, viewed as a whole, overemphasizes the role → actor relationship, and underemphasizes the actor → role one.

Alexander's new schema overcomes the above one-sidedness by introducing the crucial distinction between action and agency. The analytically established agentic processes of typification, invention and strategizing – because they operate via the three environments of action – may lead to both passive and non-passive, rational and irrational, informed and ignorant types of concrete action. In this way, Parsons' passive portrayal of actors is avoided, while his highly instructive analytical distinction between cultural, social and personality systems is safely retained.

Alexander's schema, however, needs further development. Parsons' three-system model, despite its obvious deficiencies, does relate in a theoretically coherent manner to a conceptualization of the social system in terms of the major macro-institutional orders of society: the economic (adaptation A), political (goal achievement G), social (integration I), and the pattern maintenance/socialization (latency L) subsystems. In this way the social system, as a complex set of institutionalized norms/roles, is not only subdivided into four subsystems according to the AGIL functionalist logic – each subsystem is further subdivided into four sub-subsystems according to the same functionalist logic, and so on *ad infinitum*. As I have already argued (Mouzelis, 1995b: 81–100, and chapter 1, section 1 above), this type of onion-like, system-within-system conceptualization not only reifies the four major macro-institutional orders, but also fails to create a theoretical space for autonomously constituted collective actors – actors who are not mere products but also the producers of the four institutional subsystems. In the Parsonian scheme, actors are either absent or they are portrayed as the passive outcome of structural determinations.[3]

In view of the above, Alexander's emphasis on the agentic dimensions of action leads, quite logically, to the rejection of Parsons' further subdivision of each of the four major institutional subsystems along functionalist lines. At the same time it leads to a conception of actors who have the potentiality of being, according to circumstances and the nature of their internal and external environments, both passive and active, both products and producers of the institutional orders within which they operate. However, Alexander does not spell out just *how* collective actors relate actively and/or passively to the major institutional spheres of society. How do the three-environments schema and the agency–action distinction operate on the macro-level of analysis? If Parsons has failed, for instance, effectively to connect the adaptation subsystem with such 'economic' actors as classes, interest groups, trade union organizations, etc., what type of connections does Alexander propose in the light of his own theory of action? This is a question that will have to be answered if Alexander's scheme is to be useful not only on the level of general discourse, but also on that of more specific research programmes.[4]

---

[3] For a critique of the Parsonian underemphasis of class interests and struggles as relatively autonomous mechanisms of macro-historical transformations, see Thompson, 1963.

[4] For an attempt to work out theoretically the linkages between the economic institutional subsystem and collective actors, see chapter 16.

Similar difficulties arise in respect of Alexander's discussion of the notion of cultural autonomy. I think he is perfectly correct in asserting that Parsons' three-system scheme does provide space for the autonomous treatment of cultural phenomena. He is also correct when he says that Parsons did not take full advantage of the opportunities of his scheme, and dealt with culture in only a functionalist, quasi-reductive manner. What is not very clear is how Alexander links culture with action. It is not enough to replace Parsons' values with the notion of cultural codes and narratives in order to move away from the functionalist treatment of culture.

Alexander points out that the functionalist, semiological and dramaturgical approaches constitute three different ways of conceptualizing cultural autonomy, and that all three possess 'an element of truth' (1995: 26). So far so good; but the point is to go beyond this rather obvious statement, and to provide *new concepts* with the help of which the researcher of culture will be able to move from a semiological to a sociological approach to culture and vice versa. More concretely, if the culturalist, semiological approach tends to emphasize the internal logic of culture to the extent that all external contexts (such as power struggles, interests, functional requirements, individual contingencies, etc.) are ignored, can one rearticulate the inner symbolic logic with its external contexts? What kind of concept does Alexander propose for bridging the gap between Saussure's or Lévi-Strauss's hidden codes or grammars with Parsons' or Gramsci's 'soft' cultural reductionism? The dramaturgical concept of 'aesthetic performance' is suggestive, but as used by Alexander it is rather *ad hoc* and merely descriptive. It fails to provide *analytical* insights into the precise ways in which cultural codes or narratives can be linked to their extra-symbolic contexts without committing the methodological sin of reductionism.

To remedy this, Alexander will have to start by spelling out, in much greater detail, what the actor's internal, cultural environment consists of, and how this environment is linked to concrete action via the agentic processes of typification, invention and strategizing. As Alexander rightly argues, Parsons has failed to link culture to action. But while, as I believe, Alexander is in a better position to establish effective linkages, he has not done so yet. In his more recent work, the linkages between culture and action become clearer, but the useful 'environments of action' conceptualization is abandoned (see the postscript to this chapter).

4 The theory of civil society

Concerning the third major area of Alexander's preoccupations, the author, in his important introduction to the edited volume *Real Civil Societies* (1998b), distinguishes three key definitions of civil society.[5] The earliest (civil society I, in short CSI) is linked to the eighteenth-century struggles of rising social strata against the European absolutist monarchical state. It views civil society as a residual category comprising all non-state institutions. CSII, on the other hand, places the concept within the state-versus-market controversy. It identifies the civic sphere with 'bourgeois society' as the source of exploitation for Marxists, and of 'freedom' from state authoritarianism for liberals. The third notion of civil society (CSIII) that Alexander adopts refers to a relatively autonomous institutional sphere portraying a logic quite distinct from that of the market, the state and other institutional areas.

Alexander's CSIII comes close to Cohen and Arato's attempt to view the civil society concept in terms of Parsonian theory (Cohen and Arato, 1992). As is well known, Parsons identified the societal community as the major institutional form of the integration subsystem (I) in modern, highly differentiated societies. For him, the societal community provides an integration based on a universalistic type of solidarity – a solidarity that strikes a balance between individual rights and collectively imposed obligations. As such, the integration subsystem (I) of modern societies is quite distinct from the other three major subsystems, adaptation (A), goal achievement (G) and latency (L) (Parsons, 1971). Cohen and Arato, according to Alexander, have constructed a definition of civil society that comprises all non-economic and non-state institutions. Alexander, more closely following Parsons, thinks that CSIII should be clearly distinguished not only from the economy and polity, but also from religion, kinship and science. The editor of *Real Civil Societies* differs from Parsons in three fundamental ways, however:

(i) He replaces the Parsonian fourfold AGIL division of the societal system with a rather *ad hoc* sixfold division (economy, polity, civil society, religion, kinship, science).

---

[5] As the main focus of this review is Alexander's recent work, I shall not deal systematically with others' contributions to *Real Civil Societies*.

(ii) Unlike Parsons, who links advanced differentiation with the *balanced integration* of the differentiated institutional parts, Alexander stresses the possibility of severe imbalances between subsystems. He rightly points out, for instance, that the universalistic solidarity which underlies the ideal of the societal community tends to be undermined in modern societies both by negative inputs from other subsystems (e.g. growing economic inequalities) and by non-universalistic, particularistic solidarities based on race, ethnicity, language, etc. Most of the contributions to part I of *Real Civil Societies* ('Uncivil hierarchies') make the unbalanced aspects of institutional differentiation abundantly clear.[6]

(iii) Unlike Parsons, who underemphasizes the interactive dimensions of social life, Alexander stresses that civil society, as a partially realized universalistically based solidary community, 'possesses its own cultural idiom, is patterned by a set of peculiar institutions, most notably legal and journalistic ones, and is visible in *historically distinctive sets of interactional practices like civility, equality, criticism and respect*' (1998b: 7, emphasis added).

5 The basic dilemma in the conceptualization of civil society

Alexander's conceptualization of civil society entails two basic elements. These are:

(i) the idea of an institutional sphere which, in modern, differentiated societies, is quite distinct from both the economic and political spheres on the one hand, and the religious, kinship and scientific spheres on the other.

(ii) the idea of a universalistically orientated solidary community, which is only partially realized in modern societies and which portrays relatively specific codes/values (e.g. democratic ideals), institutions (e.g. a free press) and interactive patterns (e.g. open, trusting, civil relationships).

The problem here is that (i) may clash with (ii). For instance, when Alexander talks about 'the dark and destabilizing underside of civil society' (1997: 122); or when he argues that civil solidarity is 'compromised' or 'distorted' not only by negative inputs from other

---

[6] For a similar critique of Parsons, see chapter 2, section 4.

institutional spheres but also by 'competing, more primordial definitions of community, such as race, language, nation, territory, and ethnicity' (1997: 115) – then the following question must be asked: Are those discourses or definitions of 'we-ness' that have a particularistic base (racial, ethnic, etc.) part of a civil society or not? To be more specific, Jacobs (1998: 138–61), in a very interesting contribution to Alexander's reader, analyses an actual conflictual situation where a conservative newspaper (the *Los Angeles Times*) put forward a quasi-racialist discourse in its attempt to explain black people's rioting; whereas a radical newspaper (the *Los Angeles Sentinel*) was trying to explain the riots in non-racialist terms. Do both collective actors involved (i.e. the two newspapers) belong to civil society III? Are racialist as well as anti-racialist discourses (and the associations/organizations that promote them) constituent elements of CSIII?

If yes, then 'real' civil society clashes with definition (ii). If no, if discourses encouraging a racialist, non-universalist type of solidarity are not part of civil society, then there is the problem of how to conceptualize the relationship between civil and extra-civil or anti-civil discourses and associations. Are the latter 'vestiges' of the non-differentiated traditional community, as Parsons' evolutionism partly implies?[7] Or are anti-civil discourses/associations elements that belong to the 'social' sphere but not to civil society, in which case civil society is not co-terminous with the social/solidarity sphere but only one dimension of it?

I think that the above questions point to the conclusion that Alexander, in the light of what he writes about CSIII, has two options:

— *either* to define civil society in more 'neutral' terms, in which case it becomes an arena where the dominant discourses or associations have to do with the issue of solidarity – *whether universalistic or not* – and where values and interactive patterns portray a logic that is distinct from that of the other institutional spheres (economic, political, religious, etc.);
— *or* to elect a 'positive' definition (emphasis on democracy, universalistic solidarity, civility, etc.), in which case he will have the problem of conceptually 'locating' those discourses and associations which, although 'modern' or post-traditional, promote non-universalistic, particularistic forms of solidarity.

---

[7] See, on this point, chapters 2 and 3.

As Alexander has shown in his introduction to *Real Civil Societies* (1998b: 96–114), the notion of the civil or civic is inextricably linked, both semiologically and commonsensically, with democratic and universalistic values and codes. This being so, I would rather choose the non-neutral, positive definition. In which case, one will have to differentiate clearly between the social/solidarity sphere and civil society – the latter being an analytically distinct dimension of the former. If this is done, one can argue that the decline of the less differentiated, 'traditional' community and the development of more differentiated modern social structures do not necessarily lead to a universalistically oriented type of social community (as Parsons' theory implies). It may equally well lead to a post-traditional societal community within which modes of particularistic solidarity prevail over modes of universalistic solidarity – both modes of 'we-ness' being *equally* compatible with the notions of differentiation and modernity.

Parsons linked the integration subsystem in general and the societal community in particular with a universalistic type of solidarity because, as Alexander rightly points out, he believed that there was a strong tendency for a *balance* to be established between the four major institutional spheres of modern society. On the basis of that assumption it is easy to argue that high differentiation, in modern conditions, leads to a universalistic mode of social integration that is compatible with democracy as an evolutionary universal (Parsons, 1966). But once, *pace* Alexander, Parsons' 'balance' assumption is (rightly) questioned; once it is realized that in late capitalism or late modernity 'imbalance' between spheres might not be the exception but the rule – then it becomes necessary to have conceptual tools that make it possible to study the complex articulation between particularistic and universalistic *post-traditional* solidarities.

If one looks at the real world today, it is quite obvious that particularistic forms of 'we-ness' characterize not only 'traditional' or modernizing/underdeveloped societies where clientelistic politics are dominant; they are also important in present-day developed capitalist societies where, to use Shils's typology, ideological politics prevail over civil politics (1997: 67ff). To be more specific, the post-1974 economic crisis exacerbating inequalities in the capitalist centre has peripheralized large sections of the population (within which most ethnic minorities live), and created processes of ghettoization (both for the poor and rich) – these processes leading to the dominance of particularistic rather than universalistic modes of 'we-ness'.

If due consideration is given to the above, two points become obvious. First, if one defines civil society in positive, non-neutral, quasi-utopian terms, there is a theoretical need for the construction of a more neutral and at the same time broader concept (which could still be called a social or solidarity sphere, integration subsystem, societal community). This 'neutral' concept will refer to discourses and/or associations that are predominantly non-state, non-market, non-religious or kinship-orientated, and which may adopt both universalistic *and* particularistic values and orientations.

The second point is that in order to *explain* rather than simply describe the intricate articulation between post-traditional universalistic and particularistic forms of solidarity in actual societies, *collective actors* (both within and outside the social/solidarity sphere) must be brought to the fore in the analysis. In order to explain why civil society's cultural codes, institutions and interactive patterns are stronger in some societies than others, or to understand why in some countries clientelistic or ideological politics peripheralize civil politics and universalistic modes of solidarity, one needs to put collective actors at centre-stage. Parsons, in his more historically orientated, macro-comparative writings, has failed to deal with collective actors satisfactorily. Alexander, by radically restructuring Parsons' three-system scheme, provides some very useful elements for a general theory of action. However, he needs to spell out more fully how the conceptual tools he is offering would work on the level of collective actors and the intricate games they play within the macro-institutional orders that both shape and are shaped by such games.

Conclusion

In the problem areas of action and culture, as well as civil society, Alexander's recent work contains very useful conceptual tools which help with the construction of a post-Parsonian theoretical framework for the study of the social. But for the moment, his work is rather schematic in all three areas. It provides brilliant insights, it suggests broad lines of orientation, but it lacks the kind of detailed conceptualization that is found in Parsons' highly flawed but profoundly innovative work.

More specifically in the area of action theory, it is necessary for Alexander to show how his agency–action distinction, as well as his notion of internal and external environments of action, can be useful on the macro-level of analysis, i.e. when one is trying to understand or explain how collective actors relate to the constitution, reproduction and long-term transformation of the macro-institutional orders within which they play their intricate games.

The key problem in the area of culture, of how to move from *langue* to *parole*, from the paradigmatic to the syntagmatic level of analysis, has to be spelled out more clearly and fully. Neither the semiological nor the dramaturgical approach to cultural autonomy satisfactorily provides the conceptual tools by means of which cultural codes can be linked up in a non-reductive manner with their 'external' economic, political and social contexts.

Finally, in developing his notion of civil society, Alexander will have to distinguish more precisely between civil society as a very partially realized utopian democratic project and as a post-traditional, differentiated social sphere within which a variety of discourses and collective actors (civil, non-civil, anti-civil) keep struggling for the establishment of different and often conflicting types of solidarity.

POSTSCRIPT: ALEXANDER'S CULTURAL
SOCIOLOGY

Introduction

In his more recent work, *The Meanings of Social Life* (2003), Alexander offers us a 'strong program' for the sociological study of culture: a post-foundationalist programme informed by the cultural/linguistic turn in the social sciences – as well as by structuralism, symbolic anthropology and the 'rediscovery of hermeneutics'. For Alexander, cultural sociology is quite different from the more conventional sociology of culture, in that the latter concerns itself less with cultural-symbolic structures as such and more with how other structures (social, material) exert an impact on symbolic wholes. So sociologists of culture (whether interested in the arts, religion, knowledge or ideology)

do not concern themselves with interpreting collective meaning, much less with tracing the moral textures and delicate emotional pathways by which individuals and groups come to be influenced by them. Instead, the 'sociology of' approach sought to explain what *created* meanings: it aimed to expose how the ideal structures of culture are formed by *other structures* – of a more material, less ephemeral kind. (Alexander, 2003: 5)

As already mentioned, according to Alexander, the way to move from the *sociology of culture* to *cultural* sociology is by disconnecting social from cultural structure, in other words by establishing the latter's analytic autonomy. It is only when the autonomy of the cultural object is demonstrated and fully explored that one can proceed to show how culture as 'thick description', as text, impacts on actors and institutions.

If hermeneutics or thick description in the Geertzian sense is one basic dimension of cultural sociology's strong programme, another is the structuralist analysis of codes which, in a more or less hidden manner, organize meanings and give definite form to the texture of social life. However, unlike, Lévi-Strauss's methodology, which decentres the subject and therefore views codes or abstract systemic logic as causal processes, Alexander's cultural sociology links 'causality to proximate actors and agencies specifying in detail just how culture interferes with and directs what really happens' (2003: 14). What this amounts to is that if the combination of thick description with a structuralist analysis establishes the cultural object as analytically distinct and autonomous from socio-structural objects, the author's attempt to relink cultural analysis with actors as agents enables him to avoid the essentialism found in both structuralist and post-structuralist approaches. In brief, Alexander claims that his 'structural hermeneutics' combines the rich, in-depth exploration of cultural wholes as texts with the elegant analysis of structuralist codes, while avoiding the reification of either texts or codes. This is achieved via an examination of how texts and codes are linked to real actors operating in specific institutional contexts.

1 On the conceptualization of culture

Since the focus here is on post-Parsonian developments, let us see how the author of *The Meanings of Social Life* criticizes Parsons' view of culture. As we have seen, Parsons' scheme of the cultural, social and personality systems clearly distinguishes culture from social structure, the former referring primarily to core values that are specified and institutionalized on the social-system level. In this scheme, culture ceases to be one of the four institutional subsystems (AGIL) of the social system; analytically the cultural system is seen as autonomous from the social system. For Alexander, however, this autonomy does not go far enough. Although Parsons emphasizes core values, he views them from an 'externalist' perspective. As already mentioned, he is more concerned with how values relate to systemic, functionalist requirements than with considering them in terms of codes and narratives. Hermeneutically speaking, in other words, Parsons' theorization of culture is rather weak:

Without a counterweight of thick description, we are left with a position in which culture [for Parsons] has autonomy only in an abstract and analytic sense. When we turn up to the empirical world, we find that functionalist logic ties up cultural form with social function and institutional dynamics to such an extent that it is difficult to imagine where culture's autonomy might lie in any concrete setting. The result was an ingenious systems theory that remains too hermeneutically feeble, too distant on the issue of autonomy to offer much to a strong program. (Alexander, 2003: 16)

I would add to the above justified critique that the way Parsons links culture to actors is too one-sided. There is too much emphasis on how core values, via institutionalization and internalization, affect actors' conduct, and too little on how actors construct or transform core values (see chapter 1, section 1). On that score, Alexander's conceptualization is clearly less systemic, more actor-oriented, more voluntaristic. When examining, for instance, the Holocaust, Alexander sees a transition from a 'progressive' to a 'tragic' narrative. In the former the emphasis is less on the mass murder of Jews and more on how these atrocities were part of an overall historical process which, after the defeat of the Nazi regime by the allied forces, led to a new 'progressive' era.

The tragic narrative, on the other hand, sees the Holocaust as a unique world-historical event, a 'sacred evil' which cannot be transcended by 'progressive' acts. The transition from the one narrative to the other occurred slowly (over a period of fifty years) and had a lot to do with the allies having lost control of the 'means of symbolic construction'. What this amounts to is that as the enormity of the evil became more widely known (through such mechanisms as 'personalizing' the event, producing eye-witness accounts of the mass murders, etc.), the groups that contributed most to the construction of the progressive story lost control over the 'means of persuasion' – this leading to the gradual dominance of the tragic version of events.

Moreover, in addition to referring to groups or elites operating in specific institutional spheres, Alexander (unlike Parsons) stresses the importance of asking actor-related *who*-questions: Who controls the means of symbolic construction in the mass-media institutional sphere? Who controls the 'religious orders'? Are the courts independent? Who exercises control of government policies? (2003: 102).

Notwithstanding all the above, however, the linkages between the relative autonomous cultural realm and social structure (which, according to Alexander, refers 'to actors, relations between actors and institutions') are not very clear. What are the connections between actors and institutions, or institutions and cultural structures? Precisely how do the former articulate with the latter? In what way can actors and institutions help us focus on 'causal processes'? There are no clear answers to these questions in *The Meanings of Social Life*. On the level of conceptual tools we have *juxtaposition* rather than *articulation* of codes and narratives/texts on the one hand, and of actors and institutions on the other. Parsons' treatment of culture was indeed hermeneutically feeble and oversystemic, but at least the links between the cultural and the social system were clearly spelled out. In Alexander's recent work, as well as in his previous work (see this chapter, section 3, above), they are not.

2 The environments of action

I think that in order to deal with the above theoretical weakness one should go back to Alexander's conceptualization of the environments of social action (see this chapter, section 1), a conceptualization which does not appear in *The Meanings of Social Life*.

As already mentioned, Alexander's earlier work refers to three environments of action, two of them (the cultural/code and the personality/motivational patterns) being internal to the actor, the third (the social/social network), external. Both internal and external environments of action set limits and provide opportunities for the actors involved. More specifically, actors relate to their three environments via the agentic processes of typification, invention and strategizing. This interesting scheme does establish some linkages between culture (as an 'internal' environment) and actors via the above-mentioned agentic processes. The above conceptual framework is dropped, however, in Alexander's 'strong program' of cultural sociology. As a result of this move, on the one hand his treatment of culture in *The Meanings of Social Life* is richer and linguistically more informed; but on the other, in so far as the linkage between culture and social structure is concerned, it creates more problems than his earlier culture–action theorization.

A possible reason for Alexander's abandoning the 'environment–agentic processes' scheme may have been that in *The Meanings of Social Life* he deals with culture in such a way that the 'internality' characteristic does not apply. Culture as thick description or text can be partly internalized by specific actors, but in other respects it clearly constitutes an external rather than an internal environment of action. First of all, narratives, texts, symbolic wholes can be substantiated in the form of novels, travel books, philosophical treatises, epic poetry and so on. In that sense they definitely constitute an external environment which has a direct or indirect impact on action. Moreover, *situated* actors may have motivational patterns and internalized cultural codes that are in conflict with the dominant culture in which they find themselves. Such is the case, for instance, of Muslim immigrants in Western European countries. In terms of their position in the workplace, they may comply with the normative requirements of their role, but their motivational patterns and cultural codes may be radically different from or even quite incongruent with the host country's dominant narratives and values. In that sense the dominant cultural environment is definitely 'external' to the immigrant workers; they neither internalize nor necessarily accept/respect it. As I argue more extensively in chapter 8, rather than cultural structures, it is Bourdieu's habitus (conceptualized as internalized dispositions that an actor, via various socializations, acquires and carries) which should be considered as an internal environment of action.

I think that Alexander's concept of internal and external environments of action, as well as his notion of agentic processes linking environments to actors, are valuable tools of analysis. Instead of dropping them altogether, it would be better to retain the basic scheme but *reformulate* the references to 'internality' and 'externality'. More specifically, if we consider dispositions as constituting a subject's internal environment of action, on the level of 'externality' one should refer to three rather than one external environment of action, corresponding to three types of structure: symbolic, institutional and, following Elias, figurational structures.[8]

---

[8] On the concept of figurational structures, see Mouzelis, 1995b.

To take figurational structures first, these entail relations between actors, and in that sense they approximate Alexander's social networks. Institutional structures on the other hand refer to relations between roles rather than actors. The notion of a figuration of actors, therefore, implies issues of *conflict or co-operation*, whereas that of institutions comprises *incompatibilities or compatibilities* between roles or institutional complexes. The reason why these two structural dimensions (or environments of action) should not be conflated is that they may vary independently of each other. In terms of, for instance, Marx's theory of social change, the possibilities of social transformation increase when the power relations between social classes no longer correspond to the distribution of rights and obligations as defined by law – that is, when there is a discrepancy between *de facto* power relations (figurational structures) and *de jure* normative-legal arrangements (institutional structures).[9]

On a more meso or micro level of analysis, similar discrepancies can be observed in formal organizations whenever sudden changes (internally or externally generated) create situations of 'organizational uncertainty': situations, for instance, where hierarchically subordinate actors control strategic resources and therefore acquire powers disproportionate to their bureaucratic position or role (Crozier, 1963: 193–232). In such circumstances a middle-level manager developing a sales strategy, for example, will have to take into account the firm's external-to-her/him institutional environment as well as the equally external figurational or interactive environment. These two environments both set limits to and create opportunities. Finally, the manager has to take into account the third environment external to him/her: the culture of the organization, i.e. narratives such as foundation myths or legitimizing accounts of the firm's contribution to the local or national community, philosophies of managerial ethics, theories of organizational democracy or leadership styles.

It is quite obvious that the organization's culture, described in a 'thick' manner is, partially at least, external to our manager, if not for any other reason than because s/he might be a newcomer or because s/he might find the values underlying the core cultural narratives unacceptable. It is equally obvious that there could be serious discrepancies

---

[9] On the discrepancy between *de jure* (institutional) and *de facto* (figurational) power structures in Marx and Durkheim, see Lockwood, 1992.

between the cultural, institutional and figurational structures. So in our organizational example a rhetorical focus on democratic or participative narratives could be in flagrant contradiction to the firm's authoritarian institutional structure, or on the figurational level, with the paternalistic way in which the firm's owner relates to his/her managers or workers (I will examine in a more systematic manner the linkages between actors and their environments in chapter 12).

3 Cultural narratives as second-order discourses

Another way of conceptualizing the linkages between cultural and social structures is to view cultural narratives or texts as *second-order discourses* (e.g. theories about the value of democratic rules) more or less congruent with first-order discursive or non-discursive practices as these relate to specific figurational and/or institutional structures. Let me illustrate this by returning to Alexander's analysis of the Holocaust. As already mentioned, the author of *The Meanings of Social Life* sees a long-term transition from a 'progressive' narrative concerning the mass murder of Jews by the Nazis to a 'tragic' narrative. I think that in his account of the two narratives Alexander failed to take into consideration discrepancies between cultural structures as second-order discourses, and laypersons' first-order discursive and non-discursive practices taking place within specific institutional and figurational contexts. If we focus on Germany in the early postwar period, the denazification process by the victorious allies was extremely timid, given the rising Soviet-communist threat. In this state of affairs it is plausible to assume that the progressive or even the subsequent tragic narrative did not penetrate very deeply into the various institutional spheres mentioned by Alexander. It could be that in some institutional spheres (in higher education, say, or the media) there was congruence between second-order cultural discourses and first-order discursive and non-discursive processes. Meanwhile, in other institutional spheres (let's say the judiciary or the military) there might have been marked incongruencies between the two discursive levels. On the cultural level, second-order progressive or liberal/democratic themes may have prevailed, whereas on the level of roles and institutions, first-order discursive and non-discursive practices may have retained their authoritarian, racist, anti-Semitic characteristics. More concretely, pro-Nazi 'patriotic' judges, doctors, engineers, ex-military officers, having kept up their social positions, could have paid lip-service to the progressive and later to the tragic narrative, while at the same time carrying 'internal' motivational patterns and living in an institutional and figurational environment where the old roles, the old normative requirements, were still in place.

Conclusion

Alexander's strong programme for cultural sociology treats culture in a manner that is linguistically and hermeneutically more sophisticated than Parsons' functionalist account. On the other hand, the way he conceptualizes the autonomy of the cultural sphere and its linkages with social structures lacks the theoretical rigour to be found in his earlier work. I think that in the latter, both the idea of internal and external environments of action, as well as the actor–agency distinction (which leads to the notion of the agentic processes of typification, invention and strategization) are very useful concepts which ought to be incorporated into a strong programme of cultural sociology. I have suggested a different manner, however, of conceptualizing 'externality', and argued that situated actors face not one but three external environments of action: the cultural-symbolic, the institutional and the figurational. If this is granted, then one has the conceptual means for establishing in a theoretically congruent fashion the analytic autonomy of the cultural, as well as the complex linkage between cultural and social structures (institutional and figurational).

5 | *Post-Parsonian theory II: beyond the normative and the utilitarian*

Introduction

Alexander has tried to restructure Parsonian theory by reworking the theory of culture and by exploring the connections between culture and action in novel ways. Hans Joas, on the other hand, in his influential *The Creativity of Action* (1996), tries to go beyond Parsons by putting at the centre of his analysis not the normative but the creative, not the actor but interaction.[1]

According to Joas, Parsons' early work, particularly his *The Structure of Social Action* (1937), set the foundations for all subsequent sociological attempts to construct a general theory of action. For Joas, however, these foundations are rather inadequate. They have directed the attention of social theorists to the utilitarian–normative or rational–non-rational distinction, which leads to a very restrictive conceptual framework. This framework rules out the idea that what is most distinctive about human action is neither rationality nor normativeness but *creativity*, which underlies and goes beyond the notions of the rational and the normative.

Parsons' critique of utilitarianism and his persistent attempt to show the normative basis of social order (which is to say, his one-sided concern with the rational–normative dialectic) prevented him from taking into consideration various philosophical theories of action that grapple with the issue of creativity. It also prevented him from seeing what the theorists on whom he focused (Pareto, Marshall, Durkheim, Weber and, to a lesser extent, Tönnies and Simmel) had to say about the creative, inventive aspects of action.

The Creativity of Action, in its attempt to restructure Parsons' theory of action, discusses both what the above-mentioned theorists said about

---

[1] An earlier version of this chapter appeared in the *British Journal of Sociology*, vol. 49 (1998).

human creativity and the more explicitly elaborated creativity theories to be found in the work of Herder (creativity of expressivity), Marx (creativity of production) and Castoriadis (creativity of revolution). If the above thinkers' notion of creativity was located in specific human institutions or activities (artistic, economic and politico-revolutionary, respectively), the so-called *Lebensphilosophie* of Schopenhauer, Nietzsche and Bergson saw it as underlying life in general and/or human life in particular. This broadening of scope acquired a more social/sociological form in the American pragmatist tradition (Pierce, Dewey and Mead), which conceptualized creativity as a fundamental dimension of all social action, including that of everyday social conduct.

1 Three problematic presuppositions

Focusing particularly on the American tradition, Joas points to three basic but problematic presuppositions that underlie conventional action theory. These presuppositions are clearly present in the rational-choice model but, to a lesser degree, can also be found in the Parsonian, normatively oriented alternative.

a. Teleological intentionality

The first problematic presupposition rests on the erroneous idea that an actor is always capable of purposive action. This notion results in the extremely rigid means–ends schemata seen in both neoclassical economics and in Parsons' early work. From this perspective, any action that does not fit the means–ends straitjacket (i.e. routine action, expressive action, silent contemplation, etc.) is considered residual, a 'deviation' from the norm requiring explanation. According to Joas, what this rigid conceptualization ignores is that ends/goals (whether conceptualized in utilitarian or Parsonian terms) are not static, not given 'in advance', so to speak. They are intrinsically linked in their constitution, reproduction and transformation to the *interactive situation*: if they do not always 'emerge', they are profoundly affected and constantly reproduced or transformed by actors' interactive practices.

If this point, which has been extensively developed by symbolic interactionism and ethnomethodology, is taken seriously into account, then it becomes obvious that the situation is not, as Parsons has conceptualized it, a neutral and/or immobile terrain where actors choose means in order to achieve pre-given, stable goals. The interactive situation is *constitutive* of goals and actions. It does not merely set limits to what may occur; it constantly and directly influences what does occur. To use Parsonian terminology, neither general values (at the level of the cultural system) nor institutionalized norms (social-system level), nor yet needs/dispositions (personality level) can account for social action if they are divorced from the interactive situation. Values, norms, needs/dispositions are constantly, reflexively, creatively handled, negotiated and reshaped as people interact in specific contexts in time and space.

To put it finally in more philosophical terms: as both Simmel and Heidegger have pointed out, the rigid means–ends conceptualization of action ignores the fact that human freedom may entail the opposite of purposive, strategic action. It may entail the capacity to get rid of the 'tyranny' of purposiveness; it may entail transcending the rather compulsive, never-ending setting of goals, the fulfilment of which only generates new goals, and so on *ad infinitum*.

b. Instrumental control of the body

A second problematic presupposition of conventional action theory is a too activistic conceptualization of the actor's body. The actor is supposed to be in full control of his/her body, this control entailing an instrumental self–body and body–world orientation. This activistic and, at the same time, instrumental or manipulative orientation to the body is, as Foucault has argued, a feature of the Western cultural tradition. As such it excludes the consideration of action that is predominantly characterized by passivity, sensitivity, receptivity, imperturbability, etc. It does not allow us, for instance, to consider the kind of non-activistic intentionality which releases the body from cognitive and purposive controls (falling asleep or meditating, for instance); it does not, in other words, guide us to consider seriously the great variety of non-instrumental, non-controlling ways in which we relate to our bodies.

c. The passive individual

Conventional action theory's third problematic presupposition has to do with the conception of the social actor as based on an individualistic ontology – the Western tradition of possessive individualism. This tradition, if it does not see human beings as monads, certainly under-emphasizes the extent to which the social and historical context shapes both our inner and outer selves, both inter- and intra-action. Parsons' focus on psychoanalysis and socialization/internalization does not, of course, lead to the crude essentialist construction of pre-constituted, self-contained rational actors such as we find in neoclassical economics. But just as his role players are shown as products rather than producers of the social world, so the self/personality is shown in a passive rather than an active manner, in the sense that there is an underemphasis on the complex, ongoing games that actors play not only with each other but also with themselves.

2 Constitutive theories of action and systemic theories of differentiation

Joas' critique of conventional action theory's presuppositions makes him take up an intermediate position between the rigidities of rational and normative models on the one hand, and the extreme postmodernist reaction on the other. The latter, influenced by the Continental philosophy of life rather than by American pragmatism, emphasizes creativity to the extent that normative or rational considerations are thrown overboard. *The Creativity of Action* – by stressing the notions of reflexive rather than purposive intentionality, non-instrumental rather than instrumental 'corporeality', primary sociality rather than pre-constituted individualism – argues, contra postmodernism, that human creativity does not exclude the rational or the normative, but rather combines these and other elements in ever-novel, inventive ways.

In his last two chapters Joas (1996) shows the relevance of the above insights to an assessment of ongoing sociological debates on the nature and causes of collective action (199–208), on the validity of function-alist explanations (209–22), on how to bring action-oriented socio-logical theories closer together, and on the normative linkages between the latter and democracy (223–58). With regard to collective-action theories, Joas contends that rational-choice models (e.g. Olsen's) or those based on Parsonian normative functionalism (e.g. Smelser's) are less adequate than theorizations (e.g. Touraine's approach) that explain macro-phenomena in terms of real collective actors and social movements operating within specific cultural traditions. On function-alism, he argues that it can be useful as an explanatory theory only in a limited number of cases: as a heuristic device it can help only if it avoids the conflation of function with cause, and if its rejection of methodological individualism does not introduce holistic-essentialist views of the social world.[2]

For the action/system divide in the social sciences, Joas believes that a rapprochement is possible between 'constitution theories' (i.e. theories stressing the constitutive role played by action, both individual and collective, in the construction and transformation of social phenomena) and system-oriented differentiation theories. For Joas, the extreme ideal-typical forms of the two approaches are mirror images of each other. He urgently wants to see constitution theory applied to the differentiation process of modern societies in such a way as to avoid both an over-rationalized, over-integrated image of society on the one hand, and the portrayal of actors as strictly constrained by systemic evolutionary imperatives on the other. This is to say that constitution theories should sensitize one to the contingent, constructed character of all social patterns, and to the indeterminate nature of all macro-social configurations.

Finally, constitution theory for Joas entails, at least implicitly, the notion of self-determination, and on the normative level this unavoidably links it with the notion of democratization. While Parsons argues that growing differentiation, in modern conditions, relates positively to democracy (see chapter 3), Joas reverses the problem. For him, given that growing differentiation may or may not lead to democratization, the degree and type of differentiation becomes an issue in democratic debate. Looking at the work of Luhmann, Münch, Offe and others, he asks whether growing differentiation is stoppable; and if it is, whether we should try to slow it down, reverse it, or pay less attention to the degree of differentiation and more to the way the differentiated parts have to be integrated if democracy is to be enhanced.

3 Some critical remarks

Given the density and richness of *The Creativity of Action*, it is difficult to convey here the great number of insights it offers in a variety of fields, among others in philosophy, the history of ideas, classical social theory,

---

[2] For Joas, holistic theories always entail essentialism. However, as I will argue in the last part of the book, holistic theories need not lead to essentialism.

analytically oriented sociological theory and the theory of collective movements. In all the above areas Joas shows an impressive command of the literature, as well as a capacity for establishing new connections between seemingly unrelated spheres of study. Moreover, his overall argument, that we should break out of the rational-normative strait-jacket by seriously considering the creative dimension of all human action, is very persuasive. I find his attempt to partially establish this proposition by looking, from the creativity perspective, at the work of Durkheim, Weber, Tönnies and Simmel, as well as at the more philosophical theories that were ignored by Parsons, equally persuasive.

For all that, the above strategies, although relevant and convincing, are by themselves not enough to provide an adequate alternative to Parsons' theory of action. Because if Parsons is weak on philosophy, he is very strong on sociological theory proper; on the construction, that is, of an interrelated set of conceptual tools (what Althusser called Generalities II)[3] that enable the sociologist to link social action with such other fundamental dimensions of social organization as roles, institutions, social structures, culture, personality, etc. in a theoretically and logically coherent manner. If Parsons' *oeuvre* is still relevant today; if (as in Joas' case) it is still used as *the* basic frame of reference in debates dealing with the fundamental dimensions of social life; if it is still used by sociologists as a conceptual guide that helps to raise interesting questions and to produce substantive theories (Generalities III) in numerous empirical fields, this is because it offers us not simply philosophical disquisitions about the nature of human action, but *specific, theoretically developed concepts* that an empirically oriented social scientist can use in his/her research. It is precisely on this fundamental level (on the level of heuristic tools, of Generalities II) that Joas' book is wanting.

a. Restructuring Parsons' theory of action

Let me make this central point more specific. Parsons, in his attempt to overcome the difficulties of the utilitarian theory of action, did not limit himself to mere criticisms and/or the formulation of general methodological directives. In a more positive and constructive manner he presented us with an alternative model of action, which he called

---

[3] For the concepts of Generalities II and III, see Althusser, 1969: 183–91.

voluntaristic. This is based on the interrelated concepts of unit act, values/ends, means of action, conditions of action and situation. And if one looks at his entire theoretical edifice, these five interrelated concepts are systematically linked, *however inadequately*, with the notions of institutionalization and internalization (as one moves from the cultural to the social, and from the social to the personality system); with the four functional requirements that every system has to cope with if it is to survive as such (the famous AGIL scheme); to the idea of structural-functional differentiation; to that of sociological and evolutionary universals, etc.

This being so, an effective restructuring of the Parsonian theory of action requires more than a simple critique of its fundamental presuppositions and the tentative formulation of more convincing ones. It has to go a step further and translate these insights into *specific conceptual tools* that make it possible to see, for instance, how precisely the 'rational' and the 'normative' relate to the 'creative'. If actors do not operate on the basis of rigidly set means–ends schemata, if interactive situations constitute and constantly reformulate both means and ends, what sort of conceptual tools can make this obvious, and how are such tools linked to each other and to broader macro-sociological conceptualizations? Joas does not give us any answers here. Neither does he show how interaction is linked to intra-action – i.e. to the reflexive process, the internal conversations that constantly take place within the actor's mind. In order to understand how interactions shape means and ends, it is necessary to see how an actor deals not only with other actors in interactive contexts but also with himself/herself. In other words, creativity is directly linked with both interactive and intra-active processes (see chapters 8 and 12).

b. The rapprochement between constitution and differentiation theories

The same difficulty applies to Joas' attempt, on the basis of his theory of creative action, to bring action-based constitution closer together with system-based differentiation theories of stability and change. To simply argue that it is only in their ideal-typical form that the two approaches are incompatible, and that a rapprochement is both possible and necessary, is neither sufficient nor original. Neither is it enough to provide general and equally non-original suggestions concerning the limitations of teleologically oriented functionalist explanations, the capacity of action theory for successfully linking micro with macro levels of analysis, etc.

The demanding task is to 'concretize' the action/system rapprochement by working out new concepts for overcoming some of the theoretical difficulties that Parsons' theory generates. For instance, as far as intra-societal mechanisms of change are concerned, Parsons explains the overall movement towards greater social complexity and differentiation in terms of incompatibilities or strains between the four institutional subsystems: adaptation (A), goal achievement (G), integration (I) and latency (L). As David Lockwood (1964) noted long ago, Parsons has failed to show how systemic incompatibilities between the norms and values of the institutional subsystems are linked (on the level of social integration and disintegration) with the strategies and struggles of collective actors. Do incompatibilities between economic and political or cultural norms automatically generate change? Obviously not. As Marx and others have pointed out, it depends on whether, and how, actors see these incompatibilities and contradictions, and what they do about them. Parsons, because of his overemphasis on system and his underemphasis on social integration and disintegration, fails to systematically link subsystem incompatibilities with social co-operation and conflict.

My point here is that this Parsonian weakness cannot be remedied by injecting the idea of social or class struggles (Smelser, 1985) or of economic, political, social and cultural elites (Eisenstadt, 1990b) into the Parsonian conceptual construct in an *ad hoc* manner. In addition, we will have to show what specific *theoretical consequences* the introduction of concepts borrowed from 'constitution theories' will have on such fundamental Parsonian concepts as the AGIL scheme, the pattern variables and the notion of evolutionary universals. When this is not done, theoretical rapprochement or convergence is reduced to the eclectic exercise of picking and choosing whatever one fancies from constitution and differentiation theories, without showing whether or how the new amalgam holds together; we have, in other words, *juxtaposition* rather than *articulation* of the two approaches.[4]

---

[4] For a theoretical attempt to articulate action/constitution with system/differentiation approaches, see chapter 16.

Conclusion

It is only by Joas moving – as is to be hoped, in a subsequent volume – from philosophical analysis to sociological theory (in the narrow sense of the term) that an effective reconstruction of Parsons' action theory will become possible. Giddens (1984) and, to a lesser extent, Habermas (1984, 1987) have already tried this with varying degrees of success. Joas could start with a more serious and systematic reassessment of these authors' work as a convenient way of constructing new conceptual tools reflecting his insights on the creativity of social action.

This criticism certainly does not imply that Joas' book has failed. *The Creativity of Action* succeeds, among other things, in showing the relevance of the type of project Parsons set himself. Despite the fact that Joas has not managed to bring his own ambitious undertaking to a conclusive end, he has convincingly shown that the concept of creativity should have a much more central place in sociological theorizing. *The Creativity of Action* is an important book. It should be indispensable reading not only for those interested in post-Parsonian sociological theory, but also for empirically oriented sociologists concerned with the sociology of social movements, the social structure of modern societies and the linkages between differentiation and democratization.

PART III

Agency and structure: reworking some basic conceptual tools

6 | *Social and system integration: Lockwood, Habermas and Giddens*

The distinction between social integration and system integration has been a useful tool in the empirical investigation of social transformation. The various attempts to change or transcend this well-known dichotomy relate it to some key debates in sociological theory, such as the status of functionalist explanations, the links between subjectivist and objectivist sociologies, the issue of essentialist accounts of social phenomena, etc. In the present chapter I focus on how Habermas and Giddens have tried to restructure Lockwood's distinction, and argue that their attempts have not been very successful and that it is more useful to retain Lockwood's original formulation (with some modifications).[1]

1 Lockwood

For Lockwood (1964), the distinction between social integration and system integration sensitizes the student to two different ways of viewing social wholes; in turn, these two different perspectives lead to different mechanisms accounting for social order or disorder. Social integration refers to 'the orderly or conflictual relationships between the actors', whereas system integration focuses on the compatible or incompatible/ contradictory relationships between 'the parts of the social system' (1964: 244).

Looking at a social whole from the point of view of actors and their relationships leads to investigating the problem of social order/disorder in terms of social co-operation/conflict. These are the result of the actors – on the basis of how they conceive the social world – developing strategies for defending or promoting what they consider to be their interests. On the level of system integration, the focus shifts from an agency to a systemic perspective. It is no longer the actors who occupy centre-stage, but 'system parts'.

[1] An earlier version of this chapter appeared in *Sociology*, vol. 31 (1997).

Lockwood considers that Parsonian functionalists view systemic parts in institutional terms. More specifically, in Parsons' subdivision of the societal system into four subsystems (adaptation, goal achievement, interaction and latency – AGIL for short) systemic parts are institutions: economic institutions (A), political institutions (G), legal institutions (I) and educational/kinship/religious institutions (L). It follows that the problem of social order/disorder is a matter of how congruous or incongruous certain complexes of institutionalized values/norms are with each other. For instance, in several late-developing countries, traditional patriarchal norms concerning female conduct in the latency subsystem may clash with more individualistic normative expectations in the rapidly industrializing adaptation subsystem.[2]

But for Lockwood, incompatibilities between systemic parts can also take a different form. If one looks at system integration/disintegration from a Marxist perspective, such incompatibilities take a normative/non-normative or institutional core/material substratum form. Or, as expressed in his more recent work (Lockwood, 1992), the difference is between a normative and a factual order: a *de jure* state of affairs, where values/norms regulate social conduct by defining the rights and obligations of each social role – thus leading to the constitution of a stable *status* hierarchy; and a *de facto* situation, where social conduct is primarily shaped in a non-normative, utilitarian fashion by the differential control and distribution of resources within and outside the economic sphere. (The former dimension is theorized chiefly by the Durkheimian sociological tradition; the latter by Marxism.)

While Lockwood is correct in putting this particular type of systemic incompatibility at the centre of a theory of societal transformation, the way he conceptualizes the two incompatible systemic parts creates serious difficulties. With regard to the normative/non-normative distinction, however one defines (for instance) the forces of production in Marxist theory, they obviously do entail norms, such norms portraying varying degrees of institutionalization (Mouzelis, 1993c). Moreover, when Lockwood conflates the non-normative with the utilitarian, that too creates ambiguity, since utilitarian action, as Lockwood himself admits, entails the norm of 'rationality' (1992: 357–8).

Similar difficulties arise when the distinction is expressed – as it was in Lockwood's earlier formulation – in terms of an institutional core and a

---

[2] For a discussion of Parsons' AGIL scheme along such lines, see chapter 1.

material substratum. This would imply that the latter does not entail institutionalized norms, that it is somehow ontologically different from the former.

One way of avoiding the essentialist connotations of this position is to reject the manner in which Lockwood conceptualizes systemic incompatibilities. If one starts from the premise that all system parts entail normative regulation, then there are no system parts that are 'non-normative'. System parts always refer to institutionalized complexes of norms/roles. This is true whether one looks at such institutional complexes as kinship, law and religion, or at science, technology and private property. All of the above refer to institutions; and if this is so, then system contradictions of both the Marxist and the Parsonian variety always entail incompatibilities between institutions, i.e. incompatibilities between the various kinds of *logic* of different institutionalized complexes or norms/roles.

Accepting the above premise does not necessarily entail rejecting Marx's insight that certain systemic parts are, so to speak, more durable, less 'malleable' as far as their transformation is concerned. But this varying malleability or durability of institutionalized complexes of norms/roles can be expressed without using the essentialist material/non-material distinction. It could be argued, for instance, that certain institutions are less malleable, harder to change, because powerful interest groups support them in a more or less purposive manner (see, on this point, chapter 15, section 1).

Needless to say, since institutions should not be conceptualized as reified anthropomorphic entities, the prevalence of one institutional logic over another does not come about automatically. It always entails struggles on the social-integration level of analysis, i.e. on the level of actors, their strategies and the unanticipated consequences of these strategies. In other words, as Lockwood has correctly argued, system contradictions do not result automatically in social transformation. In order to assess whether or not systemic contradictions or incompatibilities lead to social change, and/or to see what type of change, one has to focus on how actors handle contradictions, how conscious they are of incompatibilities between institutions, what they do in order to maintain or change the contradictory status quo, etc.

Take, for instance, the growing contradiction in present-day Britain between the productivity and competitiveness logic in the institutional sphere of the economy, and what Parsons (Parsons and Platt, 1973) has called the logic of cognitive rationality in the sphere of higher education. In view of the prevailing balance of political and social forces since the 1974 world economic crisis, it is not surprising that the more malleable, educational institutions have been *colonized*, to use Habermas' expression, by the less malleable, economic ones. This colonization, which took the form of the gradual displacement of the academic by a managerial logic in British universities, did not occur automatically. It entailed strategies of colonization and resistance to colonization by a variety of interest groups in and outside academia.

A final point about the varying malleability of institutional complexes: following Weber's critique of Marx's historic materialism, one should stress that it is impossible to argue in a transcultural, transhistorical, universal manner that certain (e.g. economic) institutions are always less malleable than others (e.g. religion, kinship). The degree of malleability of all institutions is an empirical question; it cannot be decided in an armchair, aprioristic manner by the construction of such misleading dichotomies as material base/superstructure (see, on this point, chapter 16).

To conclude this section, if one accepts the above, social integration refers to co-operative/conflictual relationships between actors, whereas system integration refers to compatibilities/incompatibilities between 'parts' that should always be viewed as institutionalized complexes exhibiting different degrees of durability/malleability. With this modification the social-/system-integration distinction becomes consistently analytical – leading to a view of the same social phenomena from two different perspectives. From the social-integration perspective the focus is on concrete actors and their relations/interactions in time and space. From the system-integration perspective the focus shifts to institutional complexes as a virtual order of rules/norms which, in Giddens' terminology, are instantiated only when actors draw upon them in order to act or interact in specific situations. To use an expression from linguistics, social integration refers to the syntagmatic level (concrete interactions in time and space), and system integration to the paradigmatic level (logical compatibilities/incompatibilities between rules outside time and space).[3]

---

[3] Although Lockwood is not directly concerned with it, another type of systemic contradiction that is expressed problematically is the one between a durable institution (say, private ownership of the means of production) and institutionalized discourses trying to analyse, explain, criticize or legitimate that

2 Habermas

In adopting the social-/system-integration distinction, Habermas retains Lockwood's agency/system perspective. Social integration refers to an 'internalist', agency-oriented view of the social world, whereas system integration points to an 'externalist' perspective that 'reaches through and beyond action orientations'. It is the view of an observer who examines social orientations/actions not from the point of view of the actors involved, but from that of the system and its functional requirements for maintenance and reproduction (Habermas, 1987: 117).

Given this agency/system distinction, when Habermas tackles the problem of social order he distinguishes two action co-ordinating mechanisms. From the point of view of social integration, action co-ordination is based on 'a normatively secured or communicatively achieved consensus', whereas on the level of system integration, co-ordination is based on the systemic steering media of money and power that regulate actions more or less 'automatically'. In this latter case, action co-ordination is assured by systemic mechanisms operating behind the actors' backs, so to speak, i.e. by mechanisms not entailing normatively reached agreements or mutual understanding (1987: 117ff).

institution. Marxists usually assign the former (let us call it M) to the material base, and the latter (I) to the ideological superstructure. Here also, the intuitive notion that M is more solid, less malleable than I is quite useful. But the way in which the M–I relationship is expressed, in terms of material versus ideal, creates more problems than it solves, particularly in a post-positivist, anti-essentialist phase in the social sciences, when the emphasis is on the discursive and symbolic construction of the social. How can one translate the material/ideal distinction into non-essentialist terms? By differentiating between *first-* and *second-order discourses*. Whether one looks at economic, political, religious or kinship institutions, one will find first-order discursive practices through which laypersons, on a recursive basis, reproduce these institutions, and second-order discursive practices that may be conceptualized as attempts by specialists to understand, criticize, legitimize, transform or defend them. Both first- and second-order discourses entail interpretations or theories. The basic difference between them is that the latter are 'theories about theories', second-order interpretations about the first-order interpretations that millions of laypersons use in their everyday interactions. Now although second-order discursive practices significantly influence first-order ones and vice versa, there is a sense in which the former are 'softer', more malleable than first-order practices. To take our previous example again, in non-revolutionary circumstances it is easier to change I than to change M. It is easier, for instance, in a stable capitalist society to change the theories social sciences hold about private property than to change the actual institution of private property as a set of first-order discursive and non-discursive practices of millions of buyers and sellers (see, on this point, chapter 11, section 2b).

The third step in Habermas' formulation consists of using Parsons' AGIL scheme to link system-integration mechanisms of co-ordination with what he calls the *system* (the adaptation and goal achievement subsystems) and social-integration mechanisms with the *lifeworld* (which corresponds to Parsons' integration and latency subsystems).

Adopting an evolutionary framework, the German social philosopher argues that in primitive societies there is no clear differentiation between social- and system-integration mechanisms of action co-ordination. As societies become more complex, a differentiation does develop between system and lifeworld. Modern societies show a clear differentiation between the economic, political, social and religious/educational/kinship spheres, systemic steering media co-ordinating action in the spheres of the market (A) and the state (G). In the remaining spheres (I, L), as traditional norms decline, 'problem areas' or areas of uncertainty emerge, and action co-ordination is or can be achieved on the basis of communicative rationality. From this perspective, modernity's pathology consists of the lifeworld being colonized by systemic steering media that are 'appropriate' only to the economic and political spheres. As traditional normative regulations recede, communicative co-ordination in the lifeworld is replaced by steering-media co-ordination. This results in the gradual dehumanization of the lifeworld (1987: 163ff).

This third step, where Habermas links mechanisms of co-ordination with specific institutional spheres (e.g. steering media with Parsons' A and G subsystems), leads away from the initial formulation by Lockwood. For the latter the internalist/externalist or social-/system-integration perspectives, and the appropriate mechanisms that each perspective entails (conflict/contradiction), apply to *all institutional spheres*. Whether one examines an economic enterprise, a public bureaucracy, a religious organization or a family group, one can look, following Lockwood, at all these social wholes (and their problems of order/disorder) from both a social- and a system-integration point of view: both in terms of agency (mechanisms of conflict/co-operation), and in systemic, functionalist terms (compatibilities/incompatibilities between institutionalized parts or sub-parts).

For Habermas this is no longer the case, since the externalist perspective is only linked with systemic/steering media of co-ordination operating in the A and G subsystems. This creates problems, for the simple reason that the conflation of a *methodological* distinction (externalist/internalist perspective) with a *substantive* one (steering media linked to the system, and non-steering media to the lifeworld) engenders a great deal of confusion.[4] It leads to the assumption that the externalist/functionalist perspective is appropriate only for the study of the economic and political subsystems, and the internalist perspective for the study of the lifeworld (I and L subsystems). This is patently not so because, as Habermas himself has admitted (1987: 311), communicative forms of co-ordination do play a role, not only in the lifeworld but also in the adaptation and goal achievement subsystems. Of course, Habermas may defend his position by arguing that in the latter cases the co-ordination role of communicative understanding is peripheral or subordinate to that played by the steering media. This is an empirically open question, however, given that the importance of the non-steering media in the economy and polity may vary from case to case – being extremely crucial, for instance, in industrial relations negotiations (Mouzelis, 1991a: 179ff).

Quite irrespective of the above consideration, however, labelling the A and G subsystems as the 'system' and the I and L ones as 'lifeworld' builds into the very definition of these two terms, and therefore solves aprioristically, the substantive, empirical issue of how important steering and non-steering mechanisms of co-ordination are in each institutional sphere. In that sense it may lead to the false impression that one cannot study economic and political institutions from a social-integration, agency perspective. In other words, it gives the false impression that there are no economic or political lifeworlds.

To sum up this argument, Lockwood's perspectivism (i.e. his distinction between an agency and a systemic perspective) is *logically congruent* with the mechanisms of integration he posits: co-operation/conflict is linked with an agency perspective, and institutional compatibilities/ incompatibilities with a systemic perspective. By contrast, Habermas' perspectivism (i.e. his internalist/externalist distinction) is logically incongruent with his mechanisms of co-ordination because, quite inappropriately, he locates steering-media co-ordination within economic and political institutions, and communicative mechanisms of co-ordination within the remaining institutional spheres.

---

[4] For a critique of Habermas' communicative theory along similar lines, see McCarthy, 1985 and Mouzelis, 1991a: 177–81.

3 Giddens

With Giddens (1984), the distinction between social integration and system integration moves even further away from Lockwood's original formulation. Given that Giddens' structuration theory aims at transcending the subjectivist–objectivist divide in the social sciences (see chapter 1, section 7), he rejects the agency/system or internalist/externalist distinction, and tries to use the social-/system-integration concepts as a substitute for the micro-/macro-perspective in the social sciences.

For Giddens, social integration entails mechanisms bringing about reciprocity of actors' conduct 'in circumstances of co-presence, understood as continuities in and disjunctions of encounters'; whereas system integration refers to 'reciprocity between actors or collectivities across extended time–space, outside conditions of co-presence' (1984: 376–7). This means that *co-presence* or face-to-face encounters entail social integration (i.e. processes of reciprocity not extending considerably in time–space), whereas absence of co-presence entails system integration (i.e. processes of reciprocity that do extend in time–space).

As in the case of Habermas, Giddens' formulation creates serious difficulties. His micro/macro, or rather restricted/extended time–space, conceptualization is not logically compatible with his reciprocity-achieving mechanisms. More precisely, when Giddens links a 'restricted' time–space perspective with co-presence or face-to-face encounters, he does not take into account the very simple fact that face-to-face encounters may entail macro- rather than micro-processes of reciprocity. So the face-to-face encounter between heads of state may well lead to agreements that achieve reciprocity between actors or collectivities across extended time–space. Linking the extended time–space perspective to lack of co-presence is plainly wrong, therefore. Giddens here reproduces a misconception that is quite common among micro-sociologists who link face-to-face interactions with the micro-level of analysis (Mouzelis, 1991b: 194–200).

Another difficulty with Giddens' reformulation of the social-/system-integration distinction is that his 'transcendence' of the subjectivist–objectivist divide is only decorative. He, in fact, reintroduces Habermas' internalist/externalist and Lockwood's agency/system perspective when he coins yet another distinction: between 'institutional analysis' and 'analysis in terms of strategic conduct' (1984: 288). Institutional analysis corresponds more or less exactly to how Lockwood uses system integration, and strategic-conduct analysis corresponds to Lockwood's social-integration perspective.

With this new distinction, Giddens merely reintroduces the subjectivist–objectivist divide he tried to transcend in the first place. Its reintroduction, by the back door, was quite inevitable. Giddens, an accomplished sociological analyst, was not prepared to pay the price that total abolition of this fundamental conceptual divide entails. The only effective way of transcending the subjectivist–objectivist dichotomy would be to move in a post-structuralist direction: to decentre the subject and view the social world as a flat, non-hierarchized chain or network of 'subjectless' practices, discourses or texts (see chapter 1, sections 4–6). This peripheralization of actors, as Foucault's work clearly shows, leads either to the impossibility of moving from description to explanation, or to teleological accounts of social phenomena (Mouzelis, 1995b: 45–69).

Conclusion

Lockwood's distinction between social and system integration points to two fundamental ways of looking at the social world (agency and system perspectives). These in turn point to two mechanisms useful for understanding social order and disorder: co-operation/conflict between actors and compatibility/incompatibility between institutions. If Lockwood's notion of contradiction between substratum and institutional core is translated as a systemic contradiction between more and less durable institutional complexes, then this distinction exhibits a logical consistency that is missing in its subsequent modifications by Habermas and Giddens.[5]

Habermas' reformulation of the social-/system-integration distinction retains Lockwood's agency/system perspective (internalist/externalist), but the mechanisms of integration he derives from this perspective are, in a rather confusing manner, linked with specific institutional spheres (steering media with the economy and polity, and non-steering media with the rest).

Giddens rejects Lockwood's and Habermas' internalist/externalist perspective in his endeavour to transcend the subjectivist–objectivist divide

---

[5] For an application of Lockwood's distinction in the study of macro-historical social transformation, see Mouzelis, 1990: 93–157.

in the social sciences. To do so he uses the social-/system-integration distinction to identify two types of reciprocity between actors, corresponding to restricted (micro) and extended (macro) time–space distantiation. He is not very successful. Not only is his linkage of co-presence with restricted time–space problematical, but he also has to bring back Lockwood's initial distinction in the guise of a somewhat different terminology (as analysis in terms of strategic conduct and analysis in institutional terms).

7 | *The subjectivist–objectivist divide: against transcendence*

As I have argued in chapter 1, the dominance of Parsonian functional-ism in the field of sociological theory during the early postwar period gave way to extreme fragmentation when Parsons' grand synthesis was challenged by a variety of competing paradigms (symbolic interac-tionism, ethnomethodology, phenomenological sociology, non-Marxist conflict theory, structuralism/post-structuralism, etc.). This prolifera-tion of approaches led to compartmentalization, with each theoretical tradition claiming the monopoly of truth and busily building impreg-nable barriers (methodological, epistemological and ontological) to inter-paradigmatic, open-ended communication.[1]

The 1980s and 1990s brought a reaction to the 'war of paradigms' with attempts from various quarters to overcome the fragmentation of the previous two decades. This reaction took two main forms. On the one hand, post-structuralism presupposed the radical dissolution of boundaries not only between social-science paradigms but also between social-science disciplines and sub-disciplines (economics, sociology, social psychology, anthropology, etc.), or even between the social sciences and philosophy, literature, linguistics, etc. This extreme form of theoretical dedifferentiation led to a situation where complex social phenomena were reductively explained in terms of signs, texts, 'desire', etc. (Mouzelis, 1995b: 41–68).

A more constructive reaction to fragmentation and compartmentali-zation was the endeavour to *transcend* the boundaries between existing paradigms. For instance, Giddens' structuration theory (1984) is sup-posed to provide a 'transcending' conceptual framework which draws elements from what he calls interpretative sociologies, structural socio-logies and structuralist ones. Bourdieu's theory of action or theory of practice, in an equally 'transcending' spirit, attempts to put an end to

---

[1] An earlier version of this chapter appeared in *Sociology*, vol. 34 (2000)

what he terms the 'subjectivism–objectivism' split in the social sciences (Bourdieu, 1977, 1990).[2]

My argument in this chapter is that there is a third possible reaction to the 'war of paradigms' and the ensuing compartmentalization: neither dissolution nor transcendence, but *bridge-building*. This third position presupposes that what Giddens and Bourdieu call objectivist and subjectivist perspectives in sociology are logically and analytically quite separate and not mutually reducible. This being the case, doing away with compartmentalization does not entail the creation of concepts eliminating the 'distance' between subject and object; instead, it entails the creation of concepts that show us the complex ways in which subject and object interrelate – so that in certain cases the subject–object distance disappears, but in others it does not.

Of course, theoretical rapprochement via bridge-building has been practised in the social sciences for a long time.[3] What I hope to add here is an enhancement of the bridge-building process via a constructive critique of Giddens and Bourdieu's 'transcendence' strategy. I shall try to show why that strategy failed, as well as how the fourfold typology that I propose can lead to a more effective rapprochement of conflicting paradigms – a rapprochement that fully respects the logic inherent in each theoretical tradition.

1 On the concept of social structure

A great deal of confusion in sociological theory stems from the fact that the key term *social structure* has a multiplicity of meanings. Here I shall

---

[2] When Bourdieu refers to subjectivism, he has mainly phenomenological approaches in mind, whereas when he uses the objectivism label he is criticizing Lévi-Strauss's structuralism. The subjectivism–objectivism distinction, as applied by Giddens and Bourdieu to differentiate between dissimilar or contrasting types of sociological paradigms, is rather problematic. So while it makes sense to view Parsonian functionalism as an objectivist paradigm (in the sense that it portrays subjects in a rather passive manner), it is much more problematical to label Marxist/neo-Marxist approaches objectivist. This is because in historically oriented Marxisand approaches *collective subjects* are portrayed not only as products but also as producers of their social world (see chapter 16).

[3] On various attempts to establish bridges between interpretative and macro-structural paradigms, see Alexander, 1998a: 183ff; for a bid to introduce class conflict into Parsonian functionalism, see Smelser, 1985; Eisenstadt, 1990b.

neither list the numerous interpretations of the term[4] nor indicate which is the most appropriate. Instead, by the use of a simple typology I shall briefly examine four major ways in which the concept is used in the social sciences and how these four relate to each other. This exercise in turn will allow me to develop my ideas about the subjectivist–objectivist problematic.

There is agreement among most social scientists that 'social structure' refers to a whole of interrelated parts. Disagreements derive from the various ways in which the *parts* concept and the notion of relations or *linkages* between parts have been defined.

If one starts with the common-sense distinction between thinking and 'doing', or Merton's distinction between attitudes and performance, then 'parts' can refer (in linguistic terminology) to both virtual objects on the paradigmatic level of *langue* and actual ones on the syntagmatic level of *parole*. Consider, for example, an actor with racist attitudes (virtual, paradigmatic level). In so far as these attitudes are actualized or instantiated[5] in a particular act (e.g. voting for a racist politician) or a specific interaction (beating up a black immigrant), attitude gives way to performance and we move from paradigmatic virtuality to the syntagmatic actuality of the here and now.

Concerning the second key dimension, that of linkages between parts, these can have either a social-relational or a numerical-statistical character. For example, in normative terms, the father–son role relationship in a kinship system based on Confucian values (the son is expected to express great respect for his father) entails a *social-relational* linkage between two *virtual* objects, i.e. roles on the paradigmatic level. The *actual* relationship between a father and a son in a particular Confucian community (whether or not it is congruent with normative expectations) entails social-relational linkages on the syntagmatic level: it entails concrete relationships between persons as these unfold in time and space. Another way of putting this is to say that the syntagmatic level entails *actor–actor* social-relational linkages, whereas the paradigmatic level entails *role–role* relational linkages. Of course, actors recurrently interacting with one another may fulfil the normative expectations inherent in their roles wholly, partially or not at all. In that sense, if *virtual*

---

[4] For a systematic exposition of the various meanings of the term, see Crothers 1996.

[5] On the concept of instantiation, see Giddens, 1979.

role–role relations are normative, *actual* actor–actor relations are not non-normative but simply entail different degrees of normativity.[6]

If we now look at *statistical*, or numerical, linkages between parts, here too we can distinguish between the paradigmatic and syntagmatic levels. If, for instance, one finds that racist attitudes are very pervasive in professional category A, less so in B and very low in C, we have a statistical-numerical linkage between these three categories on the paradigmatic level. If the same study is interested less in attitudes and more in performance, it may explore the distribution of racist acts (voting, violence) in the three professions. This would give us statistical linkages between parts on the syntagmatic level, with profession A perhaps having, for instance, fewer racist incidents than profession B, and B fewer than C. In other words, when we establish linkages between the three professional categories we are not interested in whether or not the three professions are related to each other in terms of, say, conflict or co-operation. We are interested only in ranking them in terms of the racist attitudes or acts of their members. In that sense the linkages between professions A, B and C do not entail social causality; they simply entail numerical-statistical comparisons effectuated by the researcher.

The distinctions between the virtual and the actual, and between social-relational and statistical-numerical linkages lead to the fourfold typology shown in figure 7.1. The figure gives us four different types of 'social structure' – all of them very common in the social-science literature.

---

[6] Radcliffe-Brown has expressed this by arguing that in so far as the concept of social structure refers to rules, these rules are recognized by social members in two ways: either in terms of 'verbal recognition' only, or in terms of actual 'observance in behaviour' (1940: 188). In linguistic terminology, the former mode of recognition relates to the paradigmatic and the latter to the syntagmatic. From this it follows that Radcliffe-Brown's notion of social structure is quite inclusive: it entails, in my terminology, aspects of both an institutional-normative and an interactive-figurational structure. More precisely, for the British anthropologist, social structure refers to a network of social relations between persons. This network cannot be observed directly, but can be constructed by the anthropologist as she/he works from the analysis of the particular and unique to that of the general and recurrent, i.e. from particular, unique interactions to 'the form of the structure' or the 'normal form' (1940: 192ff). Therefore for Radcliffe-Brown, social structure, as 'normal form', refers to social relations based on rules which one only verbally recognizes (e.g. in society X, the role of the son entails absolute obedience to the father); as well as to rules which are actually followed (e.g. in terms of concrete practice in society X, sons tend to obey their parents in issues related to work but not in those related to marriage).

Character of linkages between parts		
	Social-relational	Statistical-numerical
Virtual	1 Institutional or normative structures	3 Virtual distributional structures
Actual	2 Interactive or figurational structures	4 Actual distributional structures

(Ontological status of parts)

Figure 7.1. A fourfold typology of social structure.

a. Institutional or normative structures (box 1)

The notion of social structure as a whole of interrelated roles (which entail normative expectations) or institutions (entailing a cluster of interrelated roles) prevails, of course, through Parsonian normative-functionalist sociology. More concretely, for Parsons (1971) the social structure of a modern societal system consists of four major institutional parts or subsystems: adaptation (economic institutions), goal achievement (political institutions), integration (legal and communal institutions) and latency (kinship, educational and religious institutions) – the well-known AGIL schema. As many critics have pointed out, Parsons is more interested in how actors orient themselves to their roles (paradigmatic level) than in how they use the norms entailed by these roles to act and interact in concrete situations (Turner, 1990; see also chapter 1, section 1).

b. Interactive or figurational structures (box 2)

Here we move from the virtual level of institutionalized roles to actual relationships between actors unfolding syntagmatically in time and space. Interpretatively oriented micro-sociologists – placing less emphasis on the roles or norms of social games than on how actors use or choose not to use such norms in the syntagmatic process of playing actual games – focus on social-relational linkages between actors rather than on roles. They see these actors not as the 'puppets' of Parsonian functionalism, but as the producers and constructors of their social world (Garfinkel, 1967). Of course, given their excessive fear of reification, many micro-sociologists avoid using terms such as social structure. But inasmuch as they emphasize the importance of social interaction (symbolic interactionism), or intersubjectivity (ethnomethodology), and of actual relationships/games between situated actors, their overall approach can be said to be social-relational on the syntagmatic rather than the paradigmatic level. To use the well-known theatrical metaphor, they are less interested in players rehearsing than in players acting out their roles on the actual stage (Goffman, 1959).

Needless to say, the concept of interactive structure can apply to both micro- and macro-situations. Elias' figurational sociology, for instance, is in many respects the mirror image of Parsons' (Mouzelis, 1995b: 69–80). In his socio-historical works, Elias focuses on the actual power relations between macro-actors (classes, interest groups) as these relations evolve syntagmatically. For instance, he shows how the increasing division of labour in France and elsewhere from the Middle Ages onwards led to growing interdependence and power equalization between groups, as well as to such processes as state expansion, concentration and/or monopolization of the means of violence at the top, extensive pacification, etc. (Elias, 1978/1982). In fact, Elias sees interdependencies between actors/groups as 'the nexus of figuration, as structures of mutually oriented and dependent people' (quoted in Crothers, 1996: 51).

A similar emphasis on actor–actor syntagmatic, social-relational linkages is to be found, of course, in macro-historically oriented comparative work. From Barrington Moore's (1967) conflicting figurations of peasants, landlords, merchants and state elites during the process of modernization to Mann's (1986) power networks (economic, military or administrative), the emphasis is on social relations between actors unfolding syntagmatically in the *longue durée*.

Finally, it is worth mentioning that the 'network-analysis' research tradition provides a clear focus on interactive social structures on both the micro- and macro-levels of analysis. Researchers in this tradition are concerned with the construction and operation of social networks of both individual micro-actors (such as neighbourhood or kinship networks) and of such macro-entities as multinational corporations or nation-states (Crothers, 1996: 92–3; Diani and McAdam, 2003).

In the light of the above examples, I wish to emphasize here that, in terms of my typology, the 'actual' entails three types of interactive relationships or situations: (i) relationships that are unfolding in the here and now and can, therefore, be 'observed' by a layperson or researcher *in situ* so to speak (e.g. a sports sociologist observing unique interactions or ongoing recurrent interactions between players during a specific football game); (ii) relationships that are *intermittently*

actualized (e.g. patterns of interactive relationships between departmental managers of a firm, relationships that cease being actualized at
night or during the holiday period); (iii) patterned relationships that
have been *actualized in the past* and no longer exist (e.g. relationships
between peasants, landlords and merchants in seventeenth-century
England).

c. Distributional structures (boxes 3 and 4)

Moving now from social-relational to statistical-numerical linkages,
here social structure refers neither to actor–actor nor to role–role connections, but to statistical-numerical linkages or computations that set
out to map distributions: i.e. how social traits (virtual or actual) are
spread among one or more specific populations. Social-stratificational
studies try, for example, to measure how virtual traits (for example,
attitudes, life chances) or actual ones (income, crime rates, birth and
death rates) are distributed among social categories (professional,
gender-based, class-based, etc.).

As already mentioned, the distributional, stratificational type of
structure is statistical rather than social-relational, in the sense that
the linkages between categories entail neither the notion of conflicting
or co-operative interactions unfolding syntagmatically in time and
space (interactive or figurational structures), nor the notion of compatible or incompatible relationships between norms or institutions on the
paradigmatic level (normative or institutional structures).

To be specific, dividing up a population into statistical categories in
terms of, say, income or chances of social mobility, can indicate how
certain types of resources are distributed. It cannot explain, however, the
constitution, reproduction or transformation of such a distribution. To
move from mere measurement and description to explanation requires
moving from statistical categories to groups or collective actors who
orient themselves to normative-institutional contexts (paradigmatically)
and/or interact with each other in time and space (syntagmatically).[7]

---

[7] Since the syntagmatic/paradigmatic distinction is also central in Lévi-Strauss's
work, it might be relevant to say a few words about how the French
anthropologist's notion of structure relates to the four types of social structure
discussed above. Since Lévi-Strauss's codes or deep structures are conceptualized
on the level of *langue*, i.e. paradigmatically, they have an affinity with what I have

d. Independent variation

The fourfold typology discussed above is, of course, based on analytic distinctions. While a specific social system (whether a formal organization, village community or nation-state) entails all four social-structural dimensions in ways that exclude their absolute separation, the distinctions are nevertheless heuristically useful because the four social structures frequently vary independently of each other. Concerning, for instance, the relationship between the institutional and interactive/figurational social structures, a classic example in the sociology-of-development literature is the dissonance in semi-peripheral countries between politico-administrative institutions imported from the West and the underlying power relations between indigenous interest groups (Riggs, 1964).

More concretely: several Balkan and Latin American countries in the nineteenth century imported Western parliamentary institutions that (in certain cases) were, democratically speaking, very advanced and progressive. For instance, Greece as well as Argentina adopted universal male suffrage decades before Great Britain did so (Mouzelis, 1986: 7–15). But, given their pre-industrial agrarian economies and the concentration of political and economic power in a handful of notable families, in both countries parliamentary institutions functioned in such a way that the majority of the population was kept outside active politics (mainly via clientelistic or more coercive means). The term *oligarchic parliamentarianism* characterizes such a type of liberal-democratic regime precisely. However, it should be noted that even then parliamentary institutions were not a mere facade or dead letter. Although they did not function as they were supposed to, parliamentary institutions did have a profound impact on the organization and dynamics of the political game. So political patrons, in their attempt to buy and control the votes of their clientele, had to develop forms of competition that were quite different from those that had prevailed before the introduction of parliamentary rule (Mouzelis, 1986: 15–50). In Greece and Argentina, therefore, liberal-democratic institutional

called institutional-normative structures as well as with virtual distributional ones. There is a difference, however. Paradigmatic social structures (relational or distributional) are not as 'hidden' as those of Lévi-Strauss. As Nadel has put it, in contrast to Lévi-Strauss, 'I consider social structure, of whatever degree of refinement, to be still the social reality itself, or an aspect of it, not the logic behind it' (1962: 150).

structures on the paradigmatic level were instantiated or actualized on the syntagmatic level – albeit in such a manner that the distance or discrepancy between the normative-virtual and the actual was much greater than in those Western democracies where parliamentary institutions had grown up from within.

Finally, if institutional structures, although always interrelated, can vary independently of interactive ones, the same is true of the relationship between social-relational and distributional structures. Similar distributional structures (of virtual or actual traits) can give rise to different social-relational wholes (of the institutional or interactive type).

The relative autonomy of social-relational structures *vis-à-vis* distributional ones does not mean, of course, that there are no affinities between the two. As has been pointed out repeatedly in both the Marxist and non-Marxist literature on social class, the development of class consciousness and class organization is closely bound up with the distributional features of a social formation or society. Members of a social category sharing common characteristics (income, educational chances, social mobility, similar work experience, etc.) have a greater potentiality for moving from quasi-group to group status, from class *in* itself to class *for* itself, from an aggregation of individuals to a self-consciously organized collective actor.

2 The impasse of transcendence strategies

a. Duality of structure: Giddens' transcendence project

Having spelled out some of the major ways in which the concept of social structure has been used in the sociological literature, as well as the interconnections between them, I shall now try to show the relevance of the above to the ongoing subjectivist–objectivist debate in sociology.

As mentioned in chapter 1, the 'transcendence' strategies of Giddens and Bourdieu have, for a variety of reasons, proved unsuccessful. At the same time the concepts they have put forward (duality of structure, habitus) do provide a foundation for a conceptual restructuring that leads not to another type of transcendence, but to a closer rapprochement between the objectivist and the subjectivist camps.

For Giddens, the way to transcend the subjectivist–objectivist gap is to theorize subject–object relationships in terms of *duality* rather than *dualism*. In conventional sociology, the subject is conceptualized as being clearly separate from social structure as object. In Durkheimian sociology, for instance (based as it is on a subject–object dualism), structures are 'out there', they operate like the walls of a room, objectively constraining, setting limits to what a subject can do. According to Giddens, it is this type of separation or distance between subject and object that results in the misleading distinction between objectivist and subjectivist perspectives – a distinction that has created a great deal of sterile controversy in the discipline.

As it is well known, Giddens, following the *langue–parole* distinction in linguistics, conceptualizes structure as a virtual system of rules and resources (paradigmatic level), which are actualized, instantiated on the syntagmatic level, whenever the subject draws upon them in order to act in a concrete social context. From this point of view, structures (i.e. rules and resources) are not only constraining but also enabling. They are both means and outcome – *means* in the sense that the subject uses rules and resources in order to act and interact; *outcome* in the sense that it is via their use/instantiation that structures are reproduced. If this is accepted, then the object (structure) is not something separate from the subject. Therefore, holds Giddens, we should no longer speak of subject–object dualism, but of subject–object duality (1984: 162–74). Schematically, Giddens' theory can be presented as follows:

Structure –	*Structuration –*	*Social system*
(rules and resources on the paradigmatic level)	(the process of drawing on rules and resources via the duality of structure)	(set of interactions or patterned relationships on the syntagmatic level)

Some years ago I argued that, on the paradigmatic level, Giddens' conceptualization is satisfactory only when the subject uses rules and resources in a 'natural-performative',[8] i.e. matter-of-fact, taken-for-granted manner (Mouzelis, 1989). It becomes highly unsatisfactory in situations where the subject takes up distance from rules and resources for investigative-theoretical or strategic-monitoring reasons. To take language as an example: we have subject–object dualism when

---

[8] The notion of 'natural-performative' attitudes, in contrast to theoretical or 'hypothetical-reflexive' ones, was developed by Habermas (1984: 80–1, 122–3).

laypersons or specialists distance themselves from such rules in order to analyse, criticize or attempt to change them. In other words, the concept of duality is not adequate in cases where rules and resources (in language, kinship, political or economic institutions) operate not so much as resources but as *topics*, not so much as a means of acting but as strategic goals, as objects that the subject approaches with theoretical, critical or monitoring intent.

Giddens answered my critique directly by arguing that, as shown by phenomenology and ethnomethodology, all social conduct entails the type of 'distancing' that in my view his duality-of-structure scheme does not adequately allow for:

Even the most enduring habits, or the most unshakeable of social norms, involves continual and reflexive attention. Routinization is of elemental importance in social life; but all routines, all the time, are potentially fragile accomplishments. (Giddens, 1993: 6)

While this is perfectly true, it should not make us deny that there are *degrees of distancing*, or degrees of what one can call *paradigmatic strategying*: that sometimes theorizing and/or strategic considerations are peripheral (in which case the duality scheme is appropriate), and at other times they are dominant (in which case dualism is more appropriate). As I stressed in my initial critique of structuration theory,

the mode in which subjects relate to rules and resources always involves a mixture of practical, theoretical, and strategic-monitoring orientations – one of these being dominant at any given time. Needless to say, this dominance can change in accordance with the context. (Mouzelis, 1989: 45)

The notion of reflexivity, as used by Giddens, does not justify the elimination of the notion of subject–object dualism. For we need concepts that can make us realize that sometimes 'distancing' or paradigmatic strategying is low or peripheral, and sometimes it is high or dominant. This is to say we need a concept to emphasize that, as far as the subject–object paradigmatic relation is concerned, the situation is not constant but *variable*. This being so, the highly useful concept of reflexivity does not eliminate, but, on the contrary, *requires* the use of subject–object duality as well as dualism on the paradigmatic level. If this is accepted, it can be argued that there is a major contradiction between Giddens' structuration theory and his more empirically oriented substantive writings, where the notion of reflexivity (individual and social) plays a crucial role.[9]

Finally, it is worth mentioning here that what Giddens calls a social system and its structural characteristics comes close to what I have called relational and distributional structures on the syntagmatic level. In fact, when Giddens moves from the paradigmatic (virtual system of rules and resources) to the syntagmatic level (social system as sets of

---

[9] Giddens' second line of defence against my original critique was to point out (1993: 6–7) that

> The 'duality' of the duality structure concerns the dependence of action and structure, taken as a logical assertion, but it certainly does not involve a merging of the situated actor with the collectivity ... it is perfectly obvious that every situated actor faces an environment of action which has an 'objectivity' for him or her in a quasi-Durkheimian sense.

Although other critics have done so, I myself have never implied that Giddens merges situated actors and the environment of action. Given that he replaces one of the conventional notions of social structure with that of social system, he quite obviously can, on the syntagmatic level, deal with the situated actor–environment relation in a non-conflationary manner.

What my critique does focus on is Giddens' argument that all he implies by the duality concept is 'the dependence of action and structure, taken as a logical assertion' (Giddens, 1993: 6). The fact, for instance, that action, logically speaking, entails structure (i.e. rules and resources) – this I do accept. But I would go further and argue that, in equally logical manner, the dependence of action can be based on predominantly theoretical-strategic orientations (dualism), as well as on practical, taken-for-granted orientations (duality). In other words, even if the terms 'duality' and 'dualism of structure' do not explain the actual constitution or transformation of social systems, even if they are mere 'logical assertions', they are both necessary as conceptual tools; they are useful as means for raising sociologically relevant questions about the manner in which subjects orient themselves to rules and resources.

Finally, it is worth mentioning here Sibeon's critique of my attempt to restructure structuration theory so that one can use the concepts of both duality and dualism (2004: 101–6). For him, following Archer, the duality concept (and therefore structuration theory as a whole) should be rejected.

If one rejects Giddens' linguistically based definition of structure and adopts Archer's, then it makes sense to reject the concept of duality altogether. On the other hand, if, as I do, one considers Giddens' definition of social structure (as rules and resources on the virtual, paradigmatic level) as not conventional but legitimate, then one can argue that his duality-of-structure concept is useful – but it only covers taken-for-granted orientations to rules and resources; therefore one also needs the dualism concept to account for orientations which are based on a 'non-taken-for-granted' mode. In other words both duality and dualism, *in the context of Giddens' definition of social structure*, are useful in reminding one that a subject's orientations to virtual objects (such as social structures in the Giddensian sense) are *variable* as far as 'taken-for-grantedness' is concerned.

patterned relationships portraying structural properties), on that level the dualism between subject and object is reintroduced by the back door, so to speak. Consider the following:

To emphasize that individuals are contextually situated within *social relations* of greater or lesser span is similarly only to identify a source of constraint if it is shown how this limits their capabilities. In each case *constraint stems from the 'objective' existence of structural properties that the individual agent is unable to change.* (Giddens, 1984: 276–7, emphasis added)

The above quotation shows that whereas critics – complaining that structuration theory does not allow for subject–object variability – focus on the concept of structure, Giddens, in rejecting their criticism, points to the concept of the social system and its structural properties. But speaking of 'the "objective" existence of structural properties that the individual agent is unable to change' brings us to the clear distinction between subject and social object that is so common in what Giddens pejoratively calls 'objectivist' or structural sociology. The only difference between Giddens' position and my own is that he allows for the clear subject–object distinction on the syntagmatic level but not on the paradigmatic one. I, on the contrary, argue that the subject–object distinction should be maintained on both levels. In the paradigmatic case too, there should be a clear distinction between the subject and virtual social structures (of a relational and/or distributional nature).

b. Habitus: Bourdieu's transcendence strategy

If Giddens tries to transcend the subjective–objective divide via the duality-of-structure concept, Bourdieu attempts something similar with his concept of habitus, a notion referring to a subject's dispositions, to the generative schemata of perception, cognition and evaluation that actors acquire in the context of their varied socializations. From this perspective, these generative schemata or dispositions are for Bourdieu 'internalized social structures' or 'embodied history'.[10]

For Giddens, the subjectivist–objectivist divide is transcended because the duality-of-structure concept pertains to both the subjective

---

[10] 'The habitus, a product of *history*, produces individual and collective practices – *more history* – in accordance with the schemes generated by history' (Bourdieu, 1990: 54).

(structure is the subject's means of action) and the objective (structure is also objective outcome). For Bourdieu, the habitus notion plays a similarly 'transcending' role. As the internalization of *objective* social structures, it entails objectivity; as the subject's means of relating to others in specific social contexts in a *practical manner*, it entails subjectivity.

To put this differently: in so far as the habitus has a quasi-automatic, quasi-unconscious character, it comes close to Lévi-Strauss's hidden codes, which are 'objective' in the sense that the subject has no theoretical knowledge of them. Nevertheless, in so far as Bourdieu stresses the practical, polysemic and polythetic character of habitus – the fact that it can flexibly apply to the ever-changing contexts of the here and now – it comes pretty close to Garfinkel's ethnomethods, for instance. Using Giddens' terminology, 'objectivist' sociology (whether structural-functional or structuralist), by emphasizing external or internalized social structures, shows human beings as passive, while subjectivist sociology, by portraying actors in a more active, autonomous manner, tends to neglect the objective enablements/constraints of social structures. For Bourdieu the habitus transcends objective as well as subjective sociology, given that it emphasizes both quasi-automatic, unconscious (i.e. objective) structural or structuralist elements *and* the proactive, constructionist elements of subjectivist approaches.

However, the 'dual' nature of the habitus, like that of Giddens' duality-of-structure concept, leaves something important underconceptualized. In the case of Giddens it is *paradigmatic* strategying; in that of Bourdieu it is *syntagmatic* strategying. Let me spell out this key point in greater detail. As I have explained at some length elsewhere (Mouzelis, 1995b: 104ff), Bourdieu sees social practices as the outcome of the *positional* as well as the *dispositional* dimensions of social games. His notion of *field* (as a set of social positions that entails degrees or forms of power/'capital' in the broad sense of the term) refers to objective social structures. The habitus, however, indicates (i) that these social structures are internalized, and (ii) that these internalized social structures (as flexible, polysemic, polythetic schemata) are the means by which the subject's practices are generated. In schematic terms, Bourdieu's theory of practice takes the form: field (positional dimension) – habitus (dispositional dimension) – social practices.

What is missing from this schema is the *interactive-situational* dimension. Practices in actual social games cannot be fully explained in terms of positions and dispositions. A satisfactory explanation must also take into account the more voluntaristic, strategying interactive-situational dimension.

In reply to this criticism Bourdieu has argued that his habitus concept, given its 'dual' character, covers both the dispositional and the interactive dimension, and that the flexible, practical, 'polythetic' nature of the habitus can adequately explain the specific practices of actors. However, in so far as these practices entail rational calculations and the construction of tactical plans in the light of ongoing interactive-situational developments, the habitus – as quasi-automatic, quasi-unconscious mechanism – cannot cover both rational decision-making and automatic, not-consciously-made orientations to action.

In view of this impossibility it is not surprising that Bourdieu attempts, in various ways, to underemphasize the rational-choice, conscious decision-making aspect of social games. Neither is it surprising that he uses the notion of strategy in a highly idiosyncratic manner – stressing the fact that strategies for him have a non-conscious, non-calculating character.[11] If that is so, then what he is concerned with are not strategies as they are commonly understood, but quasi-automatic reflex reactions to the syntagmatic unfolding of social games. (For the linkages between habitus and reflexivity, see chapter 8.)

3 A concrete example: the reproduction of the LSE as a social system

Having examined Giddens' and Bourdieu's attempts at transcending the subject–object distinction, I shall now put forward a concrete example to show how the fourfold typology of social structure elaborated above – in combination with my thesis about the variability of the subject–object relationship on both the paradigmatic and syntagmatic levels – is heuristically and methodologically more helpful than the concepts of duality of structure or habitus for understanding how social systems are produced, reproduced and transformed. Having used a historical, macro-structural example in the initial section, I here shift the focus to the micro-level of analysis, taking as a case study the London School of Economics (LSE) as a social system in which both Giddens and

---

[11] See on this point, Bourdieu, 1990: 292.

myself were involved – Giddens as a director, and I as a professor in the sociology department.

a. Reproduction via the duality of structure

For Giddens, in order to understand how the LSE is reproduced/transformed as an ongoing concern, one has to use the schema *structure – structuration – social system*. More concretely: as an active LSE participant, I draw on *rules* on the paradigmatic level while performing my teaching job – such as the obligation to give a certain number of lectures/seminars/classes, to provide reading lists, to set exam papers, to mark students' examination scripts following universalistic rather than particularistic criteria of assessment, etc. At the same time I also draw on *resources*, such as the possibility of using the School's teaching facilities (allocative resources) or the power that my position gives me to decide what texts students should read, how a seminar should be conducted or what questions to set in the examination (authoritative resources). From this perspective, rules and resources (R/R) are both *means* (enabling me to do my job) and *outcome* (in the sense that every time I draw on these R/R in order to do my teaching and examining job, they are reproduced in time and space). From this point of view the LSE as a social system is reproduced by the participants (teachers, students, the director, administrators and blue-collar workers) routinely drawing on R/R via the duality of structure, in order to go on with their daily business.

However, the above scheme by no means gives a full account of how the LSE is reproduced/transformed. It leaves out of consideration what I have called paradigmatic strategying, the fact that LSE participants (from students to teachers, from low-level administrators to the director himself) orient themselves to R/R not only via the duality of structure, i.e. in a taken-for-granted manner. They often take distance from R/R for a variety of theoretical and/or strategic reasons. For instance, I as a teacher have often thought that the rule about the three-hour written examination paper at the end of the academic year, as the major or even exclusive mode of assessing a student's yearly performance, is very unfair to students who perform badly under conditions of stress. Similar cases of participants distancing themselves from existing rules can, of course, be found at all hierarchical levels.

Moreover there is a tendency, as one moves up the LSE hierarchy, for strategic monitoring orientations to R/R (i.e. dualism) to become more important than taken-for-granted orientations (duality).[12] For instance, it is the business of the School's departmental and examination boards to enquire into the effectiveness of the present examination rules. In such a situation, examination rules are less of a 'resource' and more of a 'topic'.

Given all this, the attempt to portray the social system of the LSE as the unintended outcome of participants routinely drawing on R/R in a taken-for-granted manner is like trying to explain the construction of a complex building without taking into account that such a construction involves not only the routine activities of bricklayers, but also (on the paradigmatic level) the more 'strategying' activities of architects, planners, managers, accountants, etc.

b. Reproduction via the habitus

Moving on now to Bourdieu, his scheme of reproduction (as already mentioned) boils down to *field – habitus – social practices*. Applying it to our example, the LSE can be conceptualized as a system of positions (that of teacher, student, administrator, etc.) entailing different types and degrees of 'capital'. The positions, and the rules and resources they entail, influence but, of course, do not entirely shape the participants' practices. Therefore, if my position as a professor of sociology entails rules about teaching and examining, as well as a certain amount of economic, political and symbolic capital, the way I handle the rules and the 'capital' inherent in my position has a lot to do with my habitus – with the generative schemata of cognition, perception and evaluation I have acquired in a variety of socializing contexts (mainly) before I joined the LSE (Bourdieu, 1990: 54ff).

For instance, even if I strictly follow the teaching and examination rules, my teaching and examination practices owe a great deal to my dispositions – dispositions which cannot be derived from my professorial position. From the way I move my body while delivering a lecture

---

[12] This is only a *tendency*, in the sense that in some circumstances it is not only the upper hierarchy but also the rank and file that can adopt predominantly 'distancing' strategizing orientations *vis-à-vis* rules and resources. So, for instance, during the mobilization of the 1960s, LSE students (unsuccessfully) challenged the dominance of the written examination system. On the relationship between organizational hierarchies and the duality/dualism concepts, see Mouzelis, 1991a: 67–99.

(bodily schemata of action) to the way I use basic categories of cognition and evaluation, my dispositions can be as crucial as my position for understanding my teaching and/or examining practices.

However, if Giddens' subject–object transcendence project forecloses paradigmatic strategying, Bourdieu's (as already argued) forecloses syntagmatic strategying. It occludes the fact that a full account of my teaching and examining practices at the LSE needs to include not only my position and dispositions, but also the concrete interactive situations within which I perform the main tasks of my job. In a specific seminar, for example, the interactive logic of a clash of personalities, or an emerging divergence of interests between teacher and students or between student participants, could lead to a permanently conflictual situation. In a different seminar, however, the interactive dynamic could result in institutionalized co-operation. Needless to say, my teaching strategies in the two situations would be radically different. In both cases my actual practices will be shaped by the normative logic of my position, the practical logic of my habitus/disposition and the rational-strategying logic of the unfolding interactive situation.

c. *Reproduction and the concept of strategying*

In the light of the above it becomes obvious that both Giddens' and Bourdieu's strategies to transcend the subject–object distinction fail to account for how the LSE is reproduced as an ongoing concern. The former fails because his exclusive focus on the duality of structure does not allow the researcher to take into account the various degrees of distancing or strategying that characterize the relationship of the subject to his/her paradigmatic environment of action (i.e. to *virtual* relational and distributional structures). Furthermore, Bourdieu's strategy of transcendence does not allow the researcher to take into account the varying degrees of rational-purposive strategying that characterize the relationship of the subject to his/her syntagmatic environment of action (i.e. to *actual* relational and distributional structures). It follows that the subject–object distinction is absolutely necessary in order to account for the *variability* of the participant (subject) – social-structure (object) relationship on both the paradigmatic and the syntagmatic levels.

Concretely: as a teaching member of the LSE and on the basis of my generative schemata of perception, cognition and evaluation (schemata which I acquired mainly before joining the organization), I constantly face the relatively interrelated environments of action: a paradigmatic environment of virtual objects (relational and distributional) and a syntagmatic environment of actual objects (relational and distributional).

Consider my relationship to the LSE's examination regime. To start with examination rules: although I regularly follow such rules in a taken-for-granted, uncritical manner (duality of structure), at other times – for instance, as a member of the departmental and School examining boards – I take distance from such rules. I ask questions about the effectiveness and desirability of the basic rule of yearly written examinations as the dominant mode of assessing the students' overall performance. I also question less important, more technical rules referring to invigilation, to the ways of marking scripts, of agreeing on marks with the second internal examiner, of relating to the external examiner, etc.

This applies not only to rules inherent in a set of interrelated roles (the role of examinee, internal examiner, external examiner, etc.), but also to other virtual objects of a statistical, distributional character – such as the attitudes of students or teaching staff towards the School's existing examination regime. Whether I have knowledge of such a distribution of attitudes via existing research into the matter or via more rule-of-thumb methods, I can relate to such distributional structures in either a taken-for-granted or a more strategic manner. What I want to stress here is that whether one considers the subject's relation to institutional or virtual distributional structures, the degree of 'distancing' or paradigmatic strategying can vary from very low (duality of structure) to very high (subject–object dualism).

Moving now from the paradigmatic to the syntagmatic environment of action, let us consider the hypothetical case of myself (as an LSE member occupying a professorial position and carrying a set of generative schemata of action, cognition and perception) deciding to launch a campaign to change the prevailing examinations system. To do this I try to mobilize colleagues, students and administrators, this move becoming the starting point of an ongoing game entailing three types of actors/subjects: those in favour of moderate changes (equal weight to be given to written examination and to essay work when assessing a student's overall performance), those in favour of radical changes (abolition of the written examination mode of assessment) and those in favour of the status quo. Given this unfolding game between reformers, radicals and supporters of the status quo, my actual practices in relation to this game will be shaped not only by my position or my dispositions, but also by the dynamics of the interactive situation. Given a certain balance of forces between the three groups, I might decide (together with like-minded colleagues or students) to put into action a rational-purposive plan of building alliances between reformers and radicals, while at the same time creating divisions in the conservative camp. In order to explain my engaging in this type of activity, the notion of habitus is not enough. By taking into consideration the idea that the 'examination reform' game has not only a positional and dispositional but also an interactive-situational dimension, the notion of syntagmatic strategying must be put at the centre of analysis. In other words, the subject–object distinction must be maintained, while stressing at the same time that the subjects' relationships to their syntagmatic environment of action (which entails relational and distributional structures)[13] can vary from low to high levels of rational-purposive strategying.

Finally, it is worth noting that by being an LSE participant, I am continuously confronted with both a paradigmatic and a syntagmatic environment of action. The two environments are analytically distinct, however. Not only can they vary independently of one another, but their articulation in specific contexts may lead to subject–object *paradigmatic* or *syntagmatic* dominance. In a predominantly 'contemplative' situation (for example, when my concern for the examination regime is purely 'theoretical'), the paradigmatic subject–object relation is dominant. In situations, however, where the focus is less on 'theory' or 'idle talk' and more on 'action', it is the syntagmatic subject–object relation that is uppermost. This means that there are variations not only concerning the relationship between subject and structure on the paradigmatic and syntagmatic levels (from low to high degrees of strategying), there are also variations in the articulation of the paradigmatic action environment with the syntagmatic one.

In conclusion, this hypothetical example has made quite obvious that the subject–object distinction is absolutely necessary for understanding how a social system is reproduced and/or transformed – basically because the way in which subjects relate to virtual or actual social structures is not constant but variable. Any attempt to ignore this variation (in order to

---

[13] In the case of the examinations reform example, distributional structures of actual traits would entail, for instance, rates of failure among first-, second- and third-year students.

transcend the subject–object distinction) leads to the absurd conclusion that one can explain the reproduction/transformation of a social system without taking into account that subjects often relate to social structures (virtual and actual) in strategic terms – i.e. in terms of paradigmatic and/ or syntagmatic strategying.

4 Concluding remarks: bridging rather than transcending the divide

By taking into account the fundamental distinction between paradigmatic and syntagmatic social structures (relational and distributional), as well as the notion of the variability in the relationship between subject and social structure in terms of low to high strategying, it is possible to construct a schema which, rather than transcending existing paradigms, shows some logical connections between them. Spelling out such connections does not, of course, undermine the autonomous logic of each paradigm; it simply facilitates a certain type of rapprochement between different theoretical traditions. It provides the researcher with a vocabulary or set of conceptual tools that combats compartmentalization and enhances rapprochement between different paradigms (see figure 7.2).

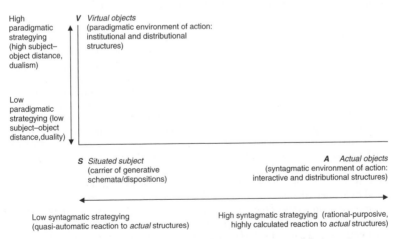

Figure 7.2. Variations in the relationship between actors and their environments of action.

In figure 7.2:

— The situated subject *S*, when involved in a social game, orients him/
herself simultaneously to *V* (virtual objects, institutional-normative
structures, distribution of attitudes, etc.) and to *A* (actual objects,
interactive-figurational structures, distributions of actual traits).
— The *S–V* dimension, referring to *paradigmatic strategying*, is variable: the more the subject is oriented to *virtual* structures (relational
or distributional) in a practical, taken-for-granted manner, the more
we have a situation of a subject–object duality on the paradigmatic
level. The more the subject, for theoretical and/or strategic reasons,
takes distance from virtual structures, the more we have a shift from
duality to dualism on the paradigmatic level.
— The *S–A* dimension, referring to *syntagmatic strategying*, is also variable. In cases where syntagmatic strategying is low or non-existent, the
subject orients him/herself to *actual* structures (relational or distributional) in a quasi-automatic manner. In cases where syntagmatic strategying is high, the subject orients him/herself to actual structures in a
highly rational-purposive, calculative manner.

If the above is given due consideration, it becomes quite clear that to
transcend the subjective–objective divide leads to the suppression of either
paradigmatic or syntagmatic strategying – i.e. to a position that ignores
the obvious multi-dimensional variability of the subjective–objective relationship.[14] What this means is that 'transcendence' (at least in the way

[14] Alexander (1998a), by using a different vocabulary, also stresses the variability of
the subject–object relationship. He begins with the very useful distinction
between action and agency. For the American theorist, the two must never be
conflated. It is agency as an analytic dimension of action which entails the
creativity, spontaneity and unpredictability spoken of by interpretative
sociologists as well as by Giddens. In this sense it is misleading to characterize the
social actor in general as knowledgeable, self-reflexive, rational, creative, etc. For
whether the agentic qualities of actors (which entail such elements as invention
and 'strategization') will lead to knowledgeable, rational, creative ways of acting
will depend on how they relate to or articulate with their environments of action.
Alexander talks about three environments of action: an 'external' one referring to
social networks formed by persons through their interactions in time and space,
and two 'internal' ones referring to cultural and motivational patterns
respectively. In terms of the subject's 'external' environment of action (which
corresponds roughly to my 'syntagmatic' one), given certain types of social
network (what I have called relational social structures), action can perfectly well
be ignorant rather than knowledgeable, irrational/non-rational rather than
rational (1998a: 218). This is to say that the subject–environment relationship

that Giddens and Bourdieu have attempted it) entails a price that is not worth paying. It means that, although it is possible and indeed useful to build bridges (like the ones proposed here) between what Giddens and Bourdieu call the subjectivist and objectivist approaches, it is not possible, without crippling distortions, to really transcend the divide.

Let me end by showing how the concepts proposed in this chapter not only show the impasses of Giddens' and Bourdieu's transcendence projects, but also can make a modest contribution towards overcoming compartmentalization and encouraging inter-paradigmatic rapprochement.

Different sociological traditions focus on the exploration of different social structures as well as on different types of relation between subject and social structure. For instance, Parsonian functionalism mainly focuses on how micro- and macro-institutional structures influence (though they do not determine) subjects as role players (social-system level) and as carriers of need-dispositions (personality-system level). Because of its passive portrayal of actors, Parsonian functionalism is compatible with the long tradition of social stratificational studies that view social structures as distributions of virtual or actual social traits among a specific population. Here, when the relationship between subject and social structure is being considered, the emphasis is on how distributional structures in quasi-Durkheimian fashion set limits to what the subject can and cannot do.

In contrast to the above 'objectivist' approaches, which place the subject at the receiving end of social determinations, the interpretative micro-sociologies emphasize that subjects are the producers rather than the products of both virtual and actual social objects; they are involved both with the construction, handling and transformation of meanings/norms/roles (micro-institutional structures) and with the construction of micro-interactive networks (figurational structures).

As to the historically oriented, Marxist tradition, here the focus is on institutional structures as well as on interactive-figurational ones. As Lockwood pointed out long ago (1964), the Marxist theory of social change, in contrast to normative functionalism, focuses not only on system integration/disintegration (i.e. on systemic contradictions and

can vary from very low or even non-existent to very high levels of experimentation, creativity and 'strategization'.

Alexander's work is an excellent example of how, via the creation of new concepts or distinctions (like that between action and agency), one can build bridges between competing paradigms (for a sympathetic critique, see chapter 4).

incompatibilities between institutional 'parts'), but also on social inte-
gration/disintegration (i.e. how actors, via conflict or co-operation, deal
with systemic contradictions). Here the subject–social structure linkages
entail collective actors/subjects who are both products and, in the long
term, producers of their paradigmatic and syntagmatic environments. It
is precisely for this reason that Marxist sociology fits neither the objectivist nor the subjectivist label – it combines both (see chapter 16).

When the differences between the above-mentioned four paradigms
are spelled out in terms of the type of social structures they explore and
the type of subject/actor–object/social structure linkages they establish,
a certain rapprochement is achieved. A set of concepts has been formulated (the fourfold typology of social structure, the notion of syntagmatic and paradigmatic variability in the subject–social structure
relationship) that can operate as a lingua franca, as a means of comparing the different logics of each of the paradigms mentioned above in a
constructive, heuristically useful manner. In such a comparative exercise, boundaries between paradigms are neither abolished (as in post-
structuralism) nor transcended (as in Giddens/Bourdieu). The internal
logic of each theoretical tradition is respected, but its claim that it
represents 'the whole truth' is seen to be unfounded.

8 | *Habitus and reflexivity: restructuring Bourdieu's theory of practice*

Introduction

A critical assessment of the relationship between the notions of habitus and of reflexivity must start with the habitus–reflexivity connection being placed within Bourdieu's overall 'theory-of-practice' scheme. For the French sociologist the habitus, as a set of dispositions (i.e. of generative schemata of cognition, perception, evaluation, etc.), is the major link between social structures on the one hand and practices on the other. Social structures, via various socialization processes, are internalized and become dispositions, and dispositions lead to practices which, in turn, reproduce social structures. It is in this way, according to Bourdieu, that the habitus transcends the subjectivist–objectivist divide in the social sciences: it is both structured and structuring, an objective product of social structures as well as the producer of practices reproducing social structures (Bourdieu, 1977, 1990). To put it schematically, we have:

Social structures (S) → Dispositions (D) → Practices (P).[1]

The SDP scheme has often been criticized as being mechanistic and deterministic or as differing very little from Parsons' oversystemic, functionalist analysis of social action (Jenkins, 1991; Mouzelis, 1995b: 100–26). Bourdieu has defended his scheme by arguing that the habitus does not automatically lead to practices and that on the contrary, it is flexible, 'polysemic and polythetic'. Rather than strictly determining practices, it operates as a limiting framework within which a great number of practices can be produced. 'The habitus, like every "art of inventing", is what makes it possible to produce an infinite number of practices that are relatively unpredictable, even if they are limited in their diversity' (Bourdieu, 1990: 63).

---

[1] For a succinct formulation of the SDP scheme and its application in the field of education, see Nash, 2003.

It is precisely this inventive flexibility that allows the habitus carrier, when s/he enters a specific field, to cope with the varied requirements that 'positions' entail. According to Bourdieu, however, this type of polythetic adaptability operates in a taken-for-granted, non-reflexive manner. In normal circumstances the habitus functions in a way that entails neither introspection nor calculation; in normal circumstances an actor's dispositions and the field's positions lead to practices without the activation of rationally based strategies. It is only when 'crises' occur, i.e. when there is a lack of fit between dispositions and positions, that reflexivity and rational strategying enter the scene. When positions change and strategies lag behind, the habitus carrier is obliged to abandon her/his taken-for-granted orientations and to adopt more reflexive, calculating modes of operation (Bourdieu and Wacquant, 1992: 131).

1 Dispositions, positions and interactions

The first objection to Bourdieu's thesis about the habitus–reflexivity relationship is that, as I argued in the previous chapter, in order to understand what role reflexivity assumes in a given field, one has to consider not only the dispositional and positional but also the inter-active dimension of the social games played within it. If a field's game entails the varied internalized dispositional structures of the players involved, it also entails not only relations between positions (i.e. in conventional sociology, the *role/institutional structure* of the game) but also the actual relations between actors (in Elias' terminology, *figurational structures*),[2] which often entail a rational, strategying dimension.

It is true of course that for Bourdieu, the carriers of dispositions who occupy specific positions within a specific field fight over the acquisition of different types of capital. But the French sociologist does not leave theoretical space for the relatively autonomous logic of the strategic/rational aspects of the fighting process. In that sense Bourdieu overemphasizes the *normative* logic of positions and the *practical* logic of dispositions and underemphasizes the *strategic/rational* logic of interactions.

To be more concrete: in a football game, for instance, each situated player, as the carrier of dispositions (acquired via various socializations),

---

[2] For a critical discussion of Elias' figurational sociology and the differences between institutional and figurational structures, see Mouzelis, 1993b.

has to pay attention not only to the rules of the game that apply to her/ his position and the position of the other players, but also to the actual interactive relations entailing different degrees of strategic/rational calculation between players. In other words, a specific habitus carrier has to take into account both the game's institutional structure (i.e. the relationships between roles/positions) and its figurational structure (i.e. the relationships between actual players). Figurational structures are not reducible to institutional structures, since there is often a discrepancy between what is demanded by a role's normative requirements and what actually happens in the context of the game's concrete interactive processes (see the postscript to chapter 4). Therefore, a field and the game related to it entail three rather than two social structures: (i) internalized dispositional structures (the habitus) based on what Bourdieu calls a practical logic, (ii) institutional structures (the system of positions) operating on the basis of a normative logic and (iii) figurational structures (systems of patterned relationships between actors) operating on the basis of an interactive and strategying logic.[3]

2 Reflexivity

If the above is accepted, rational and/or reflexive calculation does not appear, as Bourdieu argues, only when there is a lack of fit between dispositions and positions. It appears also

— when there are incongruencies between dispositional, positional and figurational structures;
— when there are intra-habitus (intra-dispositional) contradictions;
— when persons are reflexive, irrespective of how congruent or incongruent dispositions are *vis-à-vis* positions and/or figurations.

a. Reflexivity and contradictions between dispositions, positions and figurations

Consideration of the interactive-figurational dimension of social games makes it obvious that an actor's dispositions might be in conflict not only with a field's system of positions but also with its figurational

---

[3] For a concrete example of these three basic dimensions of a social game, see Mouzelis, 1995b: 101–14.

structures, with the way in which actual players rather than positions relate to each other. Let us take as an example Crozier's classical study of a formal organization where a group of actors, taking advantage of an area of 'organizational uncertainty', manage to monopolize key resources and to impose their will on their hierarchical superiors (Crozier, 1963: 200ff). In this case we have an incongruence between a *de jure* situation (constituted by the normative requirements entailed in the hierarchical system of positions) and a *de facto* situation consisting of emergent power relationships between actual interacting subjects. This means that there is a lack of fit between institutional and figurational structures. Although Crozier does not deal with the issue of reflexivity, it is reasonable to hypothesize that the actors involved (particularly those whose hierarchically superior positions gave them rights of command they were unable to exercise) became more aware both of the institutional and figurational structures of the field and of the lack of fit between dispositions, positions and figurations.

b. Reflexivity and intra-habitus contradictions

Reflexivity may focus less on interactive and more on *intra-active* processes. In other words, reflexivity may be enhanced not only when there are contradictions between dispositions, positions and figurations, but also when the subject has to handle intra-habitus conflicts. For instance, Trevor Butt and Darren Langdridge (2003) studied the diaries of the well-known comedian Kenneth Williams and found a deep contradiction between his homosexual dispositions on the one hand, and his deeply conservative, anti-libertarian mentality on the other; the latter predisposed him to consider anything related to homosexuality as 'filth'. These two fundamental aspects of Williams' habitus – both products of differing and varied socialization processes – were obviously linked to his overdeveloped reflexivity, which a reading of his diaries makes very obvious.

c. Reflexivity unrelated to contradictions

Bourdieu's emphasis on the predominantly pre-reflexive nature of the habitus and his underemphasis of the interactive dimension of social games has led him to overlook types of reflexivity that are not linked to 'crisis' situations – i.e. types of reflexivity that are features of everyday situations. The constant internal accounting that actors perform in routine social interactions (what ethnomethodologists call 'reflexive accounting') goes on regardless of whether or not the habitus is congruent with a field's positions. In fact, as Garfinkel (1967) has convincingly shown, reflexive accounting is a constitutive feature of all social encounters.

When Bourdieu argues that the habitus is highly flexible and inventive, he does not take seriously into consideration that this inventiveness, which is required by the game's constantly unfolding interactive situation, entails reflexivity. In other words, players cannot perform at all if they do not combine the taken-for-granted practical logic of their dispositions with the reflexive-calculative logic resulting from their involvement in interactive situations.

In addition to reflexive accounting, one must also bear in mind that reflexivity can be related to an actor's special disposition, i.e. to a reflexive disposition acquired not via crisis situations but via a socialization focusing on the importance of 'the inner life' or the necessity to 'create one's own goals'. For instance, growing up in a religious community which stresses meditation and inner contemplation can result in members of this community acquiring a type of reflexive habitus that is unrelated to contradictions between dispositions and positions.

Moreover, reflexivity can take historically specific forms. Giddens' and Beck's reflexive modernization, for instance, refers to a historically specific, post-traditional situation where actors find themselves obliged to reflexively create their own lifestyles, 'their own biography'. Given that in late modernity neither tradition nor collective ideologies can provide a set of goals for organizing everyday existence, individuals are 'forced to choose' – forced, that is to say, to become reflexive on matters ranging from the clothes they wear and the food they eat to the type of family they want to create. In all such cases, major or minor, broad or narrow goals are constantly constructed and reconstructed by reflexive subjects trying to fill the void left by the demise of traditional codes and early-modern ideologies (Beck *et al.*, 1994).

Finally, in late modernity reflexivity may take less activistic and more 'apophatic'[4] forms: the absence of traditionally or ideologically formulated goals may lead the reflexively orientated subject to a type of inner

---

[4] For the distinction between apophatic (negative) and kataphatic (positive) forms of reflexivity, see Mouzelis, 1999a.

exploration which, instead of consciously setting targets and rationally choosing the means to achieve them, aims at removing internal obstacles that are preventing the spontaneous emergence of personal goals. The psychoanalytic tradition is based on such types of reflexivity. The aim of analysis is not to impose on or offer the analysand pre-set goals, but rather to 'negatively' eliminate or weaken various defensive mechanisms that are obstructing the emergence of a person's 'genuine' goals. The same type of apophatic reflexivity is found in religious and spiritual traditions where the approach to the divine is achieved not by rationalistic, cognitive means but by the so-called *via negativa*. The believer turns inward in order to eliminate thoughts and/or practices that prevent him/her from becoming an 'open vessel' ready to receive the divine light (Mouzelis, 1999a: 87–90).

3 Bourdieu's conception of the subject

In the light of what has been said above, one can argue that Bourdieu's actor is halfway between Parsons' 'oversocialized' and Lévi-Strauss's 'decentred' subject. For Bourdieu, the subject relates to the former in the sense that the habitus carrier, in normal non-crisis conditions, portrays a lack of voluntarism and lack of reflexive handling of positions similar to Parsons' 'cultural-dope' actor *vis-à-vis* the role s/he plays. It relates to Lévi-Strauss's decentred subject in that Bourdieu's actor has only practical rather than theoretical knowledge of his/her dispositions. This means that at least some of the more unconscious dispositions come very close to Lévi-Strauss's 'hidden codes', which refer to the rules below the conscious surface that people follow without being aware of them.

All three authors, in different ways of course, underemphasize the agentic, voluntaristic, strategying qualities of actors. For Lévi-Strauss, anti-voluntarism relates to the structuralist attempt to abolish the subject–object distinction by decentring the subject, by going beyond or behind surface rules and norms. In Parsons, the subject–object distinction is maintained, but interaction is underemphasized[5] and players are portrayed as passive products of objective social structures (Mouzelis, 1995b: 129ff). In Bourdieu's case, finally, the subjective–objective

[5] For the underemphasis of the interactive dimension in Parsons' middle and late periods, see Turner, 1990. See also chapter 1, section 1.

divide is not abolished but transcended via a 'structurationist' strategy, which regards the habitus as pertaining to both the objective (the habitus as product of structures) and the subjective (the habitus as 'structuring' structures).[6]

It may, of course, be argued that it is unfair to criticize Bourdieu's overall theoretical scheme for lack of voluntarism. It could be objected that, unlike Parsons, Bourdieu constantly refers to actors' struggles, to their strategies aiming at the acquisition of a field's various types of capital (economic, political, symbolic, etc.).[7] But neither the struggles nor the strategies in Bourdieu's theory of practice entail rational calculation and/or reflexive handling of the norms and actions of the players. As I have argued in the previous chapter, strategies for Bourdieu do not as a rule involve rational calculation and reflexive accounting. They are generated and unfold quasi-automatically as actors, in taken-for-granted fashion, mobilize their dispositional potential within a field's interrelated positions. Therefore, in 'normal' conditions the rational, calculating, voluntaristic elements of action are absent or peripheral. For the French sociologist it is only in exceptional circumstances that, similar to reflexivity, rational strategying comes to the fore.

The most profitable strategies are usually those produced, *without any calculation*, and in the illusion of the most absolute 'sincerity', by a habitus objectively fitted to the objective structures. These strategies *without strategic calculation* produce an important secondary advantage for those who can scarcely be called their authors: the social approval occurring to apparent disinterestedness. (Bourdieu 1990: 292, emphasis added)[8]

---

[6] For a comparison of the ways in which Bourdieu's and Giddens' structurationism tries to transcend the subjective–objective divide, see chapter 7. See also Parker, 2000: 39–69.

[7] For a defence of Bourdieu's theory of practice along such lines, see McNay, 1999.

[8] It is fair to note that the absence of conscious calculation in Bourdieu's concept of strategy does not mean that his theory of practice leads to determinism. 'The idea of strategy, like the orientation of practice, is not conscious or calculated nor is it mechanically determined. It is the intuitive product of knowing the rules of the game' (Harker *et al.*, 1990: 17). But 'knowing the rules of the game' is not sufficient for playing it successfully. If a game's interactive dimension is seriously taken into account, it will be seen that what Bourdieu calls 'inventiveness' necessarily entails not only an intuitive knowledge of game rules, but also the reflexive, rational handling of such rules. For the strong linkages between interaction and 'inventiveness'/creativity, see Joas, 1996 and chapter 5.

This highly idiosyncratic, non-voluntaristic conceptualization of the notions of strategy and struggles creates some serious problems. First of all, Bourdieu's position does not sufficiently acknowledge that the degree of rational calculation and of reflexivity involved in social games is an empirical question. Quite obviously certain games (e.g. a game of chess, inter-firm competition for the acquisition of a larger market share, inter-state geopolitical struggles, etc.) require high levels of rational calculation. Other social games do not (e.g. religious ceremonies within which interactions have a strictly ritualistic character).

It should by now have become obvious that the reason Bourdieu has conceptualized strategies in a way that does not entail rational calculation and reflexivity has less to do with the rarity of rational strategying (in the current sense of the term) than with his attempt to 'transcend' the subjectivist–objectivist divide. Such transcendence implies subject–object conflation, a lack of distance between subjective dispositions and objective positions/figurations; it implies, in other words, practices being performed in a taken-for-granted, quasi-automatic, non-reflexive manner. It is only when the subjective–objective distinction is maintained that it is possible to deal in a theoretically congruent manner with cases where situated actors distance themselves from social structures relatively external[9] to them in order to assess, more or less rationally, the degrees of constraint and enablement these structures offer, the pros and cons, the chances of success or failure of different strategies, etc.

Of course, Bourdieu cannot completely avoid the above type of voluntaristic consideration in his empirical work. For instance, when he refers to the 'Don Quixote syndrome', i.e. to situations where a subject's dispositions clash with a field's positions, he does allow for the emergence of reflexivity. But he does so not because of but *despite* his conceptual framework. The latter is constructed around the idea that there is no distance between the subject as habitus carrier and social structures. Hence reflexivity and rational strategying (which entail distance) are considered as *exceptional* states of affairs. In this way the subject–object distinction is reluctantly brought back into consideration by the back door, so to speak: it does operate, but only in exceptional cases.

---

[9] Relatively 'external' in the sense that a field's institutional and figurational structures may exist before a specific actor enters a particular field and may continue after the actor's temporary or permanent exit.

Given Bourdieu's underemphasis of intra- and interaction, it is not surprising that despite his frequent reference to actors struggling for the acquisition of more capital in specific fields, the overall picture of a field or set of fields remains static – the emphasis always being on reproduction rather than transformation. As Savage *et al.* (2005: 42) put it,

there is the tendency within Bourdieu's thinking towards a kind of *latent functionalism*, where the process of reproduction seemingly allows the endless reproduction of power. Where there appear to be examples of the relatively disadvantaged improving their position, this is interpreted by Bourdieu as due to the moving of goalposts (to use the kind of metaphors he adopts), this rendering any improvement illusory. (emphasis added)[10]

4 Restructuring the SDP scheme

To summarize the above: Bourdieu's notion of the habitus and his theory of practice generally – given that it is based on the idea of transcending the subjectivist–objectivist divide – underemphasizes the rational, calculative and reflexive aspects of human action. As a result, when he deals with specific fields and the social games related to them, he stresses more their dispositional and positional and less their inter-active dimensions; more a subject's internalized dispositions and a field's positional-institutional structures and less its figurational ones; more the practical logic of dispositions and the normative logic of positions and roles and less the rational and reflexive logic of interactive situations.

The habitus concept cannot account effectively for social practices unless its connections are shown with not only positional and institu-tional but also interactive-figurational structures. The latter, because they entail notions of reflexive accounting, of calculation and of rational strategying, are indispensable for an understanding of how practices come into being and how social structures are reproduced and transformed.

---

[10] The same latent functionalism can be identified when Bourdieu refers to classes. The approach is *either* social stratificational, the focus being on how social traits are distributed within a specific population (see, on this, Mouzelis, 1995b: 114–16), *or* class is conceptualized as an 'effect' of the structuring of the various fields (Savage *et al.*, 2005). The latter definition reminds one of Althusser's and Poulantzas' conceptualization of class struggles as the effects of a combination of economic, political and ideological structures (Poulantzas, 1968).

If the above is given due consideration, it will be seen that the only way to overcome the functionalism and/or determinism which, as many critics have pointed out, characterize Bourdieu's theory of practice, is by restructuring the structure–disposition–practice (SDP) scheme so as to ensure that it takes seriously into account the reflexive, rational and voluntaristic aspects of social action and the interactive-figurational structure of social games that they entail. To be more specific, two major modifications are necessary for an effective restructuring of the SDP scheme:

(i) there must be a clear distinction between an initial phase (t_1) when social structures are internalized by the subject via socialization, and a subsequent phase (t_2) when the subject as habitus carrier is involved in a specific field and its games;

(ii) equally, there must be a clear distinction between a field's positional/institutional structures (as a set of positions or roles) and figurational structures (as a set of patterned relations between actual players).

If these modifications are made, then the SDP scheme becomes more complex, as is illustrated in figure 8.1. At an initial phase (t_1) a subject, via varied socializations, internalizes social structures (S) and acquires a set of dispositions (D). At t_2 the subject or player is situated in a specific field. S/he is confronted by and has to take into consideration the field's interrelated positions, i.e. its institutional structure (S_i). S/he also has to take into account the field's unfolding figurational structure (S_f). Practices at t_2 are the result of an articulation of dispositions (D) – acquired via the internalization of 'general' (i.e. non-specific to a particular field) social structures (S) at t_1 – of positions (S_i) and figurations (S_f) at t_2. To put this differently: players involved in a field's social game,

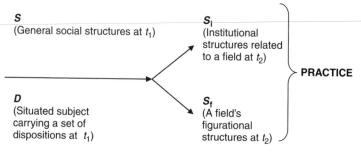

Figure 8.1. Restructuring the SDP scheme.

singly or collectively, produce practices or game outcomes by mobilizing their dispositions in the light of constraints/enablements generated by a field's institutional *and* figurational structures.

As far as reflexivity is concerned, this does not appear only when there are incongruencies between dispositions and positions, or even between dispositions, positions and figurations. As 'reflexive accounting', it is a constitutive figure of all interactive structures. Moreover, there can be pronounced reflexivity not only in situations of incongruency but also when social circumstances in general and/or a type of socialization in particular favour the development of what has been called a 'reflexive habitus' (Sweetman, 2003).

PART IV

Bridges between modern and late/postmodern theorizing

9 | Modernity: a non-Eurocentric conceptualization

Introduction

Ever since the concepts of modernity and modernization entered the sociological literature, they have been criticized for their emphatically Eurocentric nature. Whether one looks at such obvious instances as Parsonian neo-evolutionism and its applications to the study of Third World development, or at more sophisticated uses of the term in, for instance, the works of Giddens or Stewart Hall – all of them, according to the critics, manifest a strong tendency to view non-Western developmental trajectories (past, present and future) in terms of 'what happened in the West'.[1]

In the case of the Parsonian-oriented sociology of modernization, for example, the well-known ideal-typical 'tradition/modernity' dichotomy places Western societies at the modern end of the continuum, with Third World countries moving more or less rapidly up the evolutionary ladder through the diffusion of Western values, technology and capital.[2] As to Giddens (1985), who does attempt to avoid any conceptualization tainted by evolutionist and/or functionalist thinking, he too views capitalism as a major component of modernity (together with industrialism and the centralized means of violence and surveillance). This results in a situation where the non-capitalist developmental paths followed for more than half a century by the Soviet Union and other countries are considered as non-modern. Stewart Hall, although he differs from Giddens in viewing contemporary Western societies as postmodern rather than late modern, again sees capitalism as a fundamental dimension of modernity, and argues that pre-1989 Eastern

---

[1] An earlier version of this chapter appeared in the *British Journal of Sociology*, vol. 50 (1999).

[2] For an early critique focusing on the Eurocentric character of modernization studies in the so-called Third World, see Hoogvelt, 1978.

European societies constitute exceptions.[3] Finally, if one looks at purely cultural definitions of modernity, these tend to emphasize values and/or orientations that are considered to have a Western origin (e.g. belief in human progress, viewing the social world as ambiguous, evanescent, precarious, etc.); whereas, in fact, such values/orientations are neither specifically Western nor specifically modern.[4]

In the anti-Eurocentric, 'postmodern' camp the situation is even more disappointing. While its followers correctly point out the deficiencies inherent in viewing the development of humankind in terms of the Western model, when they move from critique to constructive proposals, what they have to offer is still less acceptable. By adopting extreme forms of cultural relativism, these theorists fail to differentiate features of advanced modern societies that are specifically Western (e.g. certain forms of individualism) from those which, although fully institutionalized in the West, have a more universal character. This applies both in the sense that one finds less developed forms of such features (e.g. bureaucracy, markets) in several non-European civilizations and in the sense that some of these features that critics of Eurocentrism consider Western should rather be viewed as *evolutionary universals*: as institutional breakthroughs that (whether invented or borrowed) are necessary but not sufficient preconditions for societies to move to higher levels of complexity and adaptive capacity.[5]

Failing to differentiate specifically Western from universal features of modernity, the anti-Eurocentric advocates end up with: *ethical relativism* (e.g. it is impossible to criticize non-Western cultural practices that violate basic human rights, since the notion of human rights is a Western invention); *cognitive relativism* (e.g. Western science has no *cognitive* superiority over non-Western modes of thought);[6] and

---

[3] See Hall and Grieben, 1992: Introduction.

[4] For instance those who, influenced by Simmel's urban sociology and stressing the fleeting and transient character of modern life, do not seem to realize that one finds similar orientations and interpretations in pre-modern cosmopolitan centres (e.g. Ptolemaic Alexandria).

[5] Although one can disagree with Parsons' specific list of evolutionary universals, I think that the basic concept is a sound one and extremely useful for understanding processes of modernization in the contemporary world (see Parsons, 1964a and chapter 3).

[6] For a powerful critique of these positions, see Gellner, 1992: 55ff.

Third World centrism (e.g. it is impossible to effectively criticize Western capitalism or colonialism by using 'Western' social-science concepts, etc.).[7]

Given the above unsatisfactory situation, the problem is to find a middle position between the obvious Eurocentrism of prevailing descriptions of modernity/modernization and the ultra-relativistic Third Worldist proposals that critics of Eurocentrism have to offer us. More specifically, a non-Eurocentric, non-relativistic conceptualization of modernity should be able to:

(i) accommodate forms of development where the capitalist mode of production is either strongly peripheralized (e.g. the Soviet Union and present-day North Korea and Cuba); or, without being peripheral within the economy, the capitalist logic is clearly subordinated to logics emanating from non-economic institutional spheres such as the religious (Iran) or the politico-military (Nigeria, Congo);

(ii) do the above while simultaneously showing clearly what is distinctive about modernity, what distinguishes for instance modern societies (like the United States, the Soviet Union or Iran) from pre-modern or non-modern complex, differentiated societies (such as Hellenistic Egypt, Ancient Rome, the Chinese or Islamic empires).

When (i) and (ii) are met, one can argue that Western modernity is simply one modernity among others. Although historically the first to appear and currently dominant, it is neither unique nor will it necessarily continue to be dominant in the future.

1 Modernity: mobilization/incorporation into the centre

By adopting a social-structural rather than cultural definition, we can regard modernity as the type of social arrangements that became dominant in Western Europe after the English Industrial Revolution and the French Revolution. These arrangements entailed unprecedented social mobilization that weakened people's ties with their local, self-contained, non-differentiated communities and brought them closer to

---

[7] The rapidly growing list of post-colonial studies, greatly influenced by Edward Said's *Orientalism*, provides numerous examples of this type of extreme anti-Eurocentrism. See, for instance, Williams and Chrisman, 1993.

the 'centre', i.e. integrated/incorporated them into the much wider political, economic, social and cultural arenas which, in part at least, constitute what we call the nation-state.[8]

The nation-state is historically unique in the sense that, compared to all pre-industrial states, it achieved unprecedented 'infrastructural' powers. So it succeeded in penetrating the periphery and bringing its population into centralized bureaucratic mechanisms, to a degree that was simply unthinkable in any pre-industrial social formation. In fact, pre-industrial states, however despotic, were both minute and extremely weak by comparison (in terms of size and resource-mobilization capacity) with the nation-state (Mann, 1986).

Given the seventeenth-century scientific revolution and the subsequent development of formidable technologies not only in the economic but also in the administrative, military and cultural fields, the nation-state managed to mobilize human and non-human resources to such an extent that 'segmental localism' (economic, social, political, cultural) was dramatically weakened as subjects were transformed into citizens, and as people gradually shifted their loyalties and orientations from the local, traditional communities to the 'imagined community' of the nation-state (Anderson, 1991).

2 Modernity: institutional differentiation

If one moves from a social- to a system-integration perspective, to use Lockwood's (1964) fundamental distinction, that is, from an agency to a systemic/institutional approach (see chapter 6), a second notion that can help us conceptualize modernity in a non-Eurocentric manner is that of institutional differentiation.

As Parsons and Habermas, among others, have convincingly demonstrated, modern societies have surpassed all earlier levels of structural-functional differentiation. Pre-industrial, *ancien régime* societies, despite their transcendence of the type of segmentalism that is found in tribal social formations, never achieved the separation and autonomization of institutional spheres that one sees in modernity. As Marx (1859/1964) and many others have pointed out, in the oriental-despotic type of pre-modern society, for instance, social differentiation

---

[8] For an early formulation of modernity along such lines, see Nettl, 1967; Bendix, 1969.

was limited at the top – the base or periphery consisted of highly self-contained, non-differentiated, segmentally organized communities. It is only in modernity that differentiation displaces segmentation and acquires a 'top-down' character.

By placing the concept of structural-functional differentiation at the centre of his neo-evolutionist theory of change, Parsons (1966, 1971, 1977) has done more than any other theorist to provide a theoretically sophisticated framework for the study of this fundamental process. However, the manner in which he has theorized it creates a variety of problems that do indeed, as his critics point out, lead to Eurocentrism. In this respect I think that the way out of Eurocentrism is neither the total rejection of evolutionary thinking nor the adoption of an extreme form of cultural relativism (which creates more problems than it solves). *Pace* Habermas (1987), I believe that it is necessary not merely to deconstruct but also to reconstruct Parsonian neo-evolutionism. This would, for instance, retain, in a new form, such fundamental notions as the differentiation of a social system into four subsystems (adaptation, goal achievement, integration, latency – AGIL for short), or that of evolutionary universals, as well as *combine* neo-evolutionist insights with those derived from a more Marxist-influenced historical sociology (like those of Bendix, Mann and Moore).

As I have already pointed out in chapter 2, section 3, Parsons' late work identifies four major components of evolutionary development: differentiation, integration, value generalization and adaptive upgrading. As one moves from less to more *differentiated* forms of social organization, there is the problem of *integrating* or including the more specialized roles/units into the overall social system. This requires a shift from particularistic to more abstract/generalized, universalistic values capable of subsuming under their *umbrella* the new roles/units. Once integration, via value generalization, is achieved, the social system acquires higher levels of adaptive capacity (Parsons, 1971: 26–7).

Now the difficulty with the above formulation is that differentiation, even when strongly institutionalized, does not always relate to the other three aspects of evolutionary development in the way Parsons implies. This becomes obvious if one considers that role integration or unit 'inclusion'[9] can take both *balanced* and *unbalanced* forms: the differentiated roles/institutions may be integrated in such a way that the

---

[9] Here 'units' or 'system parts' can refer both to actors and to roles/institutions.

separate logic of each of them is respected; but they may also be
included in a larger whole in an unbalanced manner so that the logic
of one differentiated unit dominates that of another. Parsons could
argue, of course, that in a case of unbalanced inclusion the process of
differentiation has failed to be institutionalized and we have *regressive*
dedifferentiation. I think this would be misleading. There is surely a
state of affairs between balanced differentiation/inclusion and dediffer-
entiation/regression – for example, the case where differentiation does
stabilize, but where one differentiated unit dominates the others without at the same time eliminating the social division of labour, i.e. without regression to segmental forms of social organization.

Let me give a concrete example. It can be argued that during the
Thatcherite era the autonomous logic of the British higher education
system (which Parsons would place in the latency subsystem) was
seriously undermined by the increased dominance of the managerial/
market logic of the adaptation subsystem. Thus *cognitive rationality*
(the value which, according to Parsons, should be dominant within the
university) was weakened by such measures as the abolition of tenure,
the adoption of managerial forms of 'quality control', the emphasis on
'market-relevant' applied courses, etc. But this state of affairs cannot
abolish the differentiation between the educational and the economic
subsystem. It does not bring the British system of higher education back
to a situation where the educational function is embedded in, for instance,
the religious and/or kinship institutions. To use Durkheimian terminology, this is not a case of regression (in evolutionary terms) from *organ* to
segment. The social division of labour is maintained, society continues
to be organized on the basis of specialized organs rather than less
specialized segments. It is simply that 'inclusion' of the differentiated
parts is achieved in an unbalanced manner: the logic of one subsystem
peripheralizes or *colonizes* that of another.[10]

a. Formal and substantive differentiation

Another way of clarifying this crucial point is to distinguish analytically
between formal and substantive differentiation. In the first we have the

---

[10] Actual dedifferentiation would consist of, for example, the kind of 'feudalizing'
tendency that is seen in declining patrimonial empires (Weber, 1925/1978:
231ff).

emergence and institutionalization of specialized units (roles, institutions, organizations). In the second the process is taken a step further in that the newly formed units achieve a high degree of autonomy: they are 'included' in the societal whole in a balanced, *multilogical* manner. This means that formal differentiation refers to the problem of the institutional *separation* of the parts, whereas substantive differentiation refers to the problem of the *autonomy* of the differentiated parts.

To revert to our earlier example, the undermining of university autonomy should be conceptualized not as a return to segmentalism (because when segmentalism prevails the problem of balanced/unbalanced inclusion, i.e. the problem of the relative autonomy of differentiated units, cannot even be raised), but as a shift from balanced to unbalanced inclusion: the basic social division of labour is maintained, but the managerial ethos, in monologic fashion, 'colonizes' the academic one. If, as Parsons has argued, functional differentiation in modern societies is linked with the development of civic, political and social rights (see chapter 2), we should not forget that in several contemporary societies (e.g. China) we have increased functional differentiation without the spread of rights. Hence the utility of the distinction between formal and substantive differentiation.

b. Value generalization

If, therefore, during the process of structural-functional differentiation inclusion can be both balanced and unbalanced, then value generalization becomes necessary only in the case of balanced inclusion. In the unbalanced case, differentiation can be institutionalized in a *particularistic* fashion: by imposing the 'less generalized' values/logic of one differentiated unit on that of another. Taking the obvious example of Japanese modernization, it can be argued that here overall integration/inclusion has been achieved not by 'value generalization' but by the ingenious adaptation of particularistic, patriarchal values which, to an important extent, have imposed themselves on all subsystems, including the economic one.[11]

Furthermore, it can be argued that even in Western European modernization, 'inclusion' has not been as balanced as Parsons implies. Thus in the post-1974 period, the dominance of neoliberal capitalism has

---

[11] On the concept of patriarchalism, see Weber, 1925/1978: 943.

meant that the economic logic of productivity has seriously undermined the autonomy of solidaristic values in the integration subsystem, and those of 'commitment' in the latency subsystem. To use another terminology: if Habermas is correct in arguing that in late capitalism the *system* (i.e. Parsons' adaptation and goal achievement subsystems) has colonized the *lifeworld*, then value generalization in the sense Parsons uses the term has not occurred. I would point out that to achieve balanced inclusion (i.e. to move from formal to substantive differentiation) is extremely difficult and rare in all modernizing trajectories, including the Western one. With reference to the latter, it is worth mentioning that during the interwar period, unbalanced, *monologic* differentiation took its most extreme form in Nazi Germany and the Stalinist Soviet Union. It is only during the brief transition from liberal to social-democratic capitalism (which reached its most developed form in the Western social democracies in the early postwar period) that one could see a *timid* development of multilogical, 'balanced' modernization.[12]

c. Adaptive upgrading

This brings us to the last dimension of Parsons' evolutionary development. If stable differentiation is not necessarily linked with value generalization, neither is the latter with adaptive upgrading. To take Asian capitalism: if by adaptive upgrading we mean the generation of resources which enable a society to avoid the typical bottlenecks of late development, then the relatively authoritarian development of the South Korean and Taiwanese type is an obvious case where 'unbalanced inclusion' (which prevents value generalization) is not at all incompatible with adaptive upgrading.

This being so, Parsons' (1964a) idea that liberal-democratic forms of government constitute an evolutionary universal, that they are a precondition for a society to achieve higher levels of adaptive capacity, is not always true. Particularly with respect to late developers it can be

[12] 'Timid' in the sense that social-democratic statism managed to achieve a high degree of solidarity, but at the price of weakening various aspects of civil society (Cohen and Arato, 1992). Also, in so far as in even a successful social-democratic regime economic capital can more or less automatically acquire cultural capital (e.g. via mass-media control), there are profound imbalances in Western capitalist societies between economic values and values derived from the political, social and cultural spheres.

said that if, in the present global environment, the shift from a command to a market economy is a precondition for higher adaptive capacity, this does not automatically apply to the political subsystem as well. So if political democratization, in more or less superficial form, is spreading to peripheral and semi-peripheral capitalist countries nowadays, as Mann (1986) has argued, this may have to do less with its structural unavoidability in conditions of late modernity than with the conjuncturally explained defeat of the Axis powers and the rise of American hegemony after World War II.

In other words, concerning late developers, quasi-authoritarian forms of government, in so far as they 'deliver the goods' (high economic growth and the limited spread of its fruits to the bottom of the social pyramid), may be more 'adaptive' in the present global environment than liberal-democratic forms of governance, which combine chronic economic bottlenecks with growing inequalities and the socio-economic peripheralization of the less advantaged classes.[13] In brief, adaptive upgrading and political democratization do not necessarily go hand in hand in the present world order.

Finally, it should also be pointed out that differentiation in general, balanced or unbalanced, democratic or authoritarian, is not invariably linked, as Parsons suggested, with adaptive upgrading. As Hobsbawm (1968) has argued, when comparing nineteenth-century Britain and Germany, it was Britain's advanced 'differentiation' in a certain direction that made it difficult for her to reorganize her industrial base when new technologies appeared; whereas the less differentiated German economy was better able to incorporate the new technologies, and so outpace Britain. This type of 'leap-frog' development cannot be accounted for by attempts to establish one-to-one linkages between differentiation and adaptive capacity.[14]

In summary, a close look at Parsons' dimensions of evolutionary development shows that they can vary independently of each other. Not only is differentiation not necessarily linked with adaptive upgrading

---

[13] See Wade, 1990; Appelbaum and Henderson, 1992. It is true, of course, that some Asian economies experienced serious difficulties in the early 1990s (Bello and Rosenfield, 1992); but however severe the difficulties, there is no doubt that, in terms of 'adaptive upgrading', the South-East Asian economies are much superior to, for instance, Latin American ones.

[14] For the view that increasing functional differentiation does not necessarily entail increasing efficiency/adaptive capacity, see Luhmann, 1982: 346ff.

but, by distinguishing between balanced and unbalanced inclusion, one can see also that value generalization does not always follow processes of inclusion.

3 Modernity: a non-Eurocentric conceptualization

In the light of the above and starting with a very general definition, modernity, as already mentioned, entails the destruction of traditional localisms and an unprecedented process of social mobilization as people are brought into the national centre. This mobilizing, 'bringing-in' process can take both autonomous and heteronomous forms. In the first case, economic, political, social and cultural rights are spread downwards; in the second, they are not. From a more functionalist-systemic point of view, modernity can be defined in terms of top-down structural-functional differentiation, as functions previously embedded in all-inclusive, multifunctional segmental units are performed by more specialized units (roles, institutions). This growing division of labour entails both monologic and polylogic forms of inclusion. In the former, the logic of one differentiated subsystem imposes its dominance on the other subsystems. In the polylogic case there is a relative balance of the differentiated parts, and it is only here that moving from formal to substantive forms of social differentiation becomes possible.

As I see it, it is the combination of unprecedented levels of (a) mobilization/incorporation into the centre, and (b) top-down structural-functional differentiation, as these two processes developed in eighteenth- and nineteenth-century Europe, which constitute 'modernity' – a state of affairs unique in human history. These unique levels of mobilization and differentiation could not have been achieved without the seventeenth-century scientific revolution that led to a kind of knowledge based, as Gellner has correctly argued (Hall and Jarvie, 1995: Introduction), on both transcultural and non-moral criteria of validation. Such knowledge was not only *cognitively* superior to all other kinds of knowledge, but its systematic application in the various spheres of production created the powerful technologies (economic, political, social and cultural) that made possible the process of large-scale mobilization and institutional differentiation discussed above.

To be more concrete: on the political level the military and administrative technologies that developed spectacularly in *ancien régime*

Europe (due mainly to geopolitical struggles between absolutist states (Mann, 1995)) are the key to understanding the destruction of political localism and the spectacular concentration at the top of the means of taxation, jurisdiction, surveillance and violence (Tilly, 1990). The nation-state, as the prototypical institutional embodiment of political modernity, would have been impossible without the development of macro-technologies of power which Weber, among others, explored in considerable depth.

Similar processes can be identified on the economic level. On the way from economic localism to the creation of relatively homogeneous, national economic arenas, the economic technologies that we associate with the Industrial Revolution played an equally crucial role. So for instance in the English cotton industry, the development of machinery which, at a certain point of technological development, could no longer be accommodated within the domestic, putting-out system of production, led to the dominance of the factory system, to the marked differentiation between economic and kinship institutional spheres (Smelser, 1962), and to a marked separation of the direct producers from the means of production – that is, led to the concentration of the means of production at the top. *This process, which is closely linked with the commodification of labour, can be seen not only in capitalist modernization, but also in non-capitalist cases* – whenever, that is, the motor force for the creation of national economic spaces and the separation of the direct producer from his/her means of production has been not the market but centralized state planning.

In the cultural sphere, the shift from local to national level was facilitated by the development of cultural technologies that made possible mass literacy and education. This, as Gellner (1996) has shown, was closely linked with the development of nationalist ideologies as people began to shift their loyalties and orientations from the local community to the 'imagined community' of the national centre (Anderson, 1991) and as modes of legitimation shifted from the royal/divine to the popular/secular (Bendix, 1978).

In the social domain, finally, the gradual transfer of major responsibility for the care of the weak and the economically destitute from the kinship unit and local community to the centrally organized welfare state was made possible by the development of administrative and surveillance techniques that, once more, led to the creation of broader, national arenas of care, health and population management.

4 Modernity and the West

It is true that modernity as described above first appeared in Western
Europe. But this should be understood in the context of the following
points. First, key institutional elements of this process can be found, in
less developed form, in several pre-industrial, non-European civilizations.

Second, it is not at all certain that the breakthrough or take-off could
only have happened in the West. It has been argued equally convincingly, I think, that the 'great transformation' could have happened at
more or less the same time in other civilizations with preconditions as
favourable as those in Europe (McNeil, 1963, 1995). If this is accepted,
one can argue that the reason that the breakthrough happened in
Western Europe had less to do with 'unique' elements (such as the
Protestant work ethic) than with the combination/timing of elements
that were not unique and could be found in several other complex
civilizations during the pre-breakthrough period.

Third, irrespective of what position one takes on the 'uniqueness of
the West' issue, it is a fact that not all but only certain elements of
Western modernity have a *transcultural* character today. These, regardless of where they were first fully institutionalized, constitute what
Parsons has called evolutionary universals. No society can advance or
even survive in the present world without acquiring the broad economic, political, cultural and social modern features discussed above.

Finally, if one deconstructs, or rather unravels, Parsons' conceptualization of evolutionary development, it becomes quite clear that differentiation, inclusion, adaptive upgrading and value generalization do
not constitute a system the elements of which always vary in the same
direction. In fact, the inclusion/integration of the differentiated parts
can take a variety of institutional forms – only one of which was actually
realized in the West. It is in this sense that Western modernity is neither
unique nor necessarily bound to prevail in the long term.

5 Variants of modernity

Let us now examine the varied institutional forms that modernity has
taken. If the articulation of a certain type of mobilization/incorporation
with high levels of top-down formal differentiation is what all modernities have in common, one way of accounting for its variant forms in a
theoretically coherent manner is to concentrate on the relationship

between the differentiated institutional spheres (in Parsonian language, the adaptation, goal achievement, integration and latency scheme – AGIL for short).

In Western modernity, the development of capitalism and the separation of the economic from the political sphere led in the post-1974 period to a situation where the logic of the market prevailed over the logic of non-formalistic democracy in the political sphere, over the logic of solidarity in the social sphere and over the logic of motivation-producing cultural autonomy in the latency sphere. This dominance was more accentuated in the Anglo-Saxon variant and less so in the so-called Rhine and Scandinavian models of capitalism (Albert, 1995; Hutton, 1995; Sapir, 2004).

If we now move from economic (A) to political (G) dominance, the Soviet type of modernization provides the most striking example of a situation where the state/party logic penetrates and abolishes, in quasi-totalitarian fashion, the distinctive rationalities of the adaptation, integration and latency subsystems (this type of modernity resembles, in structural terms, the state dominance of Nazi Germany and Fascist Italy during the interwar period). Finally, we find an attenuated variant of authoritarian modernity in most 'late-late' developing countries[15] which, although nominally capitalist, are dominated by an anti-developmental state that systematically subordinates the logic of all other spheres to the clientelistic and/or populistic logic of political domination (Mouzelis, 1994). Several African kleptocratic states provide extreme examples of this type of dominance.

Modernization processes where differentiation is marked by 'latency' dominance are best exemplified by Iran. Here the fundamentalist logic that is derived from neo-traditionalist constructions of High Islam scripturalism systematically undermines the logic and values of all other institutional spheres.

In the relevant sociological literature, the rise of religious fundamentalism in the post-communist, post-Cold War era has often been conceptualized in terms of dedifferentiation – in terms, that is, of evolutionary regression to less differentiated, quasi-segmental forms of social

---

[15] The 'late-late' label, which is used extensively in development theories, aims at distinguishing the (compared to England) relatively late European industrializers (Germany and France) from those semi-peripheral societies which experienced large-scale industrialization a century or more later (see Hirschman, 1970: ch. 3).

organization (Lechner, 1964). For reasons developed above, I consider this rather misleading. Contemporary religious fundamentalism, when fully implemented, does not portray the type of low differentiation that is found in genuinely traditional settings. There, the possible emphasis on religious values occurs in a context where the economic, political, social and cultural spheres are relatively undifferentiated. This state of affairs is qualitatively unlike that of the neo-traditional religious dom- inance that presupposes and is based on extensive formal differentia- tion of the four fundamental spheres. In fact, in post-traditional fundamentalism, the consolidation of the nation-state, the destruction of segmental localism and the formal differentiation according to the AGIL schema mean that religious dominance emerges not so much from below, but is quite forcefully imposed from above by those who control the administrative, communicative and military technologies of the modern state apparatus.[16]

Needless to say, many modernizing trajectories cannot be neatly fitted into any of the above ideal-typical categories. For instance, the modernization of Japan shows a pattern of mobilization/differentiation where the political values of democratic representation and pluralism (G) are systematically subordinated, without being eliminated, to cul- turally shaped solidaristic values (L and I) and to those of productivity/ competitiveness (A). Japanese capitalism accepts market competition, but systematically combines it with state-induced co-operation between state and capital as well as, more horizontally, between different types of capital. This co-operation, as many commentators have pointed out, is based on values which, in comparison to Western modernity, are less individualistic and more patriarchal-solidaristic in character (Woodiwiss, 1992, 1998; Berger and Dore, 1996).

On the level of differentiation, therefore, Japanese modernity por- trays a set of features that effectively combine the economic values of productivity/competitiveness (A) with the values of social solidarity (I), at the expense of effective democratic representation and political plur- alism (G). As already mentioned, this type of articulation of the four differentiated subsystems seems to provide a formula for successful

---

[16] For a different way of conceptualizing modernities which focuses on the core religious/cultural/civilizational complex of each modernity, see Eisenstadt, 1990a; Spohn, 2001.

'adaptive upgrading' in late-developing countries. It is seen in more or less accentuated form in several South-East Asian countries trying (with varying degrees of success) to follow the Japanese pattern of modernization (Woodiwiss, 1992, 1998). The relative success of this model is quite obvious if one compares it with that followed by the majority of late-developing nation-states where the dominance of an anti-developmental state systematically sacrifices the values of productivity and wealth creation, as well as those of cultural autonomy and social solidarity, on the altar of a profoundly corrupt, kleptocratic system of political domination.

Finally, within the context of Asian capitalism, one has to mention the present spectacular Chinese modernization – a modernization combining economic development led by foreign capital with authoritarian political controls. As has frequently been argued, it is highly likely that, as Chinese capitalism develops further, there will be both internal and external pressures for the opening up of the political system. Such an opening up might lead to a Taiwanese, South Korean or Japanese style of authoritarian modernity, with weak liberal-democratic political institutions providing some degree of political pluralism and democratic representation. On the other hand, the possibility cannot be excluded that, in the long term, Chinese modernity might combine effective capitalism development with political forms that continue to remain strongly authoritarian-totalitarian.

However, regardless of which modernizing route China follows – perhaps with even lower rates of economic growth than now – there is no doubt that in the decades to come a more developed China will, with its demographic weight, drastically change the global capitalist landscape. This brings us to a brief consideration of the linkages between the notions of modernity and globalization.

6 Late modernity and globalization

So far the modernity concept has been analysed in terms of fundamental transformations on the nation-state level. To what extent is this analysis relevant in a world where globalization processes articulate with the regional-local in ways that tend to bypass the nation-state level?

It goes beyond the scope of this chapter to examine the globalization phenomenon in depth. For the purposes of this analysis it suffices to point out that the 'hyperglobalization' thesis, which predicts the rapid irrelevance and decline of the nation-state, is profoundly misleading (Julius, 1990; Albrow, 1996). Although I do not agree with the opposite view that there is nothing particularly novel in the present transformation of the world economy (Hirst and Thompson, 1996), I do think that the role of the nation-state in the emerging new world order will change, but that it will not diminish in importance.

This seems to me quite obvious when looking at the strongly interventionist nature of the state in the rapidly rising Pacific Rim economies, and at the fact that developmentally oriented national governments constitute – via collaboration, antagonism or control – serious participants in the games played by multinational or transnational companies.

Not only are nation-states still the basic building blocks of the world order but, if one focuses on the global level, processes of mobilization/incorporation and differentiation can be discerned that are quite similar to those that occurred earlier on the nation-state level. Thus if during early modernity we witnessed the decline of the non-differentiated, self-contained traditional community, in today's globalized modernity we see an analogous decline, not of the nation-state but of *statism*, i.e. of the state's capacity to monitor developments taking place within national boundaries. Moreover, if the eighteenth- and nineteenth-century mobilizations incorporated large chunks of the population in the broader economic, political, social and cultural arenas of the nation-state, today's 'bringing-in' is simply taking the process a step further by creating global economic, political and socio-cultural arenas in which growing numbers of people are passive or active participants. Moreover, if the original shift from segmental localism to the construction of national arenas became possible because of the industrial and surveillance technologies of the early modern era, it can be argued that the shift from the national to the global is becoming possible because of the new information technologies of late modernity. In both cases the advent of new technologies draws people into broader social spaces, while the means of production, domination and persuasion are concentrated at the global top.

With regard to the present-day resurgence of localism/regionalism (of a non-segmental form), we could say that similar phenomena of centralization/decentralization obtained during the period of early, nation-state-based modernity. In the same way as the dominance of the nation-state, i.e. the creation of national arenas, created all kinds of local resistance, reactions or revolts on the part of those who had a stake in the status quo of the pre-nation-state, so today's creation of global arenas generates fundamentalist reactions of a nationalistic and/or religious kind in those who see their interests threatened by the globalization process. I am not saying that there are no important differences between the creation of national and global arenas, but in structural terms the global–local dialectic of late modernity does resemble the local–national dialectic of early modernity.

It is precisely for this reason that I prefer to agree with Giddens (1990) in calling the present situation *late modern* instead of *postmodern*. In this I base myself on the fact that globalization brings us a step closer to the logic of mobilization/incorporation which the advent of the nation-state and the inclusion of the population in broader economic, political, social and cultural arenas have initiated.

Conclusion

Let me summarize the main points of my argument.

(i) It is possible to conceptualize modernity in such a way as to avoid both Eurocentrism and the type of ultra-relativistic, Third Worldist interpretation of the term that views it merely as an ideological means for the further advancement of Western cultural imperialism.

(ii) Modernity refers to a type of social organization which, from a social-integration point of view, is characterized by an unprecedented level of social mobilization/incorporation into the centre; and from the point of view of system integration, by an equally unprecedented, top-down institutional differentiation. This type of mobilization and differentiation leads to the destruction of segmental localism and to the creation of broader, highly differentiated economic, political, social and cultural arenas (following the Parsonian AGIL terminology) within which the practices of individuated subjects are constituted/regulated by such institutional complexes as the nation-state (G), national markets and/or national planning agencies (A), national systems of welfare and population surveillance/management (I) and mass literacy and nationalist ideologies (L).

(iii) Although these structural features were initially fully institutionalized in Western Europe (after the seventeenth-century scientific revolution had led to the creation of powerful economic, political, social and cultural technologies that profoundly transformed *ancien régime* European societies), they constitute evolutionary universals: no society can survive today without adopting such institutional forms as the nation-state, mass literacy, etc.

(iv) The above do not lead to the conclusion that modernity equals Westernization because:

— important elements of modern institutions existed (in a less developed form) in several non-Western civilizations;
— the type of revolutions (scientific, industrial and democratic) that modernized Europe could possibly have happened first in other parts of the 'developed' pre-industrial world;
— modernization in the non-Western world took a variety of forms – some of them less effective in terms of 'adaptive capacity' than Western modernity (e.g. Soviet variants), and some probably more effective in the long term (e.g. Japanese and South-East Asian variants).

(v) One way of dealing in a theoretically coherent manner with the great variety of existing and virtual modernities is to distinguish between formal differentiation (the passage from 'segments' to 'organs') and substantive differentiation (the problem of the balanced or unbalanced relations between differentiated parts/organs). From the latter perspective it has been argued that the type of 'balanced', polylogic inclusion of the differentiated parts that Parsons saw in Western modernization (i.e. an inclusion entailing a situation where the economic logic of productivity, the political logic of democracy, the social logic of solidarity and the cultural logic of commitment/ autonomy exist without one of them dominating the others) has never been achieved in the West or anywhere else. What we see today are types of modernity where the logic/values of one (or more) institutional subsystem(s) prevail and 'colonize' the other institutional spheres. So in ideal-typical terms we can identify modernities marked by economic dominance (e.g. the Anglo-Saxon case), political dominance (the Soviet Union and Nazi Germany) and cultural dominance (fundamentalist Iran).

(vi) The most serious attempts to move from monologic/unbalanced to polylogic/balanced forms of modernity occurred in the postwar Western European democracies before the 1974 economic crisis.

To what extent these or other societies will be able to find post-Keynesian means to help themselves overcome the present impasse and thus further advance their polylogic prospects remains an open question; so does the problem of whether the globally dominant neoliberal Anglo-Saxon modernity will maintain its hegemony in the twenty-first century.

10 | *Ethical relativism: between scientism and cultural relativism*

In the previous chapters I dealt with the type of relativism which denies that modernity entails features which, under globalized conditions, are transcultural rather than Western-specific. In this chapter I deal with a related issue: I critically assess attempts to overcome the relativism that communitarian theories often entail by the adoption of an anti-relativistic strategy different from my own. In order to make my arguments as clear and concrete as possible, I focus on a single work – Amitai Etzioni's *The New Golden Rule* (1996).[1]

There are two standard critiques of communitarian theories: (i) that these theories always have authoritarian connotations, with their emphasis on the importance of communal values and order undermining individual freedoms; and (ii) that their focus on the context-bound nature of communal values results in the relativistic idea that, since every community has its own values, there is no supra-communal or extra-communal way of assessing conflicting views of the 'good' life.

1 The golden rule perspective

Communitarianism, as expounded by Etzioni (1996), attempts to overcome both the authoritarian and the relativistic critique. He responds to both with his notion of a 'golden rule' – the idea that when advocating or promoting 'community' in the modern world, one should strive to achieve a balance between *order* and *individual autonomy*. It is imbalance between these two cardinal virtues that creates difficulties: emphasis on order at the expense of autonomy leads to authoritarianism, while emphasis on autonomy at the expense of order leads to anarchy.

If this golden rule is applied, authoritarianism due to communal order taking repressive forms, undermining autonomy and therefore breaking the order–autonomy balance, cannot exist. More specifically, Etzioni is

[1] An earlier version of this chapter appeared in Lehman, 2000.

164

in favour of a voluntary social and moral order which, without being contractarian, is based on an ongoing dialogue leading to communal consensus. If *intra*-communal dialogue avoids authoritarianism, relativism, for Etzioni, can be dealt with by the notion of *inter*-communal dialogue: respect for the values and ways of life of other communities and the promotion of open-ended dialogue between them will undermine communal isolation and so encourage procedural and even substantive mechanisms of inter-communal integration. Such integrative mechanisms combat the postmodern relativistic idea that there is no common framework, no common moral vocabulary by means of which one can compare and assess the ways of life of different communities or civilizations.

In addition to the above, Etzioni argues that the values of specific communities should be compatible with the values or moral order of the 'community-of-communities', of the superordinate social entity (e.g. the nation-state or global system) within which communities are embedded. However, as he points out, this does not solve the problem of relativism but simply shifts it upwards from the community level to that of the 'community-of-communities'. Concerning this difficulty, he argues that the values of the community-of-communities should, in the last analysis, be compatible with the golden rule, with the twin cardinal virtues of moral order and bounded autonomy: 'As I see it, moral order and autonomy crown the communitarian normative account. They provide the final, substantive normative criterion this account requires' (Etzioni, 1996: 246).

According to Etzioni, this compatibility is the result of the values of moral order and bounded autonomy being 'morally compelling' and therefore self-evident. No utilitarian, consequentialist reasoning is required for their legitimation. They are accepted by people of goodwill as a matter of course – in as unmediated a manner as religious revelation is accepted by believers. In other words, the balance between the basic virtues of moral order and bounded autonomy is as manifest and morally compelling as is the value of health for the medical sciences (Etzioni, 1996: 224–47). Moreover, the golden rule is universal and applies to all communities – while at the same time, provided they do not offend it, allowing for the myriad particularistic judgements of specific communities.

I think that Etzioni's attempt to avoid the absolutism of any single value by stressing that the crucially important balance between moral order and individual autonomy will lead to a mutual reinforcement of social virtues and individual rights, as well as his dialogic approach to intra-communal communication, does indeed provide an adequate normative framework for refuting those critics who stress the authoritarian character of all communitarian theories. Where he seems to me to be rather less successful is in tackling the critique of relativism.

2 On the self-evidence of the golden rule

My difficulty with Etzioni's solution to the matter of relativism is that the virtue of a balance between order and autonomy is not as self-evident and morally compelling as he implies. To take an extreme example: in highly segmental, non-differentiated communities with low or non-existent individuation, the idea of bounded autonomy (entailing negative and positive liberties as well as the notion of self-expression) is neither self-evident nor morally compelling. The idea of the right to self-expression, or the idea of the individual having rights of his/her own, develop only in conditions of what Ulrich Beck has termed individualization.[2]

Even if we ignore such extreme examples and restrict ourselves to traditional village communities as they exist today in various parts of the so-called Third World, the contention that a moral social order, as it may be developed and defined by a specific community, should *prevail* over individual autonomy cannot be dismissed as ideological brainwashing, or as a 'misunderstanding' that can be cleared up by open dialogue, as advocated by Etzioni.

To take an example used by the author of *The New Golden Rule* himself: the father who finds a much older husband for his daughter, one rich enough to afford the dowry price, may seem to us to be 'selling his daughter' to the highest bidder (Etzioni, 1996: 245–7). But the situation may be interpreted very differently from the point of view of a culture where kinship solidarity or economic survival of the family unit takes clear precedence over the expressive needs, preferences or

---

[2] According to Beck, individualization entails three fundamental dimensions: (i) *disembedding*, or removal from 'historically prescribed social forms and commitments'; (ii) the *loss of traditional security* 'with respect to practical knowledge, faith and guiding norms'; and (iii) *re-embedding*, or reintegration into a new context, requiring a post-traditional type of social commitment (Beck, 1992: 128). See also Beck *et al.*, 1994; Beck and Beck-Gernsheim, 1996.

individual rights of family members. To put it bluntly, sacrificing the
autonomy and individual rights of a kin-member on the altar of family
solidarity may be self-evidently immoral to an American university
professor, but not at all so to an impoverished Egyptian or Bolivian
peasant. In other words, for a huge part of humankind still living in
quasi-traditional settings, the *imbalance* between moral order and individual autonomy (in favour of the former) might be more morally
compelling or more self-evident than the balance between these two
cardinal virtues. To dismiss such orientations as the result of confusion
or 'distorted communication' simply will not do. It is as unconvincing as
the Marxist argument of false consciousness that is supposed to explain
why the proletariat does not revolt.

3 Basic assumptions and difficulties of the relativist position

The above difficulties with the golden rule concept do not necessarily
result in total relativism. But I do think that, in order to overcome the
relativistic position, the focus should shift from moral and political
philosophy to sociology, and so adopt a more historically oriented
macro-comparative, evolutionist perspective. It would then be quite
feasible to show that the golden rule, without being *universally* self-
evident, does become morally compelling for a growing number of
people living in *post-traditional* contexts all over the globe.

I shall begin by looking more closely at how postmodern, relativistic
arguments are deployed. According to most postmodernist discourses,
if we take into account the social and cultural pluralism that characterizes the contemporary world – as well as the fact that what is ethical/
unethical, good/bad, valuable/non-valuable is strictly related to specific
socio-historical contexts – then we are bound to conclude that there is
no way of assessing and/or hierarchizing cultural values and modes of
life based on them. There is no foundation, no Archimedean principle,
no universal norm that would help us to stand above multiple and often
contradictory cultural codes or paradigms in order to judge which of
them is more or less good, just or true.

On a more practical level this relativistic attitude means that in our
postmodern condition, even practices that are inhuman or repulsive from
the Western point of view (such as female circumcision, infanticide, etc.)
cannot be condemned on the basis of some universal standard – whatever
that may be. On the other hand, in contrast to relativism, there is the

view that values like moral order, individual freedom, respect for basic human rights, or a combination of these, are of transhistorical, universal character, and as such can be used in the assessment or evaluation of social practices in specific contexts.

In what follows I shall develop a position which avoids the postmodern type of relativism without subscribing to Etzioni's idea that certain values (like the balance between social virtues and individual rights) are morally compelling or self-evident in a universal, transhistorical manner.[3]

Total relativism generates severe difficulties in two particular areas. First, notwithstanding the fact that values like those entailed by the golden rule are not universal, there is a very small number of human values which, because they are based on what evolutionists call biological or sociological universals,[4] are indeed universal or quasi-universal. Example: because all known human societies have a kinship system and because *homo sapiens* needs a long period of primary socialization, a certain altruism of the mother towards her biological child is to be found, as a *norm*,[5] in all socio-cultural formations from the least to the most differentiated. This statement does not necessarily lead to teleological functionalism, because one can argue that cultures/societies without such altruistic values simply could not and did not survive.[6]

Second, and more important, as Ernest Gellner pointed out long ago, the notion of total relativism assumes the existence of societies or communities that are entirely self-contained, that have no linkages whatsoever with other societies or communities. It is based on a hypothetical, non-existent world where values do not spread from one socio-cultural whole to another via trade, war, migration, etc.[7] Such a

---

[3] Etzioni does not explicitly emphasize the universal, transhistorical character of the golden rule. However, his whole argument – in so far as it does not distinguish between people still living in traditional and those living in post-traditional contexts today – implies that the balance between moral order and individual autonomy appeals to all people of goodwill. This is definitely not so.

[4] On the concept of biological and sociological universals, see Parsons, 1964a. See also chapter 3.

[5] I emphasize *norm* because, obviously, there are always discrepancies between normative expectations (as these are embedded in specific roles and institutions) and actual performance.

[6] For the theoretical elaboration of such an argument, see Dore, 1961.

[7] Of course, value-overlap or similarities between different societies is due not only to diffusion. Given similar structural conditions or systemic requirements, the same values may emerge in disconnected parts of the world. See, on this point, Parsons, 1964a.

totally compartmentalized world not only has never existed, but is the extreme opposite of what we are witnessing today, i.e. the growing interpenetration and interdependence (via globalization) of cultures, civilizations, societies, etc. The more advanced this interdependence and interpenetration, the less ground there is for postmodern relativism to stand on. It loses its footing because it is precisely the growing overlap between various cultural traditions that provides a basis both for comparison and for serious assessment/evaluation of conflicting ways of life.

4 Stepping stones towards growing socio-cultural interpenetration

The above becomes clearer if we view processes of growing interdependence or interpenetration from the perspective not of *specific* but of *general* evolution[8] – pointing out in an illustrative, non-systematic manner some of the key turning-points or institutional breakthroughs that have led to the present extraordinary 'compression' of world time and space and to the unprecedented fusion and interpenetration of cultural traditions.

(i) Starting from the city-states of antiquity, not only in Mediterranean Europe but also in Mesopotamia and Asia Minor, these minuscule socio-cultural formations were embedded in larger cultural-civilizational wholes that extended far beyond a specific city-state's walls and its military-administrative organization (Mann, 1986: 190–231).

(ii) The tendency of cultural values and norms to transcend specific juridico-administrative entities was dramatically reinforced by the shift from local, primitive religions to the so-called historic or world religions, which developed quasi-universal discourses; discourses whose abstractions made them 'detachable' from local, particularistic conditions, this increasing their appeal to millions of people across a variety of societies, polities and civilizations.[9]

---

[8] For the concepts of general and specific evolution, see Sahlins and Service, 1960.

[9] Auguste Comte, in discussing the theological stage of his evolutionist theory, is one of the first classical theorists to focus on the linkage between the growing 'abstraction' of religious belief (in the move from animism to polytheism and monotheism) and the decline of cultural localism. The linkage between growing differentiation and the emergence of 'free-floating, disembedded' religious ideas

(iii) According to Immanuel Wallerstein (1974) it was in the sixteenth and seventeenth centuries that the first 'world system' came into existence: a system of various states competing with each other in the international economic, political and cultural arenas. What was unique about this system was that no one state was strong enough to destroy inter-state economic and politico-military competition by establishing an imperial order. This 'primitive' world system was, of course, very much strengthened in the eighteenth century by the emergence of the nation-state and the shift from an inter-*state* to an inter-*nation-state* world system.

(iv) Another crucial breakthrough during the process of this growing socio-cultural interpenetration was the dominance of the capitalist mode of production in eighteenth-century Western Europe. If by 'capitalist mode of production' we do not simply mean commercialization in the sphere of trade/distribution; if (following Marx) we use the narrow definition of capitalism as the entrance of capital into the sphere of agricultural and industrial production and the consequent creation of wage labour[10] on a massive scale – then the dominance of the capitalist mode of production not only peripheralizes non-capitalist modes, but it also, together with the nation-state, systematically destroys the economic, political and cultural segmental localisms of the pre-capitalist era.

Furthermore, it dramatically advances the internationalization or globalization of the economy. If in the nineteenth century international capital was mainly oriented towards infrastructural investments (e.g. ports or railways), and in the twentieth century towards the global production of consumer goods (e.g. cars), at present, the globalization of the economy is completed by its massive entrance into the service sphere (banking, insurance, management, accounting, etc.) (Chase-Dunn, 1989).

(v) The global process of democratization after the collapse of the Soviet Union – although often superficial and extremely uneven – is another fundamental mechanism that is bringing late-modern societies closer together on the level of political, social and cultural values (Diamond and Plattner, 1996).

and values constitutes a central theme in the work of Parsons and some of his disciples (Eisenstadt, Bellah, etc.).

[10] For a systematic discussion of Marx's definition of capitalism, see Dobb, 1968: 1–32. For a debate on the meaning of capitalism and the relevance of diverging definitions in explaining the transition from feudalism to capitalism in Western Europe, see Hilton, 1976.

Summing up: world religions in the cultural sphere, the system of nation-states and the more recent trend of global democratization in the political sphere, the massive entrance of capital into the sphere of national and international production in the economic sphere – all these, as well as the technologies with which they are inextricably linked, have brought us to a situation that is the exact opposite of total societal self-containment and cultural insulation.

Today's situation creates conditions that encourage the gradual spread and acceptance of the core values of late modernity – values such as productivity and competition in the economic sphere, democracy in the political sphere, solidarity in the social sphere and individual autonomy/self-realization in the cultural sphere. The above values, as I have argued already, are certainly not transhistorical or universal, but they do appeal to the growing number of people who live in *post-traditional* settings – whether in Blairite Britain, social-democratic Sweden, authoritarian Korea or quasi-totalitarian China. It is precisely because the above values are gradually becoming global among 'late-modern' individuals that it is possible to transcend relativism and condemn the violation of human rights, whether this occurs in Israel, Turkey, Northern Ireland or China.

5 Eurocentrism

Of course, the 'politically correct' relativist may argue that the above way of founding transcultural values is clearly Eurocentric, since values relating to parliamentary democracy and entailing individual freedoms are specifically Western cultural products that have been imposed on the rest of the world via imperialism or the less violent Western-dominated mechanisms of the world market. The Eurocentrism debate is a highly complex one, and I dealt with it in the previous chapter. What I do want to point out here is that the values of democracy and of human liberties and rights – without being universal or 'eternal' in the Platonic, idealist sense of the term – transcend the narrow limits of Western European culture or civilization. As I argued in chapter 9, this is so for three reasons. First, despite the fact that parliamentary democracy and the civil, political and social rights associated with it took their most developed form in the 'West', important elements of such institutions are to be found in various non-European civilizations, past as well as present.

Second, as the historian William McNeil (1963) has persuasively argued, the types of revolution (scientific, technological, economic and political) that have 'modernized' Western Europe could equally well have happened in other 'civilized' parts of the pre-industrial world. The fact that they occurred in the West has more to do with conjunctural factors than with the uniqueness or superiority of the Western culture. Another way of putting this is to say that the fact that the breakthrough happened in Western Europe owed less to 'unique' elements (such as the Protestant work ethic) than to the combination (in time and space) of elements that were not unique but could be found in several other complex civilizations during the pre-breakthrough period (McNeil, 1995).

Finally, the modernization of the non-Western world took various forms. Some of these (e.g. the Soviet collectivist modernization) proved less 'effective' than the Western one, whereas others (e.g. the Chinese type of modernization) may, in the long run, prove more so.[11]

If we take the above into consideration, it becomes clear that values related to political rights for instance (regardless of where they became fully institutionalized for the first time) constitute what Parsons has called *evolutionary universals*: at a certain stage in the evolution of human societies they become basic preconditions if a society is to move up to higher levels of differentiation and 'adaptive capacity' (see chapter 3). As such, they have a very broad, transcultural appeal which, as I have already argued, appeals to post-traditional individuals all over the world. This does not mean, of course, that the above values are totally accepted, always respected or followed in practice. It does mean, however, that they have become a basic reference point for assessing and legitimizing or condemning political practices on a global, transcultural level.

What, therefore, distinguishes the major living cultural traditions or civilizations today is not their focus on radically conflicting values, but rather the way in which a small number of commonly accepted core values articulate with each other. For example, in the Anglo-Saxon world, at least at the level of the elites, political pluralism (as a core

---

[11] Contrary to Etzioni (1996: 234–42), I am not at all sure that 'late-late'-comers, at whatever stage of their development, can overcome the usual bottlenecks created by underdevelopment without – at least at some initial stage – a strong dose of authoritarianism (see, on this point, chapter 9, section 5).

dimension of liberal democracy) has much more weight than social solidarity. In Japan, on the other hand, the priorities are reversed. And if for Europeans and North Americans the political repression in China is totally unacceptable, for many Asians this negative feature of the Chinese regime must be seen in the light of Russia's disastrous 'democratic' revolution and of China's spectacular economic growth – a growth which, for the first time in the country's history, has freed millions of peasants from the spectre of starvation or chronic undernourishment.

Conclusion

Etzioni deals with relativism by arguing that his 'golden rule', i.e. the balance between individual autonomy and the moral, social order, constitutes a self-evident, morally compelling truth. I have argued that this is not the case, and that a more effective way of overcoming postmodern relativism is by adopting an evolutionist, macro-historical perspective. If one does so, certain values, or combinations of values (like the combination of individual autonomy and order), without being universally valid tend to have a transcultural, global appeal today for those individuals who live in post-traditional settings.

I have tried to support this claim by arguing that:

– Relativism takes into account neither the biological and sociological universals of humankind, nor the fact that societies and civilizations are not isolated, totally self-contained wholes.
– From an evolutionist point of view, the interrelatedness/interdependence of societies is dramatically increased by the emergence of world religions, the development of a system of nation-states, the penetration of capital not only into the sphere of distribution but also of production, present-day globalizing trends, etc.
– All of the above processes strongly undermine societal isolation, and create favourable conditions for the generalization/globalization of values referring to productivity (in the economic sphere), democratic freedoms and rights (in the political sphere), social solidarity (in the social sphere) and self-actualization (in the cultural sphere).
– Despite the fact that some of the above values were first institutionalized (on a large scale) in the West, they are not just Western but constitute *evolutionary* universals. As such, in different combinations,

they appeal to all individuals living in post-traditional contexts, whether in Europe, Asia or Africa.

— What, in late modernity, distinguishes various socio-cultural wholes is not so much the absolute 'uniqueness' of their values as the unique way in which a small number of common, transcultural values are related to each other.

11 | *Cognitive relativism: between positivistic and relativistic thinking in the social sciences*

Some of the issues raised by the postmodern, anti-positivist critique of the notion of objectivity are not new. The problem, for instance, of the influence exerted by the researcher's values and/or conceptual tools on a theory's empirical findings has a long history, and has been tackled, quite adequately I think, by such scholars as Weber and Elias (Weber, 1925/1978: 24–36, 285ff; Hekman, 1983; Elias, 1987a). Other problems, however, to the extent that they are part of the postmodern emphasis on the symbolic construction of all social phenomena, while not entirely new,[1] raise new issues regarding relativism, and therefore deserve more extensive treatment. I begin with a brief reference to the more conventional questioning of the notion of objectivity.

1 Objectivity and the issue of mediation

Postmodern theorists reject the idea of objectivity and 'value neutrality'[2] as it is formulated in positivist accounts of the social sciences. They

---

[1] Long before postmodernism and social constructionism, the tradition of symbolic interactionism emphasized the symbolic dimension of all social phenomena (Mead, 1934; Blumer, 1969). However, the latter's emphasis on the symbolic did not, unlike postmodernism, lead its followers to relativism.

[2] Concerning the question of value neutrality, there is the erroneous but widespread view (developed primarily by Gouldner, 1971, 1976) that Weber's notion of objectivity entails the positivistic view that values should not intrude into social-science theories; and that the German scholar developed the 'value-neutrality' view in order to enhance the respectability of the newlyborn discipline of sociology. This is not at all the case. Weber argues that values are unavoidably relevant to social-science research. When he speaks of the value neutrality of all science, he by no means adopts the positivistic thesis of an 'absence of values'. He simply argues, in refutation of *scientism*, that the social sciences, however much they develop, will never be able to bridge the 'is' and the 'ought'. In other words, Weber's value-neutrality argument is based not on a positivistic but on an anti-positivistic orientation. Sciences are value-neutral in the sense that they cannot empirically validate ultimate value judgements.

reject the notion that social researchers can orient themselves to their field of study in a value-neutral, detached manner. They argue that it is not only values (political, ethical and aesthetic), but also the vocabularies used (lay or specialized) that mediate between the researcher and the research object. Therefore researchers with different values, different lay idioms and different specialized conceptual tools must inevitably end up with different interpretations and explanations of the phenomena they study. This leads to the notion of 'equivalent narratives', to the idea that it is not possible to prove that in the case of competing theories or 'narratives' dealing with the same issues, one of them is, cognitively speaking, more valid than another.

Moreover, postmodern theory also rejects empiricism, the rather crude idea that a researcher must first of all observe social phenomena and can only then proceed to formulate generalizations. This thesis of 'first the facts and then the theory' fails to take into account that it is the theoretical problematic that has delineated a theory's subject matter in the first place, pointing out what are and what are not relevant facts, as well as how a theory can or cannot be validated.[3] All the above arguments about the mediation issue and the role theory plays in social research lead postmodern thinkers to a more or less accentuated relativist position. They lead to the conclusion that it is not possible to find a mode of assessing competing theories based on cognitive criteria of truth.

I think that one way of dealing with this type of relativist impasse is to distinguish clearly between two types of objectivity. First, there is the positivistic notion which requires the researcher at the start of the investigation to bracket or eliminate entirely all axiological and linguistic/conceptual presuppositions – i.e. to approach the object of study in an unmediated, *tabula rasa* manner. This type of 'objective' detachment (as Weber pointed out long ago) is simply not possible either in the social or the natural sciences. Different values, different linguistic mediations, different conceptual frameworks unavoidably intrude into the research process. There is not and never can be an unmediated, totally detached approach to the study of social phenomena.

However, this need not result in relativism if objectivity is defined differently, non-positivistically: as a type of self-discipline requiring the researcher, whenever there is incongruity or tension between his/her

---

[3] For an early 'pre-postmodern' version of anti-empiricism, see Braithwaite, 1964.

values or conceptual tools on the one hand and the empirical findings on the other, to adjust the former to the latter and not the other way round. It is precisely this type of self-discipline that primarily distinguishes an ideological from a non-ideological discourse in the social sciences. In both cases, of course, axiological and conceptual/linguistic concerns are related to and have an impact on the mode of construction and validation of a theory. But the crucial difference between them is that in the ideological discourse the dominant orientation requires the manipulation of empirical data so that they fit immutable value commitments. In the non-ideological discourse the researcher is prepared to do the opposite – to question values and to modify conceptual tools in the light of the empirical evidence.

Now postmodern theorists refuse to accept the concept of ideology[4] and therefore the distinction between more or less ideological approaches to the study of social phenomena. However, even while rejecting the by now unfashionable ideology term, we certainly need a way of distinguishing, for instance, the kind of discourse that Nazi social theorists produced on race from the discourses we find in today's sociology-of-race literature.[5] It is quite obvious that in the former case, objectivity, as a type of what Elias (1987a) has termed 'detachment', is totally absent, whereas in the latter it is decidedly present to different degrees. What this means is that the concept of objectivity is not synonymous with the absence of all mediation – axiological, linguistic or conceptual. It may more modestly and commonsensically mean a situation of relative detachment enabling a social researcher *first* to be aware of his/her preferences in value, linguistic and conceptual terms and *second*, be ready to constantly question the latter in the light of the ongoing empirical evidence.

This type of objectivity, particularly as far as conceptual presuppositions are concerned, is difficult but not impossible. Let us look at a classical example from the literature of industrial sociology. A team of social researchers under Elton Mayo's direction began a research project at Western Electric's Hawthorn plant. This project was initially

---

[4] Foucault, for instance, rejects the concept of ideology, both because of its Marxist, economistic connotations, and because it is based on the distinction between false (i.e. ideological) and true (i.e. scientific) knowledge. See Foucault, 1980.

[5] For the direct connection between biological and social racism and Nazi eugenic policies, see Gasman, 1971.

based on a positivistic framework: the researchers were trying to establish correlations between productivity and such variables as lighting conditions, duration of rest periods, material incentives, etc. When their empirical findings were inconclusive, they realized that the fluctuations in productivity had less to do with the variables that they were trying to measure than with the social structure of the work group and the changing relations between the workers and the researchers themselves. This led to a radical change in methodology and the conceptual tools employed, causing a marked shift from a statistically oriented positivistic approach to one based on participant observation and on a non-atomistic, holistic conceptual framework.[6]

Needless to say, objectivity in the above, non-positivistic sense is more easily achieved where researchers operate within the context of an academic community enjoying considerable autonomy *vis-à-vis* state or market pressures.

2 The postmodern critique of representation and empirical evidence

Apart from issues related to mediation, another route to cognitive relativism is via the postmodern objection to the 'mirror' or 'representation' view of social theory; to the idea that a social theory should represent, or mirror, as faithfully as possible, a social reality 'out there', so to speak. This more conventional view is based on distinguishing between the levels of 'theory' and of 'social reality'. This distinction then makes it possible to decide which of two competing theories (both dealing with the same problematic) is closer to social reality than the other by resorting to the level of 'empirical reference'; in other words, by using empirical data.

In the postmodern view this kind of theory validation is highly dubious. Since social reality, including the theories about it, is symbolically constructed, there can be no distinction between theory and social reality. Even institutions portraying 'hard' social reality – i.e. durable institutions such as that of the private ownership of the means of production in capitalism – portray (contra Marx) nothing 'material'.

---

[6] The Hawthorn studies, a co-operative five-year enterprise between the Western Electric company and a team from the Harvard Business School (1927–32) were extensively reported by Roethlisberger and Dickson, 1939.

The rules and norms of private ownership are reproduced and persist because millions of people, in a taken-for-granted, routine manner, ascribe meanings and interpret certain exchange practices in specific ways. The supposed materiality of the ownership institutions is based on nothing more than meanings, interpretations and symbols. In other words, it is not only social theorists who construct theories about the institutions of property; laypersons do so likewise every time they change currency in a bank or buy goods in the market-place. Social theories, therefore, are symbolic constructs referring to an 'empirical reality' that also consists of symbolic constructs; or, to put it differently, social theories are interpretations of interpretations; they are specialists' theories attempting to explain laypersons' theories.

Moreover, even if we consider truly material objects – trees, say, or sailing boats – these enter the world of 'social realities' when laypersons or specialists variously interpret their existence as objects of aesthetic appreciation, as resources to be used in the realization of human projects, as goods to be bought and sold in the market, as means of saving the planet from ecological disaster, etc.[7] If therefore the so-called social reality is symbolically constructed, it is as real or unreal as the theories that try to explain it. To put this in the language of textualism:[8] since society is a system of narratives or texts, the writings of social theorists are simply texts among other texts. And if everything social is constituted via language and its grammatical and syntactical rules, then distinguishing between theory and social reality does not make a great deal of sense.

This anti-representation argument is reinforced by Saussure's notion of the arbitrariness of the sign. The Swiss linguist has argued that there is no one-to-one linkage between signifier and signified. In human language, the linkage between the word as a physical sound (signifier) and the word as a concept (signified) is less important, less helpful if we want to understand the meaning attached to the word, than is the synchronic or diachronic relationship between signifiers. This means that the focus shifts from the signified and its empirical referent to the signifier and the linguistic rules governing its linkages with other signifiers. This change in emphasis from signified/empirical referent to the signifier is taken yet a step further by theorists such as Baudrillard

[7] See, on this point, Laclau and Mouffe, 1985; Laclau, 1990.
[8] On textualism, see chapter 1, section 6.

(1976, 1981, 1983) and Derrida (1978, 1981), who dismiss the former altogether and conceptualize society as a chain of signifiers, or as a set of texts that occupy all social space – with nothing social existing *hors* text.

It is on the basis of this kind of logic that postmodern theorists attempt to deconstruct any theory that tries to explain in 'representative' manner social phenomena which conventional theorists call empirical reality – a reality supposed to be 'out there', separate from theory. In actual fact, post-structuralism/postmodernism contends, there is *nothing* out there: the dualism between social reality and social theory simply does not exist. However, this point of view, as already mentioned, leads to relativism, since two theories or 'narratives' providing different explanations of the same social phenomenon cannot be assessed by the conventional method of 'empirical proof'. All that can be done is to examine which theory is more logically consistent, or which narrative is aesthetically more pleasing or politically more powerful (Foucault, 1980).

a. The modern–postmodern debate in Greek historiography

I shall illustrate the above by referring to a drawn-out debate among Greek historians, which began on the occasion of an important conference on Greek historiography in 2002 and which continues in scholarly and less scholarly writings up to the present.

In the 'modern', more conventional camp are historians who have been influenced mainly by the Marxisand French Annales school and who try to defend the distinction between theory and socio-historical reality. In the 'post-modern' camp are younger historians influenced by the linguistic, post-positivist turn in the humanities, who reject the above distinction as essentialist and therefore misleading. To quote from an author who defends the anti-foundationalist, anti-essentialist position:

> What has almost always been ignored is the textual nature of history; the fact that our past is known to us via texts – texts which are mediated by the position of the informant, by his hopes, strategies, illusions, etc. which intrude in the texts he leaves us as energetically as the social context within which he lives. It would have been desirable to have in front of us the 'real history' in order to compare it with the more or less exact representations which historiography offers us. (Exertzoglou, 2002; all quotations in this section are translations from Greek by myself)

But, he goes on to argue, such a comparison is not possible.

The above anti-representation thesis is criticized by a 'modern' historian who argues that

Social history [for the postmodern historian] is nothing but an ensemble of symbolic constructions which are embodied in texts ... Therefore, whatever refers to the past only exists within interpretations/narratives ... The battle of Athens [the civil war confrontation in December 1944], however, is not the narratives and historical accounts of it. (Theotokas, 2002: 35)

Another Marxist-oriented historian strongly supports the above critique by arguing that

What is missing [from the postmodern perspective] is the historian's double approach: to the actual beings and to the thoughts about the actual beings. These are two different levels and if one does not study them together, one misses completely the sense of historicity and temporality. (Eliou, 2002: 426)

The postmodernist retort to the above modernist position in defence of the distinction between theory and empirical reality is to point out that it is essentialist and therefore unacceptable to distinguish between 'real beings' and 'theories about them', given that both levels (that of theory and that of empirical reality) rest on interpretations and refer to symbolic constructs. In fact, there are not two levels at all but only one, that of texts and intertextuality (Exertzoglou, 2002).

This debate concerning historiography is not exactly the same as similar debates in the social sciences, but what they have in common is the anti-representation issue: to what extent the distinction between theory (social and historical) and social reality (present or past) is or is not legitimate. If the answer is affirmative, then it is possible, via the conventional procedures of empirical proof (guided of course by the researcher's theoretical concerns), to decide about the validity or non-validity of competing theoretical interpretations. If the distinction is rejected, we end up with the idea of 'equivalent' (i.e. equally valid) narratives, and we are confronted by the relativist impasse.

b. *Avoiding relativism and essentialism*

The conventional distinction between theory and social reality does have essentialist connotations in that it implies that, of the two, social reality is somehow less symbolic, less theoretical and that theory is less real, less material. The way to avoid relativism, while seriously taking into account the postmodern objection to the distinction between theory and social reality, is to maintain the two-level distinction but to conceptualize it in terms of *first- and second-order symbolic constructs.* First-order symbolic constructs (I-sc) can be conceptualized as entailing the taken-for-granted discursive and non-discursive practices of laypersons whose orientations to institutionalized rules or norms are predominantly (although not exclusively) *practical* in nature. Second-order symbolic constructs (II-sc) refer to practices of actors whose orientations to rules are predominantly *theoretical*. To use Giddens' terminology, in I-sc interpretations, laypersons orient themselves to rules and resources in terms of the 'duality-of-structure' mode – i.e. in terms of a taken-for-granted manner, a matter-of-course routine; whereas in the case of II-sc, actors as 'specialists' orient themselves to rules and resources in terms of the *dualism* mode: they distance themselves from these rules and resources in order to study or explain them (Giddens, 1984: 25–9).[9]

If this is accepted, and again taking the private-property example, two levels can be distinguished in terms of symbolic constructs. First-order symbolic constructs (I-sc) refer to the everyday, routine practices of laypersons which contribute to the reproduction of property institutions; whereas second-order symbolic constructs (II-sc) refer to the practices of theorists or 'specialists' who formulate theories and write books about property institutions. To revert to another example mentioned previously, it is possible to distinguish the 'battle of Athens' in December 1944, which entailed the first-order discursive and non-discursive practices of the combatants whose orientation was predominantly practical (i.e. to destroy their enemies and achieve victory), from the second-order practices of historians who take distance from these events in order to describe and explain them. In the first case the *predominant* mode of orientation is that of duality, whereas in the latter it is that of dualism.[10]

---

[9] For a critical assessment of the duality/dualism distinction in Giddens, see Mouzelis, 1989. Giddens, quite wrongly I think, dismisses actor–structure dualism and focuses exclusively on actor–structure duality. See also chapter 7, sections 2 and 3.

[10] I emphasize the term 'predominant' because all social practices involve both the duality and the dualism mode of orientation. For instance, as ethnomethodologists point out, even in taken-for-granted routinized conduct (duality mode) there is always a minimum degree of reflexivity (dualism). See chapter 8, section 2a.

What this means is that, if we replace the quasi-essentialist distinction between social theory and social reality with the non-essentialist one between first- and second-order symbolic constructs, we avoid the relativistic trap of 'equivalent narratives' while emphasizing that both levels entail symbols/theories/interpretations. This being so, historians and social researchers can, on the basis of their theoretical concerns, draw on empirical material linked to I-sc (e.g. statistics, personal diaries, documents produced in the taken-for-granted mode of duality, etc.) to assess the validity of their theories (II-sc). In this way the basic logic of the scientific inquiry remains the same (i.e. competing theories can be assessed both for their theoretical consistency and their empirical validity), while at the same time showing that on both levels we are dealing with symbolic constructs.

3 The 'internality' of a discipline's subject matter

If the previously discussed route to relativism was via an anti-essentialist critique of the distinction between theory and social reality, a different route rejects that distinction on epistemological rather than ontological grounds. The basic postmodern argument here is that the research object or the subject matter of a social-science discipline is *internal rather than external to the theory*. Postmodern theorists stressing 'internality' have in mind not merely the anti-empiricist reasonable argument that it is the theoretical concerns of the researcher that determine what is a relevant fact or how a theory is to be verified; neither do they refer to the well-known theme in the sociology of knowledge that there is a dialectical relationship between a theory and 'social reality' – in the sense that each impacts on the other. What they do

It is worth mentioning here that it is possible to subdivide second-order symbolic constructs into those which are constructed by theorists/specialists and are close, in terms of time or social space, to the first-order constructs they study (let us call them IIa-sc); and those constructed by theorists which are distant from the first-order constructs they study (IIb-sc). To take again our Greek example, present-day historical writings about the Greek civil war constitute IIb-sc. Systematic accounts of the civil war by historians living during the civil war period constitute IIa-sc.

Concerning social space, an anthropologist's account of an ethnic group's culture – via participant observation – is a IIa-sc. On the other hand, an industrial sociologist's theory about work groups based on questionnaires is a IIb-sc. (Concerning this last point, Collins, 2003 makes a similar distinction.)

mean by 'internality' is that the subject matter of humanistic disciplines consists of symbolic constructs which (at least partly) are constituted by discourses emanating from the very disciplines that are supposed to study them. Since a theory does not merely explain a research object external to itself, and given that in fundamental ways the theory *constitutes* its subject matter, there can be no distinction between a theory (II-sc) and its subject matter (I-sc). In that case it is impossible to use empirical data derived from I-sc for the purpose of validating or invalidating II-sc.

Consider criminology for instance. The subject matter of deviance is not external to the discipline in the way that the planets are external to astronomy. For Foucault, for instance, the subject matter of criminology has been constructed, at least partially, by discursive and non-discursive practices of specialists (criminologists, psychologists, psychiatrists, judges, etc.) who have created the 'subjectivity' of the delinquent. They have also created the distinction between the normal and the deviant – reifying along the way the phenomena to which the above distinction refers (Foucault, 1975: 206–16). This means that criminology as a discipline studies a subject matter it has to a large extent created itself. Or to put it differently: the discourses and practices of criminologists do not merely affect or regulate deviance, but in fundamental ways create and constitute the phenomenon under investigation. In view of this inextricable linkage between a discipline and its subject matter, the two-level distinction (II-sc and I-sc) cannot be maintained and, once again, cognitive relativism cannot be avoided.

a. On the construction of a discipline's subject matter

The first point to be made about Foucault's 'internality' argument is that the problem is more acute in certain disciplines (e.g. psychiatry, psychoanalysis and criminology) than in others (e.g. history and macrosociology).

Starting with historical disciplines, theories and interpretations (II-sc) about past events can influence the ways historians interpret them, but cannot affect the past events themselves (I-sc). To be more specific, the accounts by historians (II-sc) of the battle of Athens, which took place roughly sixty years ago, can have no impact on what happened during that confrontation. There is, of course, the problem of past theories (II-sc) implicated in past events (I-sc). For instance, the strategy and tactics of the two opponents in the battle of Athens were to some extent influenced by Cold War ideologies, communist and anti-communist. But this does not present additional problems for an anti-relativist historian. Current historical interpretations of the battle of Athens can and must be assessed by drawing empirical evidence from *past* first-order and *past* second-order symbolic constructs. Past I-sc might refer, for instance, to evidence drawn from participants' diaries, whereas past II-sc might refer to theories concerning the intensity of the communist and anti-communist ideologies during the civil war period. In other words, a present-day historian can avoid relativism and decide that, on the basis of empirical material drawn from past first- and second-order symbolic constructs, interpretation A of the battle of Athens is cognitively more powerful than interpretation B.

If in the case of historical events the impact of second-order symbolic constructs on past events is nil, for the study of present macro-developments it is minimal. For example, while a theory postulating growing inequalities within and between nation-states in the context of present-day neoliberal globalization may be true, false or partially true, its findings are not invalidated by the fact that the theory (as II-sc) has an impact on its object of study, i.e. on the actual inequalities (I-sc). In other words, in most cases the impact of social theories as II-sc on 'social reality' (I-sc) is not as profound as Foucault would imply. The problem remains, of course, for the kind of disciplines Foucault deals with (criminology, for instance). Here a closer look at how the French philosopher conceptualizes the links between first- and second-order symbolic constructs can give us some clues on how to avoid the relativist trap into which his arguments lead.

In his *Archaeology of Knowledge* (1972) Foucault clearly distinguishes the discursive level (with its various 'scientific' as well as moral, philosophical and legal discourses) from the non-discursive one which refers to an amalgam of elements such as institutions, techniques of regulation/surveillance, administrative measures, architectural forms, etc. (It is obvious here that by the non-discursive Foucault does not mean not discursively constructed. He simply means *extra-scientific, extra-disciplinary*.)[11] Concerning the links between them, however, there is much ambiguity in Foucault's 'archaeologically' oriented writings. In

[11] In a way, referring to institutions as non-discursive implies a certain degree of essentialism, given that institutions are symbolically constructed and therefore

some parts of his work he gives priority to the discursive level, since discourses (the *archive* as a corpus of 'discursive formations') not only give unity to the disparate elements of the 'extra-scientific', institutional level, but also constitute a given field of knowledge (Foucault, 1972: 130); for, as already mentioned, a field of knowledge is not prior to the subject matter it explores.

In other parts of his work, however, Foucault attenuates or even denies the primacy of the discursive level. For example, when discussing the principles that determine the formation of objects within a discursive formation, he distinguishes not two but three levels of analysis:

- the *discursive level proper*, which refers to disciplines such as psychiatry;
- the level of *secondary relations* formulated within the discourse itself, but entailing what psychiatrists think not so much about matters of their discipline proper, but about (for instance) the linkage between family and criminality;
- the level of *primary relations* which, 'independently of all discourse or all objects of discourse, entail linkages between institutions, techniques, social forms, etc.'.[12]

So here the non-discursive level (first-order symbolic constructs in our terminology) acquires considerable autonomy, since the distinction between primary and secondary relations implies that the institutional or power context within which social-science discourses are embedded plays a crucial role in their construction.

Such ambiguity concerning the issue of primacy disappears in Foucault's subsequent, 'genealogical' phase. At that stage there is a fusion of the discursive (II-sc) and the non-discursive (I-sc) levels. In the '*dispositif*' or discursive apparatus, discursive and non-discursive elements are linked in such a way that the problematic of primacy or determination disappears. The power/knowledge notion does not merely postulate a dialectical relationship between power and knowledge in the conventional way in which Weber, for instance, conceptualized the tension between the expert and the dilettante politician (who, because of lack of specialized knowledge, becomes the passive tool of a hierarchical inferior; Gerth and Mills, 1961: 91ff). Power/knowledge for

entail laypersons' first-order discourses. The distinction between I-sc and II-sc which I propose eliminates this kind of confusion.

[12] Quoted in McNay, 1994: 72.

Foucault denotes a situation where the knower, the specialist, derives power not only from his/her expertise, but *also and primarily* because the discursive practices of his/her discipline partly constitute the field or subject matter to be studied. It is because of their deep interconnection that no distinction between the discursive and the non-discursive, between knowledge and power, can be established – not even analytically.

This fusion leads to relativism since (as mentioned earlier) it is no longer possible to use empirical material (I-sc) from the non-disciplinary level in order to assess second-order discourses or theories (II-sc) cognitively. So two competing theories on mental disorders, for instance, cannot be empirically assessed by reference to a subject's symptoms.

This is precisely why, for Foucault, the reason for studying humanistic disciplines is not to establish how true or false they are, but to be able to spell out their power consequences, their 'material effects on docile bodies'. Once the representation principle is rejected (a principle incorporating the clear distinction between first- and second-order symbolic constructs), the criterion of truth/falsity in the assessment of competing theories is replaced by that of power/subjugation.

b. In defence of the distinction between first- and second-order symbolic constructs

The fusion between the discursive (II-sc) and the non-discursive (I-sc) in Foucault's genealogical phase is unwarranted. This is so for two main reasons. First, what Foucault calls 'object of knowledge' (the field or subject matter that a discipline is investigating) is not shaped only by practices derived from the discipline itself. It is also shaped by practices emanating from a variety of sources – some of these generating effects that contradict those resulting from the discipline proper. Consider, for example, the 'subjectivity' of the delinquent, a central object of investigation in criminology. This object is only partly constructed by the discursive practices of criminologists and of practitioners in neighbouring fields (e.g. psychologists and psychiatrists). It is also formed by discourses from the areas of literature, the theatre, films, underground subcultures, working-class organizations, left-wing parties, etc.

This being the case, the total fusion between a discipline such as criminology and one of its major objects of investigation is misleading.

It becomes even more so when we take into account the fact that within the very discipline there are conflicting paradigms, not all of which have 'subjugating' effects on 'docile bodies'. Again with criminology as an example, there are fundamental differences between a positivistic approach which constructs the normal/deviant distinction unproblematically and which, in essentialist manner, establishes correlations between crime rates and other variables (such as poverty, ethnicity, etc.); and a more interactionist, interpretatively oriented approach that leads the researcher to focus on deviant subcultures (Cohen, 1955, 1966) or on the labelling process (Becker, 1974). Both of these approaches are different from the neo-Marxist conceptual framework that links deviance to class exploitation/domination (Chambliss and Mankoff, 1976).

If this is properly taken into account, then Foucault's rather crude, one-dimensional, monolithic manner of linking social-science knowledge with domination/subjugation is seen to be misleading. This is accepted, at least indirectly, by the French philosopher himself when, in his late-late work (Foucault, 1984, 1986) he begins to speak not only of practices of subjugation, not only of 'docile bodies', but also of 'practices of freedom' and of subjects who can react reflexively *vis-à-vis* the self and the other. In view of all this, there can be no fusion of the levels of knowledge (II-sc) and of power (I-sc), and that means there is the possibility of avoiding relativism: two competing theories (on the level of II-sc), both dealing with the same issue, can be empirically assessed not only in terms of power but also in terms of truth. One can, in the light of the theoretical problematic at hand, use 'empirical data' derived from first-order symbolic constructs for the purpose of deciding which of the two theories or 'narratives' is cognitively more valid.

Conclusion

(a) Postmodern theories rightly argue that objectivity in the positivistic sense of the term – that is, as the absence of conceptual and evaluative intermediations between researcher and research object – does not and can never exist. Moreover, postmodern theorists, following a long anti-empiricist tradition, rightly argue that theory is not an aggregate result of data collection or statistical measurements. They also rightly argue that it is the researcher's theoretical problematic that indicates what is and what is not 'empirical fact' and more generally how a theory can be empirically verified.

This anti-empiricist stance must not, however, be allowed to lead to the total rejection of the process of empirical verification, a process that is based on the notion of objectivity as a self-disciplinary practice which, as Weber and Elias have pointed out, leads to a kind of 'detachment'; this detachment, in cases where there is a clash between values or conceptual tools on the one hand and empirical findings on the other, helps the researcher to avoid manipulating the empirical data to make them fit his/her conceptual and evaluative predilections. In fact, objectivity in the non-positivistic sense is what distinguishes a non-ideological from a purely ideological discourse within which data manipulation to fit value preferences is automatic.

(b) Turning to a less conventional issue, postmodern theories correctly emphasize that social phenomena are symbolic constructions, and that interpretations/theorizations are not the exclusive privilege of historians or social scientists. We see them in the interactive processes that result in the construction of everyday life – processes in which all social members are necessarily involved.

This should not, however, lead to the relativist claim that there is no theoretical and/or empirical way of comparing and assessing competing theories or 'narratives'. Comparison and assessment are desirable as well as feasible if one examines which second-order narrative is closer to first-order symbolic constructs, i.e. to what we usually call 'social reality'. Social reality, although symbolically constructed, and although to some extent affected by second-order theories trying to explain it, should not be conflated with these theories. Maintaining the distinction between first- and second-order discourses allows us to assess in relatively objective manner conflicting second-order narratives. In other words, the logic of empirical verification remains the same when we replace the quasi-essentialist 'reality/theory' distinction with the non-essentialist distinction of 'first-order/second-order symbolic constructions'.

(c) Finally, the fact that the object or subject matter of a discipline is not external to it need not lead to relativism if we remember (i) that discourses outside the discipline can also have an impact on the construction of its subject matter, and (ii) that a social-science discipline contains a plurality of often conflicting paradigms. It is precisely the plurality and contradictory character of extra- and intra-disciplinary discourses that invalidates the fusion between knowledge and power;

between second- and first-order symbolic constructs that Foucault's genealogy attempts to establish. Rejecting such a conflation of the two levels enables us to draw material from the level of first-order symbolic constructs for the purpose of examining the empirical validity of second-order discourses. It becomes possible, in other words, to assess competing theories or 'narratives' not only in terms of criteria of power and/or aesthetics, but also in those of truth.

دانش ستضاهٔ قدرت نیست(ول) در زمینه‌های متفاوت نقش(ها)

رقیب برسرکه مفهوم دارم.

12 | *Social causation: between social constructionism and critical realism*

Introduction

It must be pointed at the very start that the terms used to define the debate between social constructionists and critical realists are often misleading. They seem to imply that the differences between the two sides have to do with whether such phenomena as social structures are real or mere fictions in the minds of social scientists. In fact, the actual debate is concerned less with the 'reality' of structures than with how real social structures are constructed and what exactly they do, what kind of impact they have on social stability and change.

If we take, for instance, the exchange of views between Rom Harré and Bob Carter in a symposium published in the *European Journal of Social Theory*,[1] it is not only the critical realist Carter who believes in the real existence of structures; Harré also states emphatically that social structures, although discursively constructed, are the real products of acting agents. They both, therefore, start by accepting, ontologically speaking, the real existence of structures. They differ, however, on the way in which real structures impact on social action and interaction.

For Carter (following Bhaskar, 1978, 1989; Archer, 2000), social structures have 'causal powers', whereas for Harré only human agents have such powers. Social structures can in themselves cause nothing:

> At the end of the day I hope to show that such referents [i.e. referents of social structure expressions] are not the kind of entities that could be causally efficacious. I am not saying that there are no such things as social structures, but they are not the right kind of thing to do the sort of work that some people [i.e. the critical realists] would like them to do. (Harré, 2002: 112)

---

[1] The symposium 'Rom Harré on social structure and social change' included articles by Carter (2002), Harré (2002) and Strydom (2002), all focusing on the realism–constructionism debate.

Some pages further on in the same text Harré makes his position clearer by arguing that if critical realists, when referring to social structures, were merely content with the notion 'of patterns that might emerge in the flow of discursive acts as constraints on the actions of individuals, we would hardly have a dispute' (Harré, 2002: 147). It is plain from the above that if not all, at least some constructionists are realists in the sense that they believe in the real existence of structures and more generally in the real existence of a symbolically constructed social world.

This preliminary clearing of the ground will now allow us to focus on one of the key issues dividing the two opposing camps: the 'causal efficacy' of social structures. On this level I discern three positions, all of which seem to me problematic:

(i) the 'Harré thesis', which focuses on 'people' rather than 'structures' when reference is made to social causation;

(ii) Giddens' structuration theory, which conflates agency and structure in a way that does not allow for the idea of actors being constrained to varied degrees by structures external to them;

(iii) Archer's critical-realist thesis, which in criticizing Giddens' conflationist strategy tries to distinguish 'the causal powers of people' from 'the causal powers of structures'.

1 The Harré thesis

According to Rom Harré, as already mentioned, it is only people, not structures, that can constitute, reproduce and transform social reality. To speak about structures having causal powers is to reify social phenomena, to transform symbolic constructs into anthropomorphic entities 'doing' things. The problem with this position is that if structures cannot cause anything, neither can actors in the absence of structures. In other words, the argument that I shall develop in this chapter is that social causation always entails actors as well as internalized and external-to-a-specific-actor structures – but this entailment, contra Giddens, does not have to lead to an actor–structure conflation. Moreover, if one accepts, as Archer does, that both people/actors and structures have causal powers, it is important to stress that the causal powers of people are radically different from those of structures. It is crucial to take this difference into account if one wants to show how the two types of causal power articulate to produce social practices.

Given that the concept of social structure has several meanings, it is necessary to spell out some of the ways in which the notion is used. Harré mainly, but not exclusively, links social structures to roles and rules. He makes a clear distinction between roles/rules and people: 'Rules and narrative conventions are not causes of human action, not even formal causes. They are amongst the *tools or means* that people use to create and maintain order in their joint productions' (Harré, 1993: 56, emphasis added).

However, the distinction of people as agents and roles/rules as means becomes problematic when Bourdieu's notion of the habitus (1977, 1990) is introduced as a set of motor, cognitive, evaluative and generative schemata or dispositions which, in quasi-automatic fashion, are activated in specific social contexts. Bourdieu's habitus/dispositions are distinct from role structures (*positions*, in Bourdieu's terminology), as well as from what Harré calls people's 'personal identities'. For Harré, personal identity refers to 'the basis of the individuality and uniqueness of existence of a single human being', whereas social identity refers to 'the type of role they (people, individuals) occupy or the job they do' (Harré, 1993: 52).

Now Bourdieu's habitus as a set of dispositions is clearly distinct from both social-identity characteristics (since the latter are linked to role structures) and Harré's personal-identity characteristics (linked to the 'uniqueness' of a human being). Dispositions as 'internalized social structures' (Bourdieu, 1990: 54) are not unique but are shared by actors who have gone through similar socialization processes. In the light of the above, Harré's distinction of people as agents and role structures as means falls apart. Social actors are not only followers of rules/roles but also carriers of dispositions that are distinct from both the normative requirements of their roles and the unique features of their personal identity. To put it differently, the social games that people play have not only a role/positional but also a dispositional dimension – both dimensions being crucial for understanding the orderly or disorderly production of game outcomes. I shall make the above argument more concrete by using an example: the rugby game to which Harré refers (2002: 114).

In the course of a particular rugby match the players can carry on with the game only if they follow the basic normative expectations/rules entailed in their roles, which roles constitute the institutional structure of the game. This is to say that the rugby game has a role-institutional dimension (e.g. the specific rugby rules) which, on the paradigmatic level, players take into account when they play. As interpretative micro-sociologists have pointed out, the basic norms or rules entailed in rugby roles, contra Parsons, are not, of course, followed by the players auto-matically, in puppet-like fashion. Players use rules creatively in their interaction with other players. But as Parsons (1951) has pointed out, rules, in the form of roles/normative expectations (the institutional structure of the game), are necessary prerequisites for the realization of the game as an ongoing social whole. The complete absence of such roles/norms would make the game impossible. Therefore, in this specific example, social causation (the realization and actualization of the game, the achievement of the players' aims such as scoring a goal) is inconceivable without the entailment of both actors and institutional structures.

The rugby game has not only a *role/institutional* dimension but also a *dispositional* one. As already mentioned, each player unavoidably brings to it the set of generative schemata that Bourdieu calls habitus. These schemata (in so far as those involved are socialized in different class, educational and cultural contexts) vary from one player to another. In this way, understanding the 'actualization' or 'causation' of a specific game and its varied outcomes will have to take into account not only its institutional structure (the set of roles/rules it entails), but also the 'internalized social structures' that players carry within them (Bourdieu, 1977: 80).

To be more concrete, player A, given his/her specific dispositions (linked, let's say, to a middle-class upbringing) may adopt a more cau-tious, 'cerebral' approach to the game than player B, whose working-class socialization predisposes him/her to a more impulsive or aggressive style. Now just as the game rules are not followed automatically but are strategically handled by the players as required by the situational inter-active context, so are players' dispositions. Player B, given the coach's instructions or the reactions of team-mates, might try to control or attenuate his/her aggressive style.[2] But the fact that an agent is not passive *vis-à-vis* either rules or his/her dispositions does not mean that

[2] Some interpreters of Bourdieu's habitus argue that it entails a deterministic view of human conduct. The embodied, dispositional structures lead in a rigid, predictable, mechanistic way to specific practices that reproduce the culture and social structures internalized via socialization (Jenkins, 1991, 2000). Although Bourdieu's underemphasis on the rational-choice, voluntaristic aspects of human action make him portray actors as passive (see Mouzelis, 1995b: 104–16), I do not

the game can be played without taking roles/rules and dispositions into account. To put this differently, institutional and dispositional structures are not mere means or tools but *constitutive* elements of social causation. To repeat: social causation necessarily entails both actors and structures; it is inconceivable without actors embodying dispositions as well as following institutionalized rules/norms (McIver, 1942).

There is a third fundamental dimension of any social game (in so far as the latter is not solitary). As Harré, following the symbolic interactionist and ethnomethodological tradition (1993: 25), has repeatedly pointed out, it is impossible to understand social reality in general, and social games in particular, without putting symbolic/discursive interaction at the centre of the analysis. It is by means of the interactive dimension that one moves from the paradigmatic sphere (as a virtual order of rules and dispositions) to the syntagmatic one, the latter entailing the actualization of rules and dispositions in time and space (Mouzelis 1995b: 104–8 and chapter 7 above). As we have seen, players

think his notion of habitus is deterministic in the strict sense of the term (see Ostrow, 2000). Bourdieu has repeatedly stressed the 'polythetic', flexible, practical character of the habitus. This enables an actor to mobilize his/her stable set of dispositions in order to improvise, to play a game in a highly inventive manner (Bourdieu, 1990: 55).

It is true, however, that, as I pointed out in chapter 8, for the French sociologist, in *normal conditions* an actor's dispositions are quasi-unconscious. An actor entering a specific field or game mobilizes his/her set of dispositions in a taken-for-granted, non-reflexive manner. It is only in exceptional, 'crisis' situations (i.e. when there is a clash between dispositions and a field's positions/roles) that actors become reflexive and the voluntaristic, rational-choice dimension enters the scene. As Sweetman (2003) has recently argued, however, in late modernity it is not only in crisis situations but on a routine basis that individuals handle their habitus reflexively when they attempt to cope with constantly changing circumstances. Moreover, 'while we may not think about such things most of the time, it *is* possible to change the way we walk and talk, for example, as Bourdieu himself acknowledges in his brief discussion of "charm schools"' (Sweetman, 2003: 536).

According to Sweetman, in late modernity this type of self-management becomes routine, particularly among social strata anxious to construct lifestyles compatible with changing fashions or market requirements.

My position on the above argument is that one should distinguish between easily changeable and non-changeable aspects of an actor's habitus. It is obvious that the way we walk or talk are manipulable aspects of the habitus but, for example, the basic ways in which we perceive or experience certain social phenomena may be rather less manipulable – either because we are not conscious of such dispositions, or because, even when we do become aware of them, we are unable to change them. This type of 'deep' dispositional structures may set strict limits to social action.

do not follow game rules or even their own dispositions in puppet-like fashion; they handle them in the light of the syntagmatically unfolding interactive process. To return to our rugby example, in response to an opponent's successful strategy a player (or a team) can adopt a counter-strategy actualizing alternative opportunities offered by the game's normative repertoire and/or the player's (or players') dispositional repertoire. In other words, the same player in different interactive situational conditions might handle both rules and his/her dispositions quite differently.

Finally, in the same way that a game's rule/role dimension entails institutional structures (as well as the players' varied internalized dis-positional structures), the interactive dimension entails *relational* or *figurational* structures.[3] Here the elements or constitutive parts of structures are not rules/roles/institutions but agents; and the linkages between elemental parts are not logical/virtual (as in the case of institu-tional structures), but actual relations unfolding in time and space.[4]

So if institutional structures show us how in a specific game role A relates to role B on the paradigmatic level (e.g. how, in football, the role of the goalkeeper relates to that of the centre back), figurational struc-tures show us how a specific player, A, relates to player B (e.g. their actual relation may, within limits, be different from their normative one). This means that relational or figurational structures can vary indepen-dently from institutional structures. Moreover, the institutional structure of a game can allow for the emergence (on the syntagmatic level) of varied social relational structures. For instance, a team can adopt a strategy based on a centralized, 'authoritarian', star-dominated figura-tion of players, whereas the opposing team (or the same one on a different occasion) can opt for a participative, 'democratic' strategy leading to more decentralized relational arrangements.

A last point about the three dimensions of social games: whereas institutional and dispositional structures are constitutive elements of all 'social-causation' processes, relational structures are not. For instance, in the pursuit of solitary games or sports (e.g. cycling, jogging, etc.) we have only *intra*-active processes; *interactive processes* leading to stable social

---

[3] For the concept of figuration, see Elias, 1978, 1991; Mouzelis, 1993b.
[4] For a typology of social structures based on the paradigmatic–syntagmatic distinction, see chapter 7. For a theoretical discussion of the positional, dispositional and interactive dimensions of games, see Mouzelis, 1995b: 100–18.

relational structures are absent, but institutional and dispositional structures (i.e. rules and the actors' habitus) are always, unavoidably present.

To conclude this section, Harré, in dealing with the social causation of such social phenomena as game outcomes takes into account the role/institutional and the discourse/interactive dimension. The fact that discursively interacting players are not only rule/norm followers but also disposition/habitus carriers is ignored. This underemphasis of internalized dispositional structures can be explained by the fact that Harré's constructionist predilections make him view any 'internal state of mind' as neo-Cartesian essentialism (Archer, 2000: 89–117). Therefore, dispositions as internalized social structures have no autonomy *vis-à-vis* role structures or discursive interactions. This extreme anti-essentialist position, however, leads him to the erroneous conclusion that social causation entails only 'people' rather than, as I argue, people *and* structures (internalized and 'external' to specific actors).

2 Giddens' conflationist strategy

Although Giddens' structuration theory does not deal with the agency–structure relationship in the context of the realist–constructionist debate, there is no doubt that for him social causation entails both agency and structure. The way, however, that he brings together these two fundamental dimensions of social causation leads to a type of conflation that makes it impossible to theorize degrees of 'distance' or 'external constraint' between actors and structures.

As I have already argued in chapter 7, Giddens, influenced by linguistic structuralism, conceptualizes structures as rules and resources existing on a virtual plane (paradigmatic dimension); they are actualized, 'instantiated', when people draw on them in order to act or interact in time/space (syntagmatic dimension). In the above sense, structure is both means and outcome. It is means in that subjects use it to carry on with their daily activities, and it is outcome because each time rules and resources are actualized they are reproduced (Giddens, 1984: 169–71).

It is on the basis of this conceptualization that Giddens rejects the actor–structure dualism that is so common in conventional sociological analysis – a dualism which leads the researcher to view actors as being constrained by structures external to them. For the author of structuration theory, the actor–structure linkage entails not *dualism* but *duality*. It entails the elimination of any 'externality', any distance between actor and structure. Structure as both means (subjective dimension) and outcome (objective dimension) is 'internal' to the actor; it constitutes the two sides of the same coin. In this way the duality-of-structure schema helps us to understand the process of structuration that links *structure* (as a virtual order of rules and resources on the paradigmatic level) with the *social system* (as a set of patterned interactions on the syntagmatic level) (Giddens, 1984: 376).

Although Giddens himself does not do so, we may easily equate structuration here with the social-causation process. It is via structuration that the production and reproduction of social systems is 'caused' or actualized/'instantiated'. To take a concrete example again, institutional wholes such as rugby rules are reproduced via the duality of structure: via the fact that thousands of individual players in a routine, taken-for-granted manner use rugby rules to play their regular game. Each time they do so they reproduce and therefore strengthen this particular institutional complex.

This way of linking actors to structures is highly problematic, however. It fails to consider that actors are capable of relating to rules not only in a practical, taken-for-granted fashion but also theoretically and/ or strategically. To put it in Giddens' terminology, actors can and do relate to rules not only in terms of duality but also in terms of dualism. Very frequently actors take distance from structures (i.e. rules and resources) in order to acquire theoretical knowledge of them, or in order to construct strategies for changing or defending specific rules. Whether we look at rugby or any other institutionalized rules, these institutional complexes are not only reproduced, as implied in Giddens' structuration theory, via the actor–structure duality schema, i.e. by the fact that millions of laypersons, in taken-for-granted manner, use such rules in their everyday existence; they are also reproduced via agents (usually powerful 'macro' actors) who take distance from them in order to study, transform or defend the institutional complex to which these rules belong (Mouzelis, 1995b: 119–24 and chapter 7 above).

Rugby rules, for instance, are studied by sociologists of sport. They are also the objects of strategic interventions by 'reformers' who want to change them in a 'civilizing' direction, or by traditionalists who want to maintain the status quo (Dunning and Sheard, 1979; Dunning and Rojek, 1992). Therefore, an explanation of the constitution, reproduction and transformation of rugby rules must take into account both the relevant agents' taken-for-granted, practical routine orientation to the rules (the duality-of-structure mode), and those orientations that have a theoretical and/or strategic intent (the dualism mode).

To conclude, it is one thing to argue that social causation entails both agency and structure, and quite another to conflate the two in a way that excludes the possibility of conceptualizing agents as taking distance from structures (as rules) in their attempt to understand them better, to change them or to defend the status quo. Because Giddens' structuration theory eliminates the above possibility, it fails to give us a convincing account of how, in actual social contexts, institutionalized structures are created, reproduced or transformed. It is not therefore surprising that Giddens' structuration theory is incompatible with certain aspects of his work (for example, his theory of reflexive modernization) which focus on the capacity of agents for reflexivity and for theoretical knowledge of rules (Parker, 2000).

3 Archer's anti-conflationist strategy

Margaret Archer starts by rejecting Giddens' conceptualization of structure. She argues that Giddens conflates agency and structure in such a way that it is impossible to deal with the fundamental problem of structural constraints/enablements, and with the obvious existence of varying degrees of constraint and freedom. Because of this, structures portray no 'externality', no properties that make them distinct from those of actors/people. It is because of this conflation that Giddens cannot deal in theoretically congruent manner with the familiar notion that people tend to create social arrangements which were not anticipated and which frequently evade their control (Archer, 1982, 1990, 2000).

a. From structuration to morphogenesis

Archer puts historical time at the centre of her analysis. What she calls morphogenesis entails an initial stage, t_1, where interacting agents, in pursuing their own preferences and interests, create systems (social and cultural structures) which, beyond a certain developmental threshold, t_2, acquire properties and powers distinct from those of their initial creators. 'Cultural and structural emergent properties are held to have temporal priority, relative autonomy and causal efficacy *vis-à-vis* members of society' (Archer, 2003: 2). Therefore the move from t_1 to t_2 is a process of structural elaboration and emergence which leads (at least analytically) to a clear separation of agency and structure, a separation between actors' emergent properties and a system's emergent properties ('structural emergent properties' and 'cultural emergent properties') (Archer, 1982).[5]

Systemic emergent properties condition, but do not entirely determine social practices. Contra Althusser, actors in the morphogenetic process are not mere 'carriers of structures'. In this way the reification of structures is avoided, as is its extreme opposite seen in the interpretative micro-sociological tradition: the reduction of structures to the interactive processes between laypersons. Archer seeks, therefore, to avoid three types of reductionism:

— 'downward' reductionism (the reification of structures);
— 'upward' reductionism (the reduction of structure to interaction);
— 'middle' reductionism (Giddens' conflation of agency and structure).

b. A critique of morphogenesis

In Archer's writings, structures are relatively autonomous from agents in two different ways. First, in contrast to social constructionism, social structures have a reality that is not entirely based on or exhausted by discourse. Following the Marxist tradition Archer believes that there is, or might be, a discrepancy between, for instance, actual structures of domination or exploitation and people's perceptions, discourses and beliefs about them. Since structures pertain not merely to a discursive but also to a 'practical' world (Archer, 1982: 154–93), they can have an impact on social practices, irrespective of whether people do or do not talk, know or do not know about them.

Second, social structures portray characteristics or properties different from those of actors. For instance, one can clearly distinguish the structural characteristics of a role from the way an actor, having been socialized in a specific way, handles the role's normative expectations. Therefore, the features of an institutional role structure are not only real but also different from the features of the actors who play them. To use the distinction I developed in section 1 of this chapter, a social game has

---

[5] For the sake of simplicity, the focus here will be on structural rather than cultural properties.

a positional/role dimension that is distinct from, and *irreducible* to, the dispositional and/or the action-interaction dimension.

It is at this point that Archer's anti-conflationist strategy becomes problematic. Archer is right in distinguishing actors' causal powers from those of structures. She is also right in pointing out that actors, analytically speaking, have different properties from those of structures – i.e. that structures are autonomous from agents in the two ways outlined above. There are two problems with her morphogenetic approach, however:

— She fails to point out that the 'externality' of structures is a function not only of historical time but also of *hierarchically organized social space*.
— In linking, in her recent work (Archer, 2003), the causal powers of people with those of structures she overemphasizes intra-action (the 'internal conversation' of actors) and underemphasizes interaction (the 'external conversation' among actors).

When Archer tries to avoid agency–structure conflation by introducing a historical-time dimension into her analysis, the system created by agents in t_1 eventually reaches a certain threshold in t_2 and acquires autonomy from the initial creators. This autonomy expresses 'unanticipated consequences' and/or the inability of the initial actors to control or shape the structure emergent in t_2 in a way that will make it compatible with their own preferences and interests. When assessing the structure's autonomy from agents it is not enough, however, to focus on the linkage between the initial creators at t_1 and the emergent structural product at t_2. One should further consider how structure at t_2 links up with sets of *interacting* agents also at t_2 – interacting agents who may be different to, but are also related with the 'initial creators'.

Let me illustrate this point by taking a classical example of the 'unanticipated-consequences' syndrome: Moore's (1967) analysis of the peasantry's role in the creation of post-traditional, modern political structures. He has argued, very convincingly I think, that peasants played a crucial role in the shaping of early modernity. Whether one looks at the bourgeois democratic, the fascist or the communist route to the creation of modern political institutions, peasant mobilization was at the centre of the revolutionary process that destroyed the *ancien régime* of the societies Moore examined. On the other hand, in stark contrast to peasants' expectations and hopes, the institutional structures that eventually emerged out of the various revolutionary struggles were inimical to peasant interests. In England, Germany, Russia and China it was always the rural producers who were the major victims of the modernization process.

Therefore, in terms of Archer's morphogenetic paradigm, in t_1 we have actors (more or less 'corporate') whose intra- and inter-class interactions led in t_2 to an emergent system that was 'autonomous' from its initial creators by portraying features (e.g. the distribution of resources between rural and urban elites, etc.) incompatible with the rural cultivators' interests and hardly changeable or manipulable by them. Now it is important to note that if the emergent modern institutional structures acquired a high degree of autonomy from the peasants who contributed considerably to their creation, they portrayed a lesser autonomy *vis-à-vis* non-peasant collective actors who were more successful in creating (intentionally or not) structural outcomes more in line with their own interests. In the English and French cases, for instance, what Moore calls bourgeois classes were in this more fortunate position. To use Archer's terminology, in t_2 the emergent system of modernity was more autonomous *vis-à-vis* the dominated, peripheralized peasantry and much less so with regard to the dominant bourgeoisie. In t_2, rural cultivators play a lesser role in the reproduction and management of modern political structures than do the bourgeois classes: the post-revolutionary, post *ancien régime* structures were less manipulable from the point of view of the rural 'losers' and more manipulable, less autonomous from the point of view of the urban 'winners'.

If the above macro-historical example, with its references to classes as collective actors, seems too vague, the same point can be made by looking more modestly at a formal organization such as a business enterprise, focusing for simplicity's sake on institutional structures. The manager of the sales department – in pursuing the desired goal of increasing sales – is faced with both manipulable/changeable and non-manipulable rules. The latter may consist, for example, of a strict prohibition about pursuing sales tactics that would undermine the status or performance of other departments. Within the limits created by those rules that the sales manager is unable to change, s/he can choose from a repertoire of institutionalized sales techniques (which are the manipulable structural features of the situation) such as door-to-door promotion, television advertising, increasing sales via price reductions, etc.

Now, always in relation to the realization of the same goal, let us consider a hierarchically superior manager who, unlike the subordinate one, does have the power to change the present balance between departments by allocating more resources to sales and less to production or research and development. In that case what was non-manipulable for the sales manager becomes manipulable for his or her superior. The articulation between changeable and non-changeable structural features, between 'means' and 'conditions' in Parsonian terminology,[6] changes as we move up the corporation's formal or informal power hierarchy.

This *perspectival* approach, which leads to the serious consideration not only of *historical time* but also of *hierarchized space*, is missing from Archer's morphogenetic model. Her emphasis on the historical-time dimension is at the expense of that of social space. When she examines the agency–structure relationship, she constantly refers in undifferentiated manner to the actor(s), not to *interacting* actors or to *hierarchically placed* actors.

c. *Perspectival or methodological dualism*

Let me at this point bring together the various threads of my argument against morphogenesis, by putting forward a somewhat different account of agency–structure linkage, an account based on what one may call *perspectival dualism*.

As I mentioned in section 1 of this chapter, all non-solitary games entail actors as well as three types of structure: internalized *dispositional* structures (Bourdieu's habitus), *institutional* structures (sets of interrelated norms/roles) and relational, or *figurational,* structures (sets of interrelated actors). All structures entail features, some of which are and some of which are not manipulable by situated actors.[7] From this

---

[6] Parsons in his means–end schema distinguishes clearly the *conditions* of action, which the actor cannot change, and the *means*, which are changeable (Parsons, 1937: 44ff).

[7] To take institutional structures as an example, an ordinary player has to accept the basic rules of the game as unchangeable and non-manipulable. Within the limits imposed by the basic rules there is a repertoire of techniques from which the player can choose – these techniques constituting the structure's manipulable features. The same is true about figurational structures. From the point of view of a specific player, certain relational arrangements are changeable whereas others are not.

perspective the externality of structures must be seen within a space-time matrix.

Externality in terms of historical time

Initially, we have the distinction between internalized/dispositional structures and structures more external to a specific situated actor (institutional and figurational structures). Whereas the first are part and parcel of an agent's socio-psychological make-up, the latter are 'external' in two ways:

(i) In terms of 'unintended consequences'. As Archer has argued, interacting actors may produce structural outcomes that acquire autonomy from their creators, in the sense that the latter have not intended them and/or cannot at a subsequent stage control the emergent properties of such outcomes.

(ii) In terms of the existence of social structures before an actor enters the context that entails them and after s/he leaves this context. For instance, the role structure of the rugby game existed before a specific actor became a player and remains after s/he ceased to play the game.

Needless to say, externality of social structures in terms of (i) and (ii) does not mean that such structures are external to or autonomous from *all* actors. They are external or relatively autonomous from *specific* actors operating in specific space-time contexts.

Externality in terms of hierarchized space

If we bracket the time dimension in order to focus on hierarchically organized social space, we have to take into account that agent X, in pursuing specific goals, is faced with external institutional and figurational structures which, from his/her perspective, present a mix of manipulable and non-manipulable features or properties. This structural mix is both real and external to agent X. But despite this reality and externality, structural features change from the perspective of a more powerful agent Y who is also involved in the same space-time matrix. For actor Y, the structural mix of changeable and non-changeable features is transformed: what was non-changeable for X becomes changeable for Y.

It is precisely this type of variability that Archer does not take seriously into account. In so far as she underemphasizes it, she ascribes to the properties of structures a *fixity, an intransitivity* which they do not possess. This underemphasis leads to a partial hypostasization and reification of structural features, since the relation between agent and structure is examined in a hierarchic vacuum.[8]

I call the above approach, which tries to establish the relative autonomy of structures *vis-à-vis* actors, *perspectival* or *methodological* dualism in order to distinguish it from *philosophical* or *ontological* dualism – the latter implying that the autonomy of structures from actors has not only a methodological but also an ontological basis. Contra Archer and Bhaskar I think it is preferable to bracket the philosophical/ontological issue of whether actors and structures constitute one or two distinct realities and simply stress that it is methodologically useful:

- to avoid the actor–structure conflation which aims at the transcendence of the subjectivist–objectivist divide (see chapter 7);
- to avoid reducing structures to actors or vice versa;
- to view social reality or social practices *both* from an actor's 'internalist' perspective and from a system's 'externalist' one. Ignoring the former leads to essentialism and ignoring the latter leads to various forms of reductionism (see chapter 15).[9]

---

[8] Realists argue that the distinction between agentic and structural powers is only analytic (analytic dualism). Still, one has to show how the two types of causal powers articulate with each other. As I shall argue in section 4 of this chapter, Archer in her early work has failed to establish any linkages between the two causalities. In her more recent work (2003) there are serious problems with the way in which such linkages are conceptualized.

[9] Anthony King (1999) criticized Archer's ontological dualism by arguing that there are not two distinct realities (actors and structures) but one: people past and present and their interrelationships. I think that the shift from methodology to ontology creates more problems than it solves. If one is interested in the type of theory which provides conceptual tools (Generalities II in Althusserian terminology) useful for the empirical exploration of the social world, one should stress *methodological* rather than *ontological* dualism or monism.

To be more specific: it is much less important to decide whether structures constitute a reality different from actors; and more important to stress that actors' causal powers (in the form of a subject's decision-making, *agentic* powers – see, on this, chapter 4, section 1) are different from structural causality, which takes the form of constraints and enablements that an actor faces in specific social contexts.

Finally, I think that a more useful distinction, as far as different social 'realities' are concerned, is that between *virtual realities* on the paradigmatic level (e.g. relations between rules) and *actual* or 'instantiated' realities on the syntagmatic level (e.g. relations between actors) – see, on this crucial distinction, chapter 7, section 1. For the argument that social theory should focus less on epistemological (as in the 1970s and 1980s) or ontological issues (as in the 1990s onwards) and more on methodological ones, see Mouzelis, 1991a.

4 Articulation of agentic and structural properties

In *Being Human* (2000) Archer, as already mentioned, differentiates the causal powers of structures from those of people – but in doing so she says very little about how the two causalities articulate to produce actual practices. In *Structure, Agency and the Internal Conversation* (2003) she clearly admits this omission:

> Ontologically, 'structure' and 'agency' are seen as distinct strata of social reality, as the bearers of quite different properties and powers. Their irreducibility to one another entails *examining the interplay between them*. Hence the question has to be re-presented in this context – how do structures influence agents? In other words, how does objectivity affect subjectivity, and vice versa? Social realists have not given a fully satisfactory answer. (Archer, 2003: 2)

a. The internal conversation

Archer tries to fill the gap, so to speak, by pointing out that the missing link between structural and agentic causality is the reflexive process of 'internal conversation'. Actors have to face external situations that entail real structural and cultural constraints and enablements. The way, however, in which these constraints and enablements impinge on an actor depends on his/her internal dialogue. In the light of her/his major concerns, the actor will try to find what course of action to take. More specifically, through a process of 'internal turn-taking' in which there is continuous intra-action between an 'objective' and a 'subjective' self, the actor tries to *discern* the possible courses of action the situation offers; and then *deliberates* on the advantages or benefits and disadvantages or costs of each of them. Finally, as a result of such 'thought experiments', a mental balance-sheet is drawn up on the basis of which the actor makes a decision that may or may not consist of activating the constraints and/or enablements the situation offers (this third phase Archer calls *dedication*). The actor may also change her/his mind about the decision taken – in which case the agentic processes of discernment, deliberation and dedication, ('the three Ds') start all over again.

Archer stresses that 'people with different identities will evaluate the same situations quite differently and their responses will vary accordingly' (2003: 139). This does not mean, however, that one should conflate the situation with the ways in which actors perceive, evaluate and/or respond to it. Contra social constructionism, Archer rightly points out that the situation, as objectively shaped by cultural and structural enablements/constraints, constitutes an objective reality and, as such, should be clearly distinguished from the varied ways in which actors view it: 'Objective situations as shaped by socio-cultural properties are real; we cannot make what we will of them with impunity. If the descriptions under which they are known are wildly divergent from reality, then reality will have revenge, because the strategy for pursuing a project will be defective' (2003: 139–40).

b. Three types of reflexivity

In *Structure, Agency and the Internal Conversation*, Archer tries to account systematically for the actors' different responses to the constraints and enablements with which their situation presents them by constructing, on the basis of a series of in-depth interviews, a threefold typology of reflexive conduct: *communicative*, *autonomous* and *meta-reflexive*.

The communicative-reflexive individual portrays a type of internal dialogue that gives priority to stable personal relationships in the family, neighbourhood and local community, and so avoids projects that undermine these kinds of social arrangement. In Archer's terminology, the communicative-reflexive person will not activate, but rather evade, enablements and constraints entailing geographical and/or social mobility, being content to 'stay put'. The autonomous-reflexive, on the other hand, emphasizes in his/her internal deliberations goal achievement rather than maintenance of stable personal relationships. Instead therefore of evading, s/he activates constraints and enablements, trying to diminish the former and strengthen the latter. Finally, the meta-reflexive's internal dialogue is shaped by the fact that s/he is permanently critical of both the self and the external situation. As a result s/he is engaged in an internal process of continuous subversion, moving from one situation to the next – in this way diminishing the chances for both upward mobility and stable social relationships.

c. Some critical comments

In so far as social realists stress more how actual structures condition agents, rather than how agents handle structural constraints and enablements, there is no doubt that Archer's theorization of the internal conversation as a reflexive mechanism linking the causal powers of actors and those of structures constitutes a definitive advance. Her recent theory presents some further difficulties, however.

The externality and internality of enablements/constraints

The first difficulty has to do with the fact that the actor must face not only external but also *internal* constraints and enablements. Following Bourdieu (1990), the dispositions the subject carries are 'internalized social structures' and the result of his/her previous socializations. The French sociologist thinks that in normal conditions such dispositions operate quasi-automatically: the actor mobilizes his/her habitus in non-reflexive manner in order to act in a specific field. It is only when these dispositions clash with a field's positions that 'internal' reflexivity comes into play (see chapter 8).

As I argued in chapter 8, I do not think that this is so. An actor evinces significant degrees of reflexivity irrespective of whether there is compatibility or incompatibility between dispositions and positions. If certain dispositions are quasi-unconscious (e.g. how one perceives certain objects), others are certainly conscious and can be manipulated by their carriers (e.g. table manners; see Sweetman 2003: 536). In such cases the actor, by discerning, deliberating and eventually committing him/herself to a certain course of action activates not only external but also internal constraints and enablements. To use Alexander's terminology, actors are constantly confronted with both external and internal *environments of action*. Both internal and external environments create opportunities and limitations for situated subjects (Alexander, 1998a: 214ff).

Interaction as a second mediating mechanism between agency and structure

Archer not only neglects internalized constraints/enablements, but also fails to take seriously into account that the structure–agency mediating mechanisms are not only internal but *external* as well. In other words, we have not only 'internal' but also 'external conversations', intra-active as well as interactive processes which, by activating constraints and enablements, link structure with agency (see Craib, 1998: 4ff)

If Alexander's work helps us to distinguish internal from external environments of action (see chapter 4), Joas' *Creativity of Action* (1996) helps us realize the extent to which interaction is central for understanding how agents relate to external structural limitations and possibilities. According to Joas, while rational-choice theory emphasizes the *utilitarian* dimension of social action and Parsons the *normative*, they both neglect a third, *creative* dimension. The reason for this is that both, though in very different ways, fail to realize what a crucial role interaction plays in the production of social practices (see chapter 5).

For the author of the *Creativity of Action*, whether one considers the utilitarian means–end schemata of the rational-choice approach, or the values, normative requirements and internalized needs/dispositions of Parsonian functionalism, both models give us a very static view of social reality. They do not consider sufficiently that means and goals, values and norms are in constant flux, in constant negotiation as *interacting* actors attempt to cope with each other's strategies and counter-strategies. To take goals as an example: even when they do not emerge within the interactive situation (being given in advance), they change as the interactive process unfolds and as the actors try to adapt and readapt means to ever-changing ends. As symbolic interactionists and ethnomethodologists have pointed out, the interactive situation presents actors with problems of which the solution has to be *invented* in the here and now. 'Even if plans have been drawn up, the concrete course which the action takes has to be determined constructively from situation to situation and is open to continuous revision. Plans may place us in situations, but do not in themselves provide a comprehensive answer to the challenges of these situations' (Joas, 1996: 161).

What I would add to Joas' argument is that, as Archer has convincingly shown, it is not only the interactive but also the *intra-active* situation that has to be taken into account in exploring the creativity of action. If plans and projects, norms, values, etc. are constantly negotiated, this is due not only to interactive but also to intra-active processes. Both must be granted full consideration if we wish to understand the problem-solving dimension of social conduct. Both processes contribute to the 'invention' of solutions to the problems constantly generated by social intercourse.

Linking agency and structure
With the conceptual tools Alexander and Joas offer us it is possible, I think, both to distinguish more precisely the difference between the

causal powers of people and of structures, and to show how the two causalities articulate with each other. Concerning structure, this refers to cultural, institutional, figurational and internalized dispositional environments of action that provide limits and opportunities for situated subjects. Concerning agency (to use Archer's terminology), this entails processes of discernment, deliberation and dedication (2003: 102–3) that activate or 'deactivate' internal and external constraints and enablements. What links the two causalities, what makes them a *unitary process*, is the continuous flow of intra- and interaction, of internal and external 'conversations' that lead to specific decisions and to practical outcomes.

If this conceptual framework is accepted, a major task for an anti-conflationist, 'agency–structure' theory would be to explore the connections between intra- and interaction. If, for instance, 'autonomous reflexivity' entails a highly disciplined, strict relationship of the 'subject self' with the 'object self', does this lead to a similarly disciplined and strict relationship between the agent and his/her children or colleagues? Is it possible to be strict with oneself and highly indulgent of one's children, spouse or neighbours? What are the conditions when there is symmetry or homology between intra- and interaction, and when are intra- and interaction asymmetrical?

Questions like this, crucial for understanding agency–structure linkages, are not being asked in Archer's work. I think the main reason for this is that the interactive dimension plays a rather subsidiary role in her conceptual framework. This marked peripheralization of interaction in her earlier writings (1982, 1990, 2000) takes the form of neglecting the social space of hierarchically placed interacting agents; in her more recent work (2003) it shows itself by the overemphasis of intra-action and underemphasis of interaction as the mediating mechanisms between agency and structure.[10]

---

[10] I shall try to make the above critical point more specific by taking an example from Archer's *Structure, Agency and the Internal Conversation*. In this book (which, as already mentioned, is based on a number of in-depth interviews), one of the subjects questioned was Eliot Wilson, a former university lecturer who changed career in mid-course by moving from academia to the antiquarian book trade, an activity he performs solo from his home. Archer, quite correctly, classified him as typically 'autonomous-reflexive' who portrays such typical features as contextual discontinuity (moving from one career to another), thinking and making up his mind on his own, flexible and accommodative ethics of fairness and decency *vis-à-vis* family and friends, etc.

Conclusion

Cultural, institutional and figurational structures entail constraints and enablements that are real and external to situated actors. Contra social constructionism, the 'externality' thesis does not lead to a reification of structures if actors are located within a *space-time* matrix:

— In terms of *historical time*, as Archer's morphogenetic theory states, actors may produce structural outcomes that subsequently acquire autonomy from them (via the emergence of unintended consequences or other mechanisms). The same autonomy/externality obtains whenever the structures (cultural, institutional and figurational) of

> In deciding to move from the academic to the antiquarian field, Eliot had to consider not only the, to him, 'external' environments of action (e.g. the institutional/role structure of the university, the figuration of the organization's power relationship, the culture and philosophy of the teaching profession, etc.), but also his own internalized dispositional environment of action – an environment which also presents the actor with enablements/constraints. For instance, Archer tells us that, before taking up the antiquarian book trade, Eliot taught first at Oxbridge and then at a red-brick university. It is not clear from Archer's account whether Eliot simply disliked teaching and the academic environment, or whether he made the move to the antiquarian book trade because of failure to move up in the academic hierarchy. If the latter is true, his decision to change career might be related to dispositions such as cognitive schemata inimical to abstract thinking, or emotive schemata encouraging aloofness rather than the kind of sociability entailed in teaching. This type of disposition or habitus constitutes *internal* constraints/enablements which, together with the *external* ones (related to the university's cultural, institutional and figurational structures), are always taken into account by agents trying to make up their minds about a radical change in their life course.
>
> Archer rightly points out that 'The lives of "autonomous reflexives" tend to move through a variety of *modi vivendi* as a result of learning about themselves and their society, whilst also coping with the inevitable quota of intervening contingencies' (2003: 244). Learning about oneself means, of course, being reflexive about one's own dispositions. It means taking into account the internalized constraints and opportunities of our dispositional make-up.
>
> Another point it is important to stress here is that being autonomous-reflexive does not mean that only intra-active processes mediate between agency and structure. Unless one is autistic, interactive as well as intra-active mechanisms will always mediate between agentic capacities and structural constraints/enablements. Moreover, this is true whether one considers macro- or micro-time. Whether one looks at long-term processes leading to decisions fundamental for one's life-course or at routine, day-to-day ones, both intra- and interactions, internal and external conversations mediate between agency and structure. This is too obvious to need further development.

a social whole exist before an agent's entrance into it, and may persist after her/his exit.

— In terms of *hierarchized social space*, following what I have termed *perspectival* or *methodological dualism*, what is external/ autonomous for an actor who can only mobilize meagre resources, can be less external/autonomous for one who, when involved in the same context or game, is able to mobilize more resources. Therefore, the 'externality' of structures is a function not only of historical time (e.g. the emergence of 'uncontrollable' structural outcomes as we move from t_1 to t_2), but also of hierarchized social space (e.g. non-manipulability of a game's structures as we move from 'high' to 'low' hierarchical positions).

Both Harré and Archer, for different reasons, do not sufficiently take into account the *dispositional* dimension of social games: the fact that actors are carriers of internalized structures that present them with *internal* constraints and enablements. Harré, because of his extreme anti-essentialism, does not allow for any autonomy of dispositional structures from ongoing discursive interactions. Archer, on the other hand, underemphasizes dispositions because, for her, structural constraints/enablements are always external to the actor.

Archer, contra Giddens' conflationist strategy, rightly points out that people's causal powers are distinct from those of structures (analytical dualism). However, whereas in her early work she does not show how the two causalities are linked, in her late work she focuses only on intra-active mediating mechanisms (on the 'internal' conversation of agents). She does not, therefore, seriously consider the interactive dimension (i.e. 'external' conversations) as the other major mediating link between agency and structure.

The structure–agency controversy can be settled neither by conflating *à la* Giddens the two dimensions, nor by examining the linkages between agents and structures in a hierarchical vacuum. The neglect of interactions between hierarchically placed agents, i.e. the neglect of the fact that social outcomes result from the strategies of interacting actors who often possess different amounts of economic, political, social or symbolic capital, leads either to reductionism or to the partial hypostasization of structures. If social constructionists, as Archer has pointed out, tend to reduce structures to the discursive practices of interacting agents, social realists, by neglecting the hierarchical dimension of social life, ascribe to social structures a fixity which they do not possess – and in that respect reify them.[11]

The necessary preconditions for a theoretically congruent linkage of agency to structure are:

— to bracket the philosophical/ontological issue of dualism and to give greater stress to perspectival or methodological dualism;

— to distinguish clearly between the external and internal environments of action (i.e. between external and internal structural constraints/enablements actors have to face);

— to stress, contra Giddens, that actors can relate to structures (internal and external) both in a taken-for-granted way (duality) and in a more reflexive, strategic manner (dualism);

— to see both intra- and interaction as mediating mechanisms between agentic and structural causal powers;

— to relate social structures not to 'the actor' or 'actors', but to *hierarchically placed interacting* actors (past and present).

In brief: social causation as a unitary process entails the articulation via mediating mechanisms of intra- and interaction of the causal powers of agents (discernment, deliberation and dedication) and those of structures (internal and external constraints/enablements).

---

[11] For another kind of intermediate position between realism and constructionism, see Burkitt, 1999: 88ff. Sayer (1997) distinguishes between strong/unacceptable and weak/acceptable forms of constructionism. I think that, in the light of my critique of Archer, one can make a similar distinction between weak/legitimate and strong/methodologically illegitimate forms of realism.

PART V

Towards a non-essentialist holism

13 | *Grand narratives: contextless and context-sensitive theories*

In this and the following chapters (14–16) I take an intermediate, 'bridging' position between conventional, holistically oriented macro-sociological theories and postmodern approaches which reject all holistic theories and conceptual frameworks as always entailing essentialist connotations. It is worth emphasizing once more that the notion of holism in this and the following chapters is not used in a way which entails the 'methodological individualism versus collectivism' debate; nor does it raise the ontological issues of the emergence and the reality of causal powers of social structures (as in chapter 7). *Rather than focusing on philosophical issues, it simply raises the methodological question of whether or not it is possible to study social wholes (such as formal organizations, communities, nation-states and global formations) in a non-essentialist and, at the same time, non-fragmentary, overall manner.*

Postmodern, anti-foundationalist discourses have developed two major criticisms of holistic theories. If a distinction is made between substantive theories and conceptual frameworks,[1] the first critique stresses the over-ambitious and often deterministic character of the former, whereas the second critique points to the essentialist connotations of the latter.

1 'Grand narratives': context-sensitive and insensitive

In this case the postmodern attack concentrates on positivistically oriented theories aimed at producing generalizations or 'laws' that are supposed to be universally valid in all social situations regardless of time

---

[1] As I will argue in section 2 below, paradigms or conceptual frameworks (Gen. II in Althusserian terminology) refer to a set of conceptual tools which 'map out the problem area and thus prepare the ground for its empirical investigation' (Nadel, 1962: 1).

or space. The critics point out that such transhistorical, transcultural generalizations, whether they focus on the structure of kinship, the dynamics of revolutionary movements or the nature of religious phenomena, are wrong and, in addition, their pseudo-scientific pretensions lead (as in the case of 'scientific' Marxism) to all sorts of authoritarian practices (Lyotard, 1974).

Leaving aside the complex issues of the linkages between social theories and authoritarian politics, if for postmodern critics 'grand narratives' mean universally valid *substantive* theories rather than conceptual frameworks, their objections, although not very original,[2] are fully justified. Theories which, because of their universal scope, do not take seriously into account the historical and cultural contexts in which the phenomena being studied are embedded, are more often than not either trivial or wrong. Concerning triviality, social-science textbooks are littered with platitudes such as: 'other things being equal, the more complex societies become, the greater the need for co-ordination'; or, 'under modern conditions, the more literate peasants become, the more they are exposed to mass media and the more they are orientated to the outside community' (see Rogers, 1969: 81). On the other hand, when universal theories manage to avoid such trivialities and tell us something interesting, i.e. something we did not know about the social world, they are wrong; their universal and contextless scope does not allow specification of the conditions in which the statements put forward are valid and those in which they are not.[3] It is scarcely surprising therefore that

---

[2] For a 'pre-postmodern' critique of such theories, see Mouzelis, 1971: 76–84.
[3] To make this important point as clear as possible, consider the following propositions.

  (i) 'The greater the need for group inclusion among individuals in an interaction, the greater the need for predictable responses denoting group involvement and activity.'
  (ii) 'The level of need for symbolic and material gratification in an interaction is a partial and additive function of the intensity of needs denoting group inclusion and predictability in the responses of others' (Turner, 1990: 206).

  Statement (i) needs no comment; it is perfectly true but trivial. Statement (ii) is true only in certain conditions; however, these conditions are not specified. Thus one may have 'needs denoting group inclusion and predictability in the responses of others' without the need for symbolic or material gratification in the interaction. This would be the case for individuals who form a group not for gratification derived from the actual interaction, but for purely instrumental/strategic reasons (say, in order to blow up a bridge in enemy territory).

general, contextless theories about nationalism, bureaucracy or the state have a great affinity with essentialism. They tend to be based on the assumption of some basic substance which remains unaltered in all historical and socio-cultural contexts – a substance which the universal theory can capture.

The postmodern critique of grand narratives, although justified when it addresses positivistically oriented contextless theories, does not take into account that *not all grand narratives (i.e. broad holistic theories) are of the positivistic kind.* While, for instance, Marx's historic materialism (which asserts the dominance of the economic or material base in all social formations) is indeed trivial or wrong,[4] Moore's holistic analysis (1967) of how the outcomes of specific landlord–peasant struggles are systematically linked with three different routes to political modernity (the democratic, fascist and communist) is neither trivial nor wrong; or at least not wrong in the sense of contextless, vague and indeterminate generalizations. In Moore's work, despite its broad and inclusive scope, the *space-time context* is taken seriously. The theory of the three modernizing trajectories is based on a very extensive knowledge of the history and culture of specific societies (China, Russia, Britain, Germany, etc.). It is also based on a variety of theoretical insights drawn in non-*ad hoc* manner from Marxist political economy and Weberian comparative sociology.

It is true, of course, that with this type of grand but theoretically sophisticated and empirically grounded enterprise, historians specializing in one or two of the cases examined will invariably complain about inaccuracies, about the failure to take properly into account primary

---

I think that most of Turner's propositions, once stripped of their positivistic jargon, fall into the category of statements that are either trivial or wrong. Therefore the idea that this type of generalization (once 'tested' and refined) can constitute a solid corpus of knowledge to which other scientists can add new propositions of a cumulative nature is plainly a chimera, a dream which never has and never will come true. The innumerable attempts by positivistically oriented social scientists to build such 'laws' have led precisely nowhere. Their overall result is a mosaic of propositional statements that neither connect cumulatively, nor tell us anything much about social action we do not know already.

[4] It is trivial when one tries to 'save' historical materialism by conceptual devices like Althusser's 'determination in the last instance'. It is wrong in the sense that, in several pre-industrial societies, social struggles over the means of domination are more important than struggles over the means of production. On this, see Giddens, 1981.

sources, etc.[5] However, empirical weaknesses of this kind do not, as in the case of contextless theories, render the enterprise useless. They simply provide the setting for debates which may lead to either the refinement or the partial rejection of the initial thesis. It is through such dialogic processes that cumulative knowledge emerges. There is no doubt, for instance, that Moore's work and the complex debates related to it have deepened our knowledge, *not of revolution in general*, but of the American, French, Russian and Chinese revolutions (Smith, 1983).

It is precisely this kind of deepening that is completely absent in the positivistically oriented, contextless 'grand narratives'. Whether one looks at the sweeping nineteenth-century evolutionary schemes such as those of Spencer or Comte, or the twentieth-century statistically sophisticated attempts to build pseudo-scientific laws via the correlation of decontextualized 'variables', in all these cases historical context is either completely ignored or not taken seriously into consideration; in the latter case, the past is simply 'looted' as grand-theorists pick and choose indiscriminately from various historical periods or societies in order to fill their preconceived theoretical boxes.[6]

To put the above in a nutshell, the postmodern critique fails to differentiate between two very distinct types of substantive holistic theories: (i) the positivistic, contextless generalizations that aim at the construction of evolutionist laws or statistically based law-like correlations, and (ii) the *context-sensitive* grand theories which post-positivist comparative/historical sociology offers us.[7] The postmodern total rejection of all holistically oriented grand theories throws out the baby with the bathwater. In so doing it turns its back on politically and socially vital issues with which only a holistic, broadly focused theory can deal. These are issues such as the present growing inequalities within and between nation-states, the massive peripheralization of whole populations and the rapid ecological deterioration that the present neoliberal globalization tends to generate. At a time when the sudden opening up of world markets and the ensuing imbalance between capital and labour has created problems that urgently require serious analysis, the postmodern indiscriminate rejection of holistic theories encourages social

---

[5] On this point, see the Appendix.
[6] See, for instance, McLeland, 1961; Rostow, 1961; Hagen, 1962.
[7] For a review and critical assessment of historical sociology, see Skocpol, 1984.

scientists to wallow in uncritical, narrow-minded self-indulgence. It is urgent, therefore, to rigorously defend the type of holistic theories which, on the basis of theoretically sophisticated conceptual tools and context-sensitive empirical research, attempt to give us *synthetic overall accounts* of the social trajectories leading to the global order/disorder into which we are all unavoidably drawn (for a defence of 'grand' historical sociology, see the Appendix).

2 Holistic conceptual frameworks: open and closed

Conceptual frameworks, in contrast to substantive theories, do not so much tell us things we did not know about the social world, but rather how to look at or investigate it. They provide the indispensable lenses for looking at the subject matter in a non-empiricist, theoretically relevant manner. As Althusser has pointed out, they are tools (Gen. II) rather than end-products (Gen. III) of the process of theory production. By presenting interesting problems for analysis, by pointing out the proper mode of investigating such problems (e.g. what is and what is not a relevant 'fact'), by specifying effective ways of verifying empirical statements, in all these ways conceptual frameworks prepare the ground, as it were, for the production of substantive theories. This means that when assessing conceptual frameworks, the key criterion is less that of truth and more that of heuristic *utility*: whether the proposed conceptual tools are useful or not, and how much they can help the researcher handle the 'raw materials' (Gen. I) in order to produce a substantive theory that is theoretically congruent and empirically sound.

The postmodern critics of holistic conceptual frameworks point out that holistic paradigms are not innocent, neutral tools. In the same way that material technologies are not neutral in their consequences, so conceptual technologies exert their own effects. More specifically, holistic conceptual frameworks lead the user to view the social world in an essentialist and/or reductive manner. This means that instead of simply 'preparing the ground' for the empirical investigation of the social, they tend to generate in aprioristic manner the end-product or solution as well. In that sense holistic frameworks are dead ends, invariably leading to *closure* rather than *openness*. They put up walls and obstacles rather than providing bridges for the open-ended investigation of social phenomena.

Here again, if one looks at the major holistic frameworks existing in the social sciences today, there is much validity in the postmodern critique.

a. *The Marxist closure*

Consider for instance the now out-of-fashion Marxist political economy. The all-pervasive thesis of the primacy of the economic/material basis is not merely a substantive theory to be empirically investigated, but is built right into the major conceptual tools Marxism offers us. For instance, when Marxists define the state as the instrument of the dominant classes (Miliband, 1969) or, in systemic terms, as an institution that copes with the enlarged reproduction of capital (Brunhoff, 1978) or, finally, as a social space where class struggles unfold (Poulantzas, 1978), all these conceptualizations lead to closure. At best they simply leave cases that do not fit the Marxist conceptual framework out of the field of empirical investigation, and at worst they lead to aprioristic, ready-made, wrong solutions. To focus on the former, the Marxist conceptualization of the state as an instrument of the dominant classes rules out the investigation of cases where those who control the means of domination are more powerful than those who control the means of production; or, to put it in functionalist/systematic terms, the Marxist framework cannot account for cases where the reproductive requirements of the state and polity prevail over the reproductive requirements of the economy.[8] In other words, defining the state in class terms leads to a reductive closure: it obstructs rather than facilitates the open-ended examination of the complex and varied relationships between those who control the means of production and those who control the means of domination. Reductive closure in turn leads to essentialism. It leads to the transformation of the complex, open-ended struggle between collective actors into pre-determined relationships between actors with pre-constituted identities and interests.[9]

b. *The Parsonian closure*

If the Marxist holistic paradigm leads to a closure related to the linkages between economic and non-economic spheres, Parsonian functionalism, the major holistic framework in the postwar social sciences, produces a closure in the actor–system dimension. Here, contra Marxism and following Weber, no institutional sphere or subsystem enjoys an a

---

[8] For a development of the above argument, see Mouzelis, 1990.
[9] On different types of essentialist and/or reductive explanations in Marxist theory, see chapter 15, section 1. See also Mouzelis, 1980.

priori privilege over another. If one leaves aside what Parsons says about the 'cybernetic hierarchy',[10] the relationship between institutional spheres becomes a matter of open-ended empirical investigation. The Marxist economic-primacy closure, however, is replaced by a different conceptual closure generated by the marked *system*–actor imbalance that one sees in Parsons' middle and late work. As I argued more extensively in chapter 1, whether one looks at how Parsons subdivides the social system into four subsystems (adaptation, goal achievement, integration and latency), or at how he relates the cultural to the social and the personality levels of analysis, the highly complex conceptual tool kit he offers us results in an investigation of how systems or subsystems shape actors' practices rather than the other way round. *Who*-questions are neglected, actors being portrayed as passive products of structural-functional determinations. In this way social systems in general and 'society' in particular become a mysterious entity pulling all the strings behind the actors' backs.[11]

To sum up: if social reality, as postmodern theorists assert, is symbolically constructed, the two major holistic paradigms referred to above both lead to a different type of closure: the Marxist political economy framework leads to the hypostasization of the economy whereas Parsonian structural functionalism to that of the social system. Given the above essentializing tendencies of the Marxist and Parsonian holistic conceptual frameworks, tendencies that have been pointed out not only by postmodern but also by numerous more conventional social theorists, the reaction, or rather over-reaction, of the former is to reject all holistic paradigms and to abandon all efforts to replace them by more open, less essentialist ones.

Contra postmodern theorizing, a major thesis developed in this book is that such a rejection is unwarranted. In the same way that substantive holistic theories (when context-sensitive) are not necessarily wrong or trivial, holistic conceptual frameworks are not inherently closed or essentialist. As I shall argue below, non-essentialist, open-ended holistic conceptual frameworks are both possible and necessary if we are to understand and eventually transform in an emancipatory direction the global situation in which we are all unavoidably involved.

[10] For the concept of 'cybernetic hierarchy', see chapter 16, section 2a.
[11] On system essentialism, see chapter 15, section 1a.

3 Non-essentialist holism: three types of openness

The main objective of an open, non-essentialist holistic paradigm should be to facilitate a social researcher's study of social reality – particularly relatively self-contained social entities such as communities, nation-states, global or post-national formations – in a non-compartmentalized, non-fragmented, all-inclusive manner. This all-inclusiveness does not mean that the division of intellectual labour within the social sciences should be abolished. It simply means that *bridges* should replace the insurmountable methodological *walls* that exist today between competing paradigms. It means overcoming the present theoretical fragmentation and compartmentalization, *not by abolishing the specific logic of each different theoretical tradition, but by developing conceptual tools that will make inter-paradigmatic communication possible; conceptual tools that will enable us to translate the language of one tradition into that of another.* More specifically, an all-inclusive holistic framework entails openness in three different dimensions: an action–system (chapter 14), a micro–macro (chapter 15) and an inter-institutional dimension (chapter 16).

14 | *The actor–structure dimension: anti-conflationist holism*

Introduction

Inclusiveness in the action–structure, or action–system, dimension means that a holistic framework should encourage the researcher to look at social phenomena both from an actor's 'internalist' perspective and from a systemic 'externalist' one.[1] This means, in Lockwood's well-established terminology, that a social whole should be studied from both a *social-integration* and a *system-integration* perspective: both as a figuration of actors related to each other in conflictual and/or co-operative terms, and as a system of interrelated 'parts' (or institutional subsystems) logically compatible or incompatible with each other (see chapter 6). Any attempt to disregard the imperative of combining in a *balanced* fashion an action/internalist and a system/externalist perspective leads to either a trivial or a distorted analysis of the phenomena under investigation. An open holistic framework, as far as the action–system problematic is concerned, does not only reject the exclusive focus on one of the two perspectives, it also rejects attempts aiming at:

- the a priori subordination, or the derivation of the one perspective from the other (as in Parsons' oversystemic middle and late work – see chapter 1, section 1);
- the 'transcendence' of the action–system distinction via various conflationist strategies (as in Giddens' structuration theory – see chapter 7);
- the abolition of the action–system distinction altogether (as in various structuralist and post-structuralist approaches – see chapter 1, sections 4–6).

---

[1] For the internalist/externalist distinction, see Habermas, 1987.

1 Structures and actors

As I dealt extensively with the action–structure linkages in the previous chapter (as well as in parts II and III), here I shall bring together the various threads of my position rather briefly and schematically.

a. Methodological remarks

A holistic conceptual framework must have an anti-conflationist orientation. It must help the social researcher to conceptualize structures and actors as analytically distinct realities portraying different types of causality. Structural causality entails limitations and enablements which can be activated by actors involved in some specific game or social system. Actors' causality on the other hand entails activation of a subject's agentic powers.[2]

Methodological dualism

The type of dualism which stresses the analytic separation of actors and structures is not linked directly or indirectly to philosophical dualism, which refers to essentialist dichotomies of the body/mind type or to interminable debates about the ontological differences between actors and structures (see chapter 12, section 3).[3] Methodological dualism is *analytic*, in the sense that it stresses the necessity to view the same social

---

[2] According to Alexander, agentic powers refer to processes of typification, invention and strategization (see the postscript to chapter 4). According to Archer they refer to processes of discernment, deliberation and dedication (see chapter 12, section 4).

[3] For an agent–structure theory which stresses more philosophical/ontological and less sociological theoretical conceptualizations, see Wight, 2006. I think that Wight's emphasis on ontology and his lack of emphasis of the theoretical tradition that Parsons initiated in the postwar period – a tradition which theorizes in a rigorous and *logically coherent* manner such basic concepts as values, norms, institutions, etc. (see, for instance, chapter 1, sections 1–3) – has led him to an *ad hoc* type of theorizing. For instance, Wight adopts quite uncritically Bhaskar's typology of 'four planes of activity'. These are:

'1. Material transactions with nature (resources, physical attributes, etc.)
2. Inter–intra subjective action (rules, norms, beliefs, institutions, etc.)
3. Social relations (class, identity, production, etc.)
4. Subjectivity of the agent (subjectivity, identity, etc.)' (Wight, 2006: 174).

This typology plays a crucial role in the author's overall theory. Despite this the constituent elements of each of the four planes are very poorly theorized.

processes or social practices both from the point of view of actors and from that of systems. In the former case, one raises questions related to reflexive accounting, interpretative understandings, strategic interactions, social conflict and co-operation; in the latter case, one explores the conditions of existence (or functional requirements) of social wholes, as well as the logical compatibilities or incompatibilities between their institutional subsystems.

The space and time dimension

Social and cultural/symbolic structures, although created by actors, may be relatively autonomous from them. This autonomy can be clearly seen when actors are located within a space-time matrix. In terms of historical time, actors in an initial phase can more or less unintentionally produce emergent outcomes (institutional, figurational and symbolic structures) which, in a subsequent phase, escape their control.

Social structures are also autonomous from specific, situated actors if not only historical time is taken into account but also hierarchized space. If we consider actors involved in the same game but who possess different amounts of economic, political, social or cultural capital, we realize that structures have no fixity. The enablements and constraints that they generate vary according to the actors' power position. Structures whose main features are unchanging from the point of view of actors with small amounts of capital can be more manipulable from the point of view of more powerful actors involved in the same game.

To repeat: dualism sensitizes the researcher to the relative autonomy of structures *vis-à-vis* actors, not only in terms of emergent, unintended consequences of action but also in perspectival terms: what constitutes an autonomous structure for modestly powerful actors can be less autonomous for more powerful ones.

From this it follows that when one talks about linkages between actors and structures in an interactive vacuum, one essentialistically ascribes a fixity to structures which they do not possess. In order,

Concerning, for instance, plane 2, of inter–intra subjective actions, what precisely are the relations between rules, norms and institutions? Or why is identity appearing as part of both social relations (plane 3) and subjectivity of the agent (plane 4). Is there an overlap or does 'identity' have a different meaning in the two planes? Etc.

For the argument that social scientists pay too much attention to ontological and epistemological problems and too little to social-theoretical ones, see Mouzelis, 1991a.

therefore, to avoid structure essentialism, it is important to stress the non-fixity of structures in terms both of historical emergence (unintended consequences) and of hierarchically placed interacting subjects (see chapter 12, section 3).

b. A typology of structures

Institutional and figurational structures

Having established the utility of the analytic separation between actor causality and structural causality, it is necessary to spell out what the two terms entail, as well as how the two causalities articulate to produce concrete social practices or outcomes.

If by structure we mean a whole of interrelated parts, we have two major types of social structure: institutional and figurational. The first refers to a system of interrelated roles or institutions; the second to a whole consisting of interrelated actors.

As I argued more extensively in chapter 7, section 1, institutional structures as a virtual system of norms and roles entail, on the paradigmatic level, a set of rights and obligations inherent in a given social position. Figurational structures, on the other hand, as a system of relationships between actors, operate on the syntagmatic level. The move from the virtual to the actual, from the paradigmatic to the syntagmatic, often entails a *décalage* between the *de jure* role-linkages and the *de facto* relationships between concrete actors. For example, hierarchically superior actors may have less power than hierarchically subordinate ones who, in *de facto* manner, may control important strategic resources.[4]

---

[4] For a concrete example of a discrepancy between institutional and figurational structures, see Crozier, 1963: 193–232; Mouzelis, 1978: 134–48.

Lockwood (1992) makes a very interesting comparison of the ways Durkheim and Marx view social structure. For Durkheim, who sees social structure mainly in status terms, social structure consists of hierarchically organized status positions whose rights and obligations are legally defined and legitimized by the prevailing societal values and norms (in our terminology, institutional structures). For Marx, on the other hand, the focus is less on social status and more on power relations (figurational structures). According to Lockwood, at the centre of the Marxist view of social structure, groups are struggling over control of the means of production and over the benefits such control bestows. From this perspective, social transformation is facilitated when there is a discrepancy between class and status, between *de facto* power relations and *de jure* formal arrangements (Lockwood, 1992: 178ff).

Distributional structures: virtual and actual

In the social sciences the term social structure is also used to refer to the distribution of traits among a specific population. In that case the linkages between the elements of the system are neither role-relational nor actor-relational, but statistical. The distinction between the paradigmatic-virtual and the syntagmatic-actual applies as well, however. One can distinguish virtual distributional structures from actual ones. Thus a virtual distributional structure may refer to the distribution of attitudes among a number of people (e.g. politically conservative attitudes); whereas an actual distributional structure may refer to the distribution of specific acts (e.g. voting for a conservative party).[5]

Symbolic or cultural structures

If institutional structures entail relations between norms/roles/institutions, and figurational structures relations between concrete actors, cultural or symbolic structures refer to linkages between symbols – between values, beliefs, scientific ideas, ideologies, etc. For Parsons the cultural system, as already mentioned in chapter 1, consists of core values which, via institutionalization, become role requirements on the level of the social system, and via internalization, needs/dispositions on the personality system level.

In the above sense, cultural structures as symbolic wholes are analytically distinct from social structures (both institutional and, I would add, figurational), as well as from internalized dispositional ones. The autonomy of cultural from social structures is justified by the fact that the two can vary independently of each other. For instance, in my postscript to chapter 4 it was argued, regarding Alexander's analysis of the Holocaust, that in early postwar Germany second-order liberal or progressive discourses on the cultural level may have been incongruent with first-order anti-Semitic discursive and non-discursive practices which persisted in specific institutional spheres.

Cultural structures as such, contra Alexander, do not constitute internal environments of action (they only do so when internalized in the form of dispositions). The externality of cultural structures becomes obvious if one considers cases where a social system's value and belief systems are not fully known (as in the case of a 'newcomer') or not fully internalized (as in the case of an immigrant who accepts the normative

---

[5] On virtual and actual distributional structures, see chapter 7, section 1c.

requirements of his/her work role but rejects the general cultural orientations of the host country).

Needless to say, cultural/symbolic structures constitute an external environment of action but operate on the virtual, paradigmatic level. The move from the virtual to the actual, from the paradigmatic to the syntagmatic often entails, in addition to concrete cultural practices, the 'materialization' of the symbolic. For instance, scientific ideas in their applied form may lead to the construction of new instruments or machinery; artistic ideas can materialize in the form of paintings or sculptures; religious beliefs in the form of monuments, relics and other holy objects, etc.

Dispositional structures

Bourdieu, more than any other social scientist, has theoretically developed the notion of dispositions or habitus. Habitus entails a set of generative schemata of bodily movements, cognition, emotion and evaluation which, in a more or less taken-for-granted manner, contribute to the production of social practices. I critically examined Bourdieu's theory of practice in chapter 8. Here I would like to return to his idea that the habitus, as a set of dispositions that an actor carries, is the result of her/his various socializations. As such, dispositions are formed via the internalization of cultural and social structures.

The habitus notion is very useful as a conceptual tool to help the researcher trying to build bridges between conventional approaches and more recently developed fields of inquiry, such as the sociology of emotions and of the body.[6] Emotions and bodily movements or postures, to the extent that they are not idiosyncratic (i.e. to the extent that they result from the internalization of social and cultural structures), may be seen as aspects of the habitus, as aspects of an actor's internal, dispositional environment of action. As such they entail constraints and enablements that a player activates in specific games or in specific institutional fields.

The habitus notion can also bring closer together structural and structuralist paradigms.[7] Structuralism's 'hidden codes', for instance,

---

[6] For an introduction to the sociology of the body and of emotions, see Burkitt, 1999. See also Elias, 1987b; Kemper, 1990; Jackson, 1993; Craib, 1995.

[7] For the distinction between structural and structuralist sociologies, see Giddens 1984: 207.

entail paradigmatic and syntagmatic rules which actors follow with no theoretical knowledge of them. They may be conceptualized as dispositions which are not conscious, and which the actor automatically activates when engaged in such activities as cooking, building a hut, writing a novel, making a film, and so on.

Finally, ethnomethodology's 'deep rules' – whether they refer to taken-for-granted ontological assumptions about the social world or to more mundane techniques facilitating intersubjective communication (like the 'etcetera principle', for example) – can be conceptualized as dispositions that enable actors to move from *langue* to *parole*, from the paradigmatic to the syntagmatic. Therefore Lévi-Strauss's hidden codes and Garfinkel's ethnomethods, as quasi-unconscious dispositions, bring structuralist and ethnomethodological analysis closer to the more conventional analysis of roles or social positions that is to be found in Parsonian structural functionalism or Bourdieu's theory of practice.

Moving now to the problem of the relationship between internal/ dispositional and 'external' structures, as was the case with the analytic autonomy of social *vis-à-vis* cultural structures, here too an actor's dispositions can vary independently of both social and cultural structures. For example, a newcomer to a community may carry dispositions that could clash with communal values or the major normative requirements of the communal role structure. This incompatibility may, of course, persist even when the newcomer has achieved the status of established member. Parsons' assumption that the cultural, role/positional and dispositional dimensions of a social whole will tend to be compatible with each other, rather than contradictory, is quite unwarranted. The above three dimensions may vary independently – and this means that the degree of compatibility or incompatibility between the cultural, the social and the dispositional is an empirical matter.[8]

The habitus, as a set of 'internalized social structures',[9] constitutes an internal environment of action. In terms of structural causality, however, it operates in a way that is similar to the various external environments of action: it offers a set of internal enablements and

---

[8] For a concrete example of how dispositions, role/positions and interactive situations can be both compatible and incompatible, see Mouzelis, 1995b: 162–5.

[9] As internalization of 'objective' structures (social and cultural), the elements of the habitus are shared by all subjects who have experienced similar socialization processes (Bourdieu, 1977: 80).

constraints that the actor may or may not activate in the pursuit of his/her goals.[10]

c. The agentic powers of actors

As mentioned in chapter 4, Alexander usefully distinguishes between action and agency. Contra interpretatively oriented micro-sociologists, he argues that agency is an analytic dimension of human action; it refers to the capacity of an actor to be knowledgeable, reflexive, creative, etc. These agentic powers vary from one actor to another. Certain actors are highly knowledgeable, reflexive and creative, whereas others are less so or are simply ignorant, non-reflexive, non-creative, etc.

The American theorist goes on to identify three fundamental agentic powers (varying in intensity from actor to actor): typification, invention and strategization; Archer, on the other hand, in dealing with the actor's causal powers, refers to those of discernment, deliberation and dedication. Alexander's conceptualization of agentic powers places greater emphasis on the varying capacity of actors to be (on the basis of their typifications) inventive strategists. Archer, on the other hand, stresses more the discerning, deliberative, decision-making capacities of human beings (see chapter 12, section 4a).

2 On the linkages between the causal powers of actors and of structures

a. The intra- and interactive dimensions

Having examined the causal powers of actors (typification, invention and strategization or discernment, deliberation and dedication) and those of structures (enablements/limitations of cultural, social and dispositional structures), it remains to show how the two types of causal powers link up with each other. The lynchpin between structures and actors is intra- and interaction: the self–self internal intra-actions and the self–other interactions which simultaneously take place in a specific context. In the interrelated discursive processes of intra- and interaction, self and other use their agentic powers in order to take into

---

[10] On dispositional structures in relation to figurational and institutional ones, see chapter 12, section 1. On dispositional structures as an internal environment of action, see the postscript to chapter 4.

account limitations (with varying degrees of accuracy), and activate the enablements inherent in their internal and external environments of action. In a nutshell: discursive intra- and interactive processes link the causal powers of actors to those of structures.

The above can be represented by the diagram in figure 14.1. In this, box 1 points to institutional, virtual-distributional and symbolic/

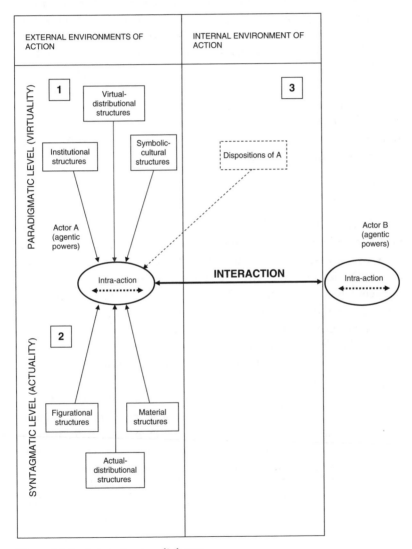

Figure 14.1. Actor–structure linkages.

cultural structures *external* to the situated actor A on the *paradigmatic* level; box 2 points to environments of action *external* to A on the *syntagmatic* level (figurational, actual-distributional and material structures); and box 3 locates actor A's *internal* environment of action on the *paradigmatic* level (dispositional structures). Both internal (in dotted lines) and external environments of action set limits and provide opportunities for actor A. What links actor A's agentic causal powers to the structures' causal powers are the discursive processes of intra- and interaction (bold lines). Actor A in pursuing a project mobilizes his/ her agentic powers (say, of discernment, deliberation and dedication), in order to assess the limitations and activate the opportunities that his/ her various environments of action provide. Bringing together A's agentic powers with the structural limitations and enablements of his/ her environments of action requires constant internal accounting, as well as syntagmatic unfolding of the interactive situation as A reacts to B's strategies and vice versa.

b. A concrete example

The above will be made clearer by an example. I shall take the hypothetical case of the sales manager mentioned in chapter 12, section 3b. Our sales manager (actor A), in launching his project of increasing sales, has to compete for resources with the manager of the research and development department (actor B). The latter also wants more resources in order to expand her department's activities. In this competitive game, both actors, in mobilizing their agentic powers, must first of all take into account the firm's role and *institutional* structure – the rights and duties of their own roles as well as those of their subordinates and their hierarchical superiors.

They will also have to take into account the actual power relations between departments. The R&D department, given that it employs many scientists, wields more informal power than the sales department, since its surveillance by hierarchically superior line-managers is difficult if not impossible. In other words, given that B's department occupies a social space not easily controllable, there is a marked discrepancy between formal and informal organizational structures, between *de jure* institutionally defined rights and obligations (paradigmatic level) and *de facto* power relations as these unfold in time and space (*figurational* structure on the syntagmatic level).

Our two competitors have further to take into account the current distribution of resources among the firm's numerous departments (*actual distributional* structure); as well as the distribution of organization members' attitudes to A's and B's demands (*virtual distributional* structure) – attitudes which are more favourable to A than to B.

Finally, as far as external environments of action are concerned, the two competitors must also consider the organization's cultural traditions, which stress the firm's responsibilities for the well-being of all employees, its civic role in the broader community, its preference for the long-term development rather than quick profits, etc. (*symbolic* structure on the paradigmatic level).

Moving now from the symbolic-paradigmatic to the *material-syntagmatic*, we note that A and B have at their disposal an array of material artefacts (communication equipment, computers, transport facilities, research laboratories, etc.), which also set limits as well as create opportunities in their struggle for the acquisition of more resources.

While all the above constitute A's and B's external environments of action, both will also have to take into account their *internal environments* of action: the *dispositions* which, when activated, again create enablements and constraints. Actor A, being socialized in a more traditional aristocratic milieu, has a self-image of the 'laid-back' gentleman-manager who rather looks down on formal qualifications and values ascription rather than actual achievements. This entails practical dispositions which comprise a capacity for friendly relationships, a relaxed ethical code, limited cognitive but developed aesthetic propensities, etc. Actor B, on the other hand, being of lower-middle-class background and upwardly mobile, has an ideal image of the self-made, highly qualified, hard-working person with practical dispositions, leading to instrumental rather than expressive, specific rather than diffuse, orientations to colleagues,[11] and cognitive rather than intuitive approaches to problem-solving, etc.

A and B, involved as they are in a zero-sum competitive game, have to mobilize their agentic powers of action. In Archer's terms, by using their varying capacities for discernment they will assess the limitations and affordances that their external and internal environments of action generate. Moreover, after an intra-active process of deliberation, they

[11] For the instrumental–expressive distinction, see Parsons, 1951: 81–3. For the specificity–diffuseness distinction, see Parsons, 1951: 65–6.

will weigh the pros and cons of various courses of action, and settle finally for a specific strategy (dedication). This strategy may, of course, change in the light of the other's counter-strategy. More specifically, A may opt for a strategy which aims at building an alliance with the manager of the production department. B, in reaction to A's move, may then try to obtain the support of the firm's board of directors. Subsequently A, in reply to B's reaction, mobilizes the rank and file to support his own cause, etc. It is by means of such intra- and interactive processes that the causal powers of actors (discernment, deliberation and dedication) are linked with the causal powers of structures (constraints and enablements).

15 | *The micro–macro dimension: anti-essentialist holism*

Introduction

An adequate holistic framework should provide conceptual tools for overcoming the compartmentalization that prevails today between micro- and macro-sociologies – the former rejecting all macro-theories as elaborate reifications, the latter dismissing micro approaches as myopic, reductive or empiricist. As already mentioned, a holistic framework should not aim at abolishing the division of labour within the social sciences between micro and macro empirical studies; it should rather transform the present 'walls' into 'bridges'. This means that macro-theoretical statements, for instance, should be constructed in such a way that it is possible to provide 'micro-foundations' – even if the theory itself does not do so. Therefore, when studying problems that become visible only when one focuses on such macro-entities as social classes or nation-states, it should be possible to move from macro- to meso- and micro-levels of analysis. For example, in the examination of the overall power structure of a multinational organization, a holistic framework should enable the researcher to establish bridges 'downwards', showing how social games taking place at the top of the organizational hierarchy link up with games taking place in the national, regional or local contexts. The focus of the research effort can, of course, be on a single level of analysis, but it must always allow another researcher to use the relevant research findings while moving 'upwards' or 'downwards' in a theoretically consistent manner.

A first step for establishing better communication between micro- and macro-levels of analysis is to distinguish between justified and unjustified critiques of each other's conceptualizations.

1 Strong and weak types of essentialism

Interpretative micro-sociologies as well as the social-constructionist turn in the social sciences have sensitized us to the methodological traps of essentialist theorizing. There has, however, been a great deal of over-reaction to the essentialist tendencies of conventional macro-sociology – in the sense that the distinction between writers who genuinely reify social phenomena (strong essentialism) and those who do so only apparently or superficially (weak essentialism) is often ignored. The latter, for purposes of expositional convenience, are simply using *metaphors* which, when challenged, can be translated into action/interaction or discursive terms, whereas the former are not.

a. System essentialism

Parsonian functionalism provides examples of both weak and strong versions of essentialist theorizing. As pointed out by numerous critics, Parsons' conceptual framework, despite claiming to provide founda-tions for a voluntaristic theory of action, loses the early voluntarism of, for instance, *The Structure of Social Action*, as he proceeds to his middle (*The Social System*) and late periods (*Societies: Evolutionary and Comparative Perspectives*). In the course of the latter two phases the social system is increasingly conceptualized in such a way that agency is downgraded, interaction ceases to be at the centre of analysis and the overall focus is on how systemic wholes shape actors' conduct, rather than on how actors construct, reproduce and transform social systems. This attempt to derive action from system is seen both in Parsons' AGIL scheme and in his conceptualization of the linkages between the cul-tural, social and personality systems (see chapter 1, section 1).

Weak system essentialism :   منزل حاج بر هني. جاح بر هنز

Starting with the latter, as already mentioned, Parsonian analysis typically begins at the cultural-system level which entails a set of core values conceptualized in highly abstract fashion. On the way from the cultural to the social system, values (via institutionalization) become less abstract and turn into the more specific normative requirements inherent in social roles. Finally, via internalization, norms and norma-tive requirements become part of the personality system's needs and dispositions. During this complex process the direction of influence is always from the cultural (core values) to the social (roles, norms), and from the social to the personality level (needs, dispositions) – never the other way round. We are not encouraged to ask actor-related questions such as who contributed most to the construction of the core values, or whose interests they primarily serve; how precisely actors handle their roles in actual contexts of social interaction; or in what ways actors mobilize their dispositions in the complex games in which they are involved. In the absence of such questions, <u>core values become essences floating in the air, so to speak</u>.

It may, however, be argued that in this case we have weak essentialism – in the sense that the approach leads to one-sided rather than erroneous conclusions. All we need to do to avoid viewing values as disembodied entities is to combine system with social integration: to show how incompatibilities/compatibilities between <u>institutional subsystems</u> (for instance) are linked to <u>co-operation/conflict</u> between actors.

Strong system essentialism (1): $AGIL$

If we move from the cultural-/social-/personality-system triad to Parsons' AGIL scheme, weak essentialism is replaced by strong essentialism. In this case the approach is not merely one-sided but also profoundly misleading. In the AGIL scheme the actors, especially collective actors, tend to disappear, while anthropomorphic, agentic characteristics are ascribed to structures.

More specifically, each of the four subsystems (adaptation (A), goal achievement (G), integration (I) and latency (L)) refers to all norms or normatively regulated processes that contribute to the solution of the social system's four functional problems or requirements. So, for instance, the adaptation, or economic, subsystem comprises all norms and normatively regulated processes that cope with the problem of acquiring the resources necessary for the system's functioning. The goal achievement, or political, subsystem, on the other hand, subsumes all norms and processes dealing with how resources should be combined for the social system's goals to be achieved. In both cases the grouping together of norms and processes follows a systemic-functional rather than an actor-related logic. Norms are placed in the analytical 'adaptation' category, not because they relate to specific economic actors, but because they contribute to the social system's resource-acquisition requirement.

We see the same systemic, functionalist logic in Parsons' further subdivision of each subsystem into four sub-subsystems (a, g, i, l) – this procedure leading to an overall picture of society as a kind of Russian doll, each of its systems containing subsystems that are further subdivided into increasingly less inclusive sub-subsystems. In this complex theoretical construction, actors – and particularly collective actors as the producers of social systems and subsystems – tend to disappear altogether, while at the same time anthropomorphic characteristics are ascribed to entities that do not have decision-making capacities or agentic powers. For instance, the subdivision of the adaptation subsystem into four sub-subsystems, one of which is labelled g (goal achievement), simply transforms the economic sub-subsystem into a collective entity with goals. Now social wholes (like groups, formal organizations or communities) can indeed have goals – but an analytical category (like the economic institutional subsystem) cannot.

Strong system essentialism (2): teleological functionalism

Another form taken by system essentialism occurs when a functionally oriented theorist, having banned actors from the analysis, resorts to teleological-functionalist explanations. In such a case, functional requirements or social needs are more or less automatically transformed into social causes. In terms of our previous distinction between actor causality (agentic powers) and structural causality (enablements/constraints), we have the methodologically erroneous transformation of the latter to the former causality.

A final remark on the teleological type of essentialism: teleological explanations are not to be found only in Parsonian functionalism; we see them as well in structuralist and post-structuralist approaches. Althusserian Marxism, for instance, often resorts to teleological explanations (see Mouzelis, 1978: 49–55), and so does Foucault in some of his analyses.[1] More generally, whenever actors are portrayed passively

---

[1] Consider for instance Foucault's reference to the 'disciplining' of the working classes in France:

> The moralisation of the working class wasn't imposed by Guizot, through his schools' legislation, nor by Dupin through his books. It wasn't imposed by the employers' union either. And yet it was accomplished because it met the urgent *need* to master a vagabond floating labor force. So the objective existed and the strategy was developed, with ever growing coherence, but without it being necessary to attribute to it a subject. (Gordon, 1980: 114, emphasis added)

> It seems to me that this teleologically oriented functionalist analysis is very similar to Parsons' way of dealing with social processes and their operation within specific subsystems. According to Parsons, for instance, the latency (L) subsystem entails the twin requirements of 'tension management' and 'pattern maintenance'. With society seen as a whole, these twin requirements refer to a societal system's

or disappear altogether there is a very strong temptation to resort to teleological explanations.

However, as Merton (1963: 19–85) pointed out long ago, functionalist analyses do not have to be teleological. For instance, raising questions about the necessary but not in themselves sufficient conditions of existence of a social whole (functional requirements), as well as about actual or counterfactual conditions that enhance or weaken its internal cohesion, constitute legitimate issues of social analysis. When putting forward such systemic, 'externalist' questions, the emphasis is on the social whole → participant relationship. This is a one-sided functionalist approach (weak essentialism), but it does not necessarily lead to teleological functionalism (strong essentialism).[2]

need for motivating its members in such a manner that they go on performing their roles in ways that ensure goal achievement and overall adaptation and survival. All social processes contributing to the requirements of tension management and pattern maintenance (e.g. processes referring to the socialization of children, religious practices, educational training, etc.), irrespective of the groups in which they are located, are brought under the latency label, since they all contribute to the same social need.

If instead of 'subjectless practices' one posits subjectless social processes, instead of 'objectives', system requirements, and instead of the 'construction of subjectivities', socialization, the methodological similarities between Foucault and Parsons become quite striking. Both underemphasize agency, and as a result both have to resort to teleologically oriented functionalist explanations.

Of course, there are also major differences between the two approaches. Parsons' analysis is more 'neutral', in the sense that it assumes a benign modern societal system that motivates human beings to follow the normative expectations entailed in their roles. Foucault, on the other hand, views modern society more critically and negatively, stressing subjugation rather than socialization, resistance rather than deviance, etc. Such substantive differences notwithstanding, there is remarkable similarity in the basic mode of explanation. For despite Foucault's avowed hostility to functionalism, his key notion of subjectless practices fulfilling domination/subjugation 'objectives' unavoidably leads to teleological forms of functionalist explanation.

[2] Functionalist explanations become illegitimate when *necessary* conditions of existence become automatically *sufficient* conditions (teleology); or when the social whole → participant relationship is conceptualized in such a way that one cannot move in a theoretically consistent manner from a system- to a social-integration approach – i.e. when it is not possible to ask questions about how participants are both influenced by and influence social wholes themselves. In the latter case, social wholes become essences (see Mouzelis, 1995b: 127–31). For an extreme form of this type of system essentialism, see Luhmann, 1982. For a critique of Luhmann along similar lines, see Mingers, 2002.

b. Actor essentialism

In system essentialism, actors either disappear or, in an attempt to derive action from system, they are portrayed as passive products of structural determinants. This leads to reification (turning institutional structures into things or essences), to anthropomorphism (turning institutional structures into decision-making actors) and/or to teleologically oriented functionalist explanations (turning functional requirements into causes).

In actor essentialism the above underemphasis of actors is replaced by their portrayal as *pre-constituted* decision-making entities, whose identities and interests are not socially constructed in the process of social development but given in advance via logico-deductive reasoning. This type of armchair rationalism can take different forms.

From statistical categories or quasi-groups to groups

A frequent form taken by actor essentialism is turning statistical categories into decision-making entities. What this amounts to is the transformation of a quasi-group[3] (i.e. a number of individuals who, because they share certain common characteristics, have the *potential* of organizing themselves) into an already formed group capable of setting goals and pursuing strategies.

This jump from potentiality to actuality, from quasi-group to group status, cannot but lead to strong essentialism. It is conducive to a situation where an imaginary decision-making collective actor is constructed by social scientists who pay less attention to the institutional realities of the case (realities often thwarting the potential from becoming actual) and more to logico-deductively derived conceptions of society as consisting of well-organized collective actors (classes, social movements, interest groups) whose agentic powers are given in advance. In this profoundly essentialist view of collective action, once it is known what social traits people have in common, and once 'obvious' assumptions are made about the 'rational', utility-maximizing tendencies of human beings, the degree of self-organization of this set of

---

[3] For the concept of quasi-groups, see Ginsberg 1956: 12–15. It should be noted here that not all statistical categories constitute quasi-groups. A statistical category which comprises all people with red hair, for instance, is not a quasi-group, because it has very low chances of becoming a group.

individuals sharing common traits follows more or less automatically, as well as the collective goals they are (or should be) pursuing.

An obvious illustration of the above is the way in which Marxists or Marxisand social historians use the concept of the bourgeoisie. In analyses of the so-called 'bourgeois' revolutions, the bourgeoisie is often portrayed[4] as a well-organized, self-aware collective actor with clear goals and specific strategies for their implementation. To take the French Revolution as an example, a major tendency in classical Marxist accounts is to interpret it as a struggle between a declining feudal class and a rising bourgeoisie which was eventually to overthrow France's *ancien régime*. As pointed out by many critics (from Cobban, 1967 to Furet, 1978), in the period preceding the events of 1789 there was no such thing as a self-aware bourgeoisie struggling to overthrow France's *ancien régime*. This makes perfect sense when it is remembered that (as pointed out by both Marxist and non-Marxist social scientists) the institutional structures of merchant capitalism were highly compatible with feudal forms of social organization; and that industrial capitalism, which does indeed undermine feudal relations of production, was rudimentary or non-existent in pre-revolutionary France.[5]

In the light of the above it becomes clear why a theory that assigns the key role in the French Revolution to the bourgeoisie is wrong. It cannot be otherwise, based as it is on a conceptual framework that ignores the institutional realities of the late eighteenth-century French social formation. It is important, however, to make some qualifications to the above critique. Contra the position of interpretative micro-sociologists, to speak of the bourgeois class as a collective actor with a key role in social transformation does not automatically lead to strong essentialism. The transformation of a 'bourgeois' quasi-group into an organized, decision-making collectivity is indeed a historical possibility, but its actual existence cannot be established by purely logico-deductive analysis.

---

[4] By using the term 'often' rather than 'always' I want to indicate that when historians and social scientists (whether Marxist or not) speak of 'bourgeois revolutions' they do not necessarily imply a bourgeois collective actor playing a central role in the revolutionary process. 'Bourgeois revolutions' for them may stand for a social upheaval that can create favourable conditions for the development of industrial capitalism and a bourgeoisie as a collective actor in a post-revolutionary situation.

[5] On the development of the capitalist mode of production (which entails a massive entrance of capital into the sphere of both agricultural and industrial production), see Dobb, 1968: 1–32; Hilton, 1976.

It can only be established by an analysis combining theoretical sophistication with empirical research on the level of both social and system integration. This presupposes asking and empirically investigating complex questions about the historical institutional contexts within which quasi-groups are transformed into groups,[6] as well as questions about the latter's internal cleavages, their relations with other groups, the interactive social games in which they are involved, and so on. It presupposes, in other words, moving from a rationalist analysis that views actors' identities and interests as given to one that attempts to show empirically how actors' characteristics are ongoing symbolic constructions.

To return to our previous example, if institutional realities precluded the existence of a self-aware, well-organized bourgeoisie in eighteenth-century France, post-revolutionary developments presented more favourable structural conditions for the emergence of such a collectivity. Even Sarah Maza, who in a recent publication writes about the 'myth' of the French bourgeoisie during the 1750–1850 period, admits that there is one major exception to her thesis: during the Bourbon Restoration (1815–1830) there was a group of prominent liberal politicians who tried 'to make a bourgeois class central to the history and politics of France' (Maza, 2003: 5). Although these first attempts at the development of class organization and consciousness were very limited, once industrial capitalism became dominant in the late nineteenth century, the existence of a well-organized industrial bourgeoisie ceased to be a mere myth, an essentialist construction of Marxist historians. Of course, such a collectivity was not then, and neither is it now, a monolithic entity. Classes as organized collectivities attempting to promote the interests of their members are extremely complex social constructions with a variety of features that do not fit the ideal-typical metaphor of a rational actor single-mindedly and unitarily pursuing clearly defined interests. Instead they exhibit internal cleavages among the elites, weak linkages between the represented and representing, oligarchic tendencies within bureaucratized organizations, goal displacement mechanisms, and so on.

It is true that frequently, depending on the specific problematic, the macro-historian or sociologist is obliged to use 'shortcuts', in the form

---

[6] Groups portray institutional and figurational structures, whereas quasi-groups do not. On the concept of institutional and figurational structures, see chapter 7, sections 1a and 1b.

of (for instance) metaphors[7] describing a collective subject in unitary fashion. Such simplification may be quite unavoidable if the given problematic entails a high level of abstraction. But if the macro-analyst were to be challenged by demands for micro-foundations, the only effective answer would be a *translation* of the metaphor into concrete action or interaction terms. So, for instance, a statement about the bourgeoisie 'sabotaging the government's welfare policies' should be translated into a statement citing concrete mechanisms, concrete inter-active practices between (let us say) representatives of employers' associations, government officials, trade unionists, etc.

To conclude: strong actor essentialism is avoided to the extent that reference to the metaphor of the unitary actor is simply a convenient expository device (necessary in order to deal lucidly with a highly complex situation); and to the extent that, if challenged, micro-foundations can indeed be provided.

The pre-constituted character of actors' identities and interests

What was methodologically illegitimate in the previous type of actor essentialism was the a priori transformation of statistical categories or quasi-groups into decision-making collectivities. A second type of actor essentialism ascribes characteristics to actual groups or collective actors which they do not have, characteristics that are derived purely from aprioristic theorizing.

A classical example of this type of essentialism is the Marxist theory about the proletariat's 'historic mission': the revolutionary overthrow of capitalism and the eventual creation of a non-alienated socialist/communist social order.

As in the previous case, this type of essentialism turns its back on the macro-historical development of institutional realities, and ascribes to the proletariat, as a collective actor, a revolutionary goal that is entirely the result of logico-deductive reasoning that takes the following form: rapid technological developments generate growing contradictions between the forces and relations of production; on the level of actors this systemic incompatibility is supposed to create a growing polarization as the means of production are concentrated in fewer and fewer hands and wages tend to fall to the minimum compatible with the

---

[7] For the use of metaphors in the social sciences, see Rigney, 2001; Lopez, 2003.

continued reproduction of commodified labour. Such conditions are seen to result in not only the development of class organization, but also that of a revolutionary class consciousness.

Of course, Marx and certain of his disciples have clearly pointed out that the above schematic analysis operates on the *mode-of-production*, ideal-typical level. Examination and explanation of specific historical developments requires looking at the more concrete *social-formation level*, which entails combining the logico-deductive with a more 'historico-genetic' approach.[8] When this is done it will be seen that a concrete social formation entails several modes of production, articulated in such a way that one is dominant; it will also be seen that 'tendential laws' may be neutralized or even reversed by counter-tendencies brought to light by empirical research.

Qualifications of this kind are often ignored by Marxist historians or social scientists, with the result that the essentialist ascription of revolutionary, anti-capitalist goals to the proletariat prevails.[9] Meanwhile, obvious institutional developments pointing to the actual reformist orientations of working-class movements and organizations, such as the formation of a welfare state or the passage from Fordist to post-Fordist forms of organization resulting in the numerical preponderance of white-collar workers, are ignored. Finally, concerning the present, the marked imbalance between the extraordinary mobility of capital and the relative immobility of labour in the globalized economy is not taken into account by those who still insist on the essentialist notion of the proletariat's revolutionary mission. From their point of view, developments such as the decline of working-class organizations, the growing political apathy of voters and the development of catch-all political parties are simply transitory phenomena which cannot possibly alter the emancipatory 'march of history' towards an anti-capitalist revolution led by a *deus ex machina* proletariat.

---

[8] For the distinction between a mode of production and a social-formation analysis, see Labica 1971; Hindess and Hirst, 1975; Mouzelis, 1978: 41–6.

[9] For a critique of Marxism along such lines, see Laclau and Mouffe, 1985. The two authors, in their attempt to transcend Marxist essentialism, reject the distinction between agency and institutional structure. However, this rejection (which one also finds in structuralist and post-structuralist writings; see chapter 1, section 4) creates more problems than it solves. For a critique of Laclau and Mouffe's position along such lines, see Mouzelis, 1988a.

It is worth mentioning here that researchers focusing on 'discourse analysis'[10] are in extreme reaction to system essentialism. Laclau and Mouffe (1985), the two main theorists of this approach, reject both the actor/institutional-structure distinction and most conventional sociological categories, replacing them with a vocabulary drawn from semiotics, Lacanian psychoanalysis and post-structuralist theory. I have critically examined their approach elsewhere (Mouzelis, 1988a). Here I would like to focus on their anti-essentialist inspired rejection of the actor/structure dichotomy.

For the two authors any reference to institutional structures leads to essentialism. Institutions are the result of discursive practices taking place in a plurality of political and social spaces that are characterized by openness, fragility and precariousness. This being so, the notion of the constant articulation and disarticulation of practices renders any reference to institutional structure redundant.

To start with, contrary to Laclau and Mouffe's position, institutions are not always fragile and precarious. While they are always symbolically constructed, and reproduced and transformed by discursive and non-discursive practices, they can be extremely durable and in this way set strict limits to actors, as well as offering definite enablements. It is easy to show that, from the point of view of situated subjects operating in a specific hierarchized social space and historical time, there are always institutional arrangements that are more easily and directly affected by their practices than others. With respect to the latter, these often evince such resilience and continuity that their extremely slow overall transformation can be seen only in the very *longue durée*.

Consider, for instance, the separation of the ruler's and of a civil servant's public position from his/her private fortune.[11] This institutional separation of the 'private' from the 'public' within the Western European state took centuries to be firmly consolidated and today seems pretty well irreversible. To all intents and purposes, therefore, this institutional/structural feature, together with other structural features of equal durability and resilience (for example, the institutions of

---

[10] For an introduction to discourse analysis, see Howarth, 2000. For the application of its conceptual tools to the empirical analysis of concrete cases, see Howarth *et al.*, 2000.

[11] On the differentiation between state and royal household in England, see Barker, 1944; Elton, 1953.

private property, markets and money, the institutional separation between management and ownership in modern corporations, and so on) constitute a core which enters the subjects' social milieu not as something to be negotiated or radically transformed, but as an incontrovertible given, as a relatively unshakeable, durable institutional terrain[12] which both limits and makes possible specific articulatory practices – the intended or unintended consequences of which may seriously affect more malleable and fragile institutional arrangements. The fact that laypersons and even social scientists tend sometimes to reify a social formation's durable institutional orders (i.e. in Lockwood's terminology, that they tend to overemphasize system integration and to underemphasize or ignore social integration) does not render them less durable; on the contrary, the 'natural attitude' towards them enhances their durability.

Given the above, the neglect of the actor/institutional-structure distinction leads *either* to a superficial analysis that views articulatory practices and their underlying logic in an institutional vacuum *or* to an analysis that reintroduces institutional analysis by the back door. It is not, therefore, surprising that when Laclau and Mouffe try to deal with such complex phenomena as the long-term development of capitalism they resort to such 'conventional' social categories as commodification, division of labour, civil society, etc.[13] This of course produces a conceptual dualism: the more conventional vocabulary employed does not fit their more theoretically worked out concepts of articulating practices, of the underlying logics of equivalence and difference, of empty or floating signifiers, etc.[14] In brief: Laclau and Mouffe either will have to exclusively use the new conceptual categories in analysing concrete situations, or, if they want to combine the old with the new conceptual

---

[12] Needless to say, the use of a topographical metaphor does not entail strong essentialism.

[13] For a critique along these lines, see Geras, 1987.

[14] Concerning the discrepancy between conventional and post-conventional concepts, Laclau argues for

the displacement of the research emphasis from mainly sociological categories, which address the group, its constitutive roles and its functional determinations, to the *underlying logics* that make these categories possible. It is in this sense that we have spoken of the underlying logics of equivalence and difference, of empty and floating signifiers and of myths and imaginaries. (Howarth *et al.*, 2000:x1) tools, they will have to spell out the linkages between the two. They have done neither the one nor the other.[15]

2 Interpretative sociologies: obstacles to micro–macro bridges

Interpretative micro-sociologies, by stressing the relative autonomy of actors and the centrality of interaction, have overcome some of the difficulties presented by Parsons' paradigm. However, the way they have conceptualized actor autonomy and interaction centrality creates new obstacles for the construction of a holistic theory aimed at establishing action–system balance and/or micro–macro linkages.

a. Action–system imbalance

As far as action–system linkages are concerned, interpretatively oriented micro-sociologists consider that since the social world is created by actors, its exploration should be exclusively by means of an 'internalist', action perspective. They reject a systemic-externalist orientation on the grounds of essentialism. They contend that to speak about social systems (micro or macro) and their 'needs' or reproductive requirements is to turn the actors' ongoing symbolic constructions into things or into mysterious entities operating over and above concrete, interacting agents; it is to invent substances that exist only in the fertile imagination of social scientists. The fact that social needs or functional requirements can be translated as conditions of existence is, of course, left out of the account.

As well as the interpretative sociologists' excessive fear of reification, which ignores any 'horizontal' linkage between actor and system, this same extreme anti-essentialism also creates obstacles 'vertically' along the micro–macro dimension. Concepts referring to collective actors such as classes, social movements or even large-scale organizations[16]

---

[15] Another type of over-reaction to essentialism in which discourse analysis theorists indulge is to replace the supposedly essentialist notion of 'objective' economic interests with the notion of identity. More generally, there is a tendency among postmodern theorists (particularly post-Marxist ones) to replace the economic with the political and the cultural.

[16] David Silverman, for instance, has argued that it is essentialist to talk about formal organizations having goals. Only individual actors can have goals. For a critique which holds that organizational goals can be translated into action/interaction terms, and that therefore one can avoid strong essentialism, see Mouzelis, 1969.

are viewed with great suspicion: their projects, strategies or overall goals are seen to be as fictitious as systemic needs and functional requirements. It is argued that since only individuals can have goals and adopt strategies for their realization, to ascribe such characteristics to macro-collectivities is at best a vague metaphor and at worst another form of essentialism. The only reality worth exploring is the reality of interacting individuals on the micro-level of analysis. To move on from micro to macro would mean moving to a much more complex situation made up of a myriad of micro-situations.[17] Following an empiricist logic, it is often argued that it is safer to first explore the 'ground floor', so to speak (i.e. the micro-world of laypersons in such contexts as a church, a hospital or a business organization), before proceeding to the 'upper' floors. First 'micro-foundations' and then, if at all, a broader focus on such macro-phenomena as large-scale societal transformations.

b. Face-to-face interaction as micro

A different but related obstacle to establishing micro–macro linkages is the widespread idea among micro-sociologists that face-to-face interaction corresponds to the micro-level, whereas institutional structures entail a macro-level type of analysis. Goffman, for instance, tried to establish the specificity of the 'interaction order' by stressing that such an order can be derived neither from macro-structures (the 'macro-institutional order') nor from individual agency. This leads him to link the *sui generis* 'interaction order' with the type of micro-situations he has so successfully explored. In these situations one finds 'ground rules' which emanate from the interactive situation itself – particularly from the 'presentational needs' of the social self (Goffman, 1983). It follows that such rules are absent when one leaves the micro- for the more macro-level of analysis. Various commentators have entered the debate about how one might distinguish the 'interaction order' from the 'institutional order'. While some of them disagree with Goffman on a variety of issues, they all seem to accept linking the 'interaction order' with micro and the 'institutional order' with macro.[18]

---

[17] For the view that macro-phenomena consist of a myriad of micro-encounters or micro-situations, see Collins, 1981a, 1981b.

[18] Concerning this debate, see Rawls, 1987, 1988; Fuchs, 1988, 1989.

The assumption 'interaction = micro' is not limited to Goffman's work. From Cicourel and Garfinkel to theoretical writings on the nature of intersubjectivity and empirically oriented studies, the misconception that face-to-face interaction entails micro-analysis is well entrenched. Peter Blau, for instance, in an attempt to differentiate between micro- and macro-sociology, argues that the former 'dissects the internal dynamic processes underlying social relations, whereas macro-sociology analyses influences on social relations exerted by external structural constraints and opportunities ... Durkheim's social facts' (Blau, 1987: 84). Later, in the same work, the author makes his position clearer by arguing that the macro-structural approach is not interested in 'social interaction between individuals' (1987: 97). But if this is so, where does one fit the interaction between very powerful individuals who can literally shape or transform social institutions? For instance, face-to-face interactions between heads of state (interactions which, among other things, may also entail 'ground rules' like those mentioned by Goffman) may lead to outcomes that affect millions of people – or which, to use Giddens' terminology, may 'stretch widely in time and space'. This type of macro-interaction is never taken into account by interpretatively oriented sociologists. The latter focus exclusively on *laypersons*, on *everyday* activities, *routine* encounters, and suchlike. The perfectly commonsensical idea that encounters may be non-routine, that activities that are not humdrum may also be worth studying, that face-to-face interaction among powerful individuals could entail deci-sions which may literally transform the globe – such considerations tend not to be found in any of the interpretative sociologies. It is as if micro-sociologists, in reaction to the conventional 'great men' accounts of history, have so much veered to the other extreme that, when consider-ing the micro–macro issue, they have become blind to the *hierarchical dimension of social life*, to the fact that *actors contribute very unequally to the construction of social orders*.

Finally, it must be stressed that if interaction can be both micro and macro, the same is true of institutional structures. To take another example from the educational sphere, the micro-interaction between lecturer and students in a seminar takes place in a micro-context entail-ing micro-institutional structures. The seminar's institutional structure would refer not only to the relevant set of interrelated roles (lecturer, students, paper-giver, commentator, etc.), but also to the type of 'ground rules' and informal 'local' understandings that emanate as the

seminar game is in progress. In other words, the seminar's social structure comprises institutionalized rules, some of which are general (and
found in other seminars of the same type), and some of which are
specific to a particular seminar. What it is important to stress here is
that the distinction between emergent rules or roles and those that are
'constituted from above' can also be applied when the focus is on micro,
meso or macro social wholes. This being so, let me emphasize again that
a fundamental rule for avoiding micro–macro blockages is always to
keep in mind that the interaction–institution distinction can only be
useful if seen to operate on both micro- and macro-levels. Micro and
macro social systems must be studied from both interaction-agency *and*
institutional-systemic perspectives.

To conclude this section, interpretatively oriented micro-sociologies,
by over-reacting to Parsons' systemic emphasis and trying to avoid the
type of essentialism (weak or strong) to which his conceptual framework is prone to lead, have created three types of roadblock to an
overall, multilevel exploration of social wholes.

First, their rejection of all systemic concepts (micro and macro), their
exclusive concern with an actor-internalist perspective, often results in
their neglecting those aspects of social reality of which actors (or at least
some actors) are not aware, aspects which a systemic-externalist inquiry
can more easily bring to the fore. This being so, it is not surprising that
their research in specific interactive contexts has been criticized for only
yielding results that are 'obvious', or obvious at least to those directly
involved in such micro-situations.

Second, the tendency of interpretatively oriented micro-sociologists
to reject as mere reifications all macro-concepts (whether systemic or
collective-action ones) creates obstacles to the establishment of open-
ended, two-way linkages between their own concerns and those of
macro-sociologists – the latter focusing on the constitution, reproduction and transformation of whole social orders or formations. In other
words, the type of vertical blockages created by the interpretative
micro-sociologists' excessive fear of reification/essentialism often
results in 'navel-gazing' or social myopia. At the same time it undermines any systematic attempt to link micro to macro, to provide, for
instance, micro-foundations for developments on the macro-historical
and macro-comparative levels of analysis.

Third, the erroneous linkage of micro with face-to-face interaction
and macro with institutional structures disregards the obvious

methodological guideline that <u>on all levels</u> of analysis (micro, meso and macro), social phenomena should be regarded in terms of both <u>action/interaction</u> and in terms of <u>institutional</u> structures. The linkage of the micro with interaction and the macro with institutional structures creates confusion and leads away from a multidimensional exploration of the social world.

3 Three guidelines for bridging micro and macro approaches

In the light of the above and with the aid of the social-/system-integration distinction, we can formulate three rules for helping to avoid essentialism while establishing linkages between micro- and macro-levels of analysis.

a. Avoiding essentialism: a balance between social- and system-integration perspectives

It is important to look at all social wholes (micro, meso and macro) from both social-integration/disintegration and system-integration/disintegration perspectives – both as figurations of actors establishing co-operative or conflictual relationships with each other, and as sets of interrelated institutions portraying varying degrees of compatibility or incompatibility.

Underemphasis or elimination of the actor/social-integration perspective results in system essentialism. When action is derived from systemic considerations (as in Parsons or Luhmann), this typically leads to the <u>reification</u> or hypostasization of institutional structures and/or to <u>teleological</u>-functionalist explanations. When, on the other hand, the actor/social-integration perspective is overemphasized, either institutional/systemic contradictions are ignored, thereby producing (as in interpretatively oriented micro-sociologies) trivial, 'obvious' findings, or, as in <u>utilitarian theories</u>, the identities and <u>interests of actors</u> are taken as <u>given</u>. This means that there is no examination of how actors operating in concrete and evolving institutional contexts construct their identities and interests. Instead, the actors' attributes are derived in advance logico-deductively. This leads to actor essentialism, to the fabrication of fictitious actors or to fictitious characteristics of real actors.

A balanced approach stressing the importance of both social- and system-integration analysis is also necessary because these two dimensions of all social wholes do not always vary in the same direction. For instance, high levels of social integration (entailing the absence of intense social conflict between actors) can co-exist with low levels of system integration entailing serious incompatibilities or contradictions between institutional subsystems.[19]

[19] I have already dealt with the possible discrepancies between institutional structures (relations between roles/institutions) and figurational structures (relations between actors) (see chapter 14, section 1b). Here I shall illustrate a similar discrepancy by referring to a historically oriented example, i.e. to the types of social organization that prevailed in Western European societies before and after the 1974 world economic crisis.

The early postwar period has been seen (correctly, I think) as the golden age of social democracy. During that period it became possible to a great extent to combine the major social-democratic goals of capitalist growth, relative social justice and political democracy. In Parsonian systemic terms, during this period the logic and values of wealth generation in the adaptation subsystem combined in balanced fashion with the logic of democratic-power creation in the goal achievement subsystem, the logic of solidarity in the integration subsystem and the logic of value maintenance/commitment in the latency subsystem.

Leaving Parsons for Lockwood, this equilibrium on the system-integration level corresponded, in terms of social integration, to a balance of power between capital and labour – mediated by state corporatism. This relatively balanced situation was shattered by the 1974 economic crisis and was succeeded by an era during which the market logic of productivity and competitiveness subordinated the rationalities of the other three subsystems. This led to greater authoritarianism in the political sphere, increasing inequalities and marginalization in the social sphere and growing anomie and disorganization in the cultural sphere.

With respect to social integration now, this systemic disequilibrium or contradiction was handled in such a way that the balance of power between labour and capital gave way to a marked imbalance in favour of capital. Mainly on account of an economic globalization that took a neoliberal form, capital, having much greater mobility than labour, became the dominant player and pushed the latter into a highly vulnerable and defensive position. This, in turn, resulted in such well-known phenomena as downsizing, massive marginalization, large-scale unemployment and/or job insecurity.

In terms of Lockwood's social-/system-integration distinction, the pre-1974 period was marked by a high degree of system integration (i.e. by a strong compatibility between the rationalities of the four institutional subsystems) and a medium degree of social integration (i.e. by state-mediated class conflict). In the post-1974 period, system integration has been low, given the marked disequilibrium between the economic/market logic, on the one hand, and the political, social and cultural rationalities, on the other. As to social integration, at any rate at the macro-level, this is medium to high, because industrial conflict has been significantly reduced. But the social integration achieved in this way is not the negotiated, consensual kind; it is a social integration imposed from above, by the dominant players dictating a 'social peace' on their own terms. This peace is

b. Social and system integration: from juxtaposition to articulation

The second guideline concerns the methodological requirement for moving from the *ad hoc juxtaposition* of the social- and system-integration approaches to their *articulation* in such a way that the move from one to the other is accomplished logically and in a theoretically coherent manner.

To this end it is necessary to stress not only the impossibility of conflating or reducing the one to the other, but also the necessity of being constantly aware of the complex linkages between systemic contradictions, social conflicts and social change. Systemic contradictions between institutional subsystems do not, contra Parsons, automatically lead to social change; neither, contra Althusser, are they bound to lead to class struggle. Incompatibilities and contradictions do increase the chances for the emergence of both social conflict and social transformation, but such developments can be weakened or aborted by ideological manipulation or brute repression. Whatever the outcome, whenever systemic contradictions/incompatibilities are identified in a social formation one should always ask actor-related *who*-questions on the level of social integration. For instance: what specific form do systemic contradictions take in terms of the actors' everyday existence? Who perceives them, who fails to do so, and why? How are the actors' relatively correct or false perceptions linked to attempts at the transformation or defence of the institutional status quo? Under what conditions do system incompatibilities enter the lifeworld of laypersons in such a way that they activate organized forms of reaction to them, and under what conditions are contradictions and incompatibilities ignored or experienced in passive isolation?

This type of questioning is useful in two ways. It avoids hypostasizing systemic contradictions, and at the same time it discourages the logico-deductive fabrication of fictitious actors who are supposed to be rationally oriented with pre-given fixed interests and reactions to institutional incompatibilities.

> achieved at the price of marginalizing a large section of the population that can neither organize easily nor obtain the active support of the declining trade union movement. It is therefore justified to characterize the post-1974 social peace arrangements as a coerced type of social integration, where the marginalized suffer in 'isolation and silence', unable to translate their suffering into collective organization and action (Mouzelis, 1999c).

While *who*-questions ensure that there is a passage from system- to social-integration analysis, the move is more successful (i.e. more theoretically congruent) if the institutional subsystems are mapped in such a way that there is not mere *juxtaposition* but effective *articulation* between the systemic and the actors' perspectives. Let me illustrate this crucial point with an example.

In chapter 4 it was argued that neo-functionalists have tried to cope with Parsons' underemphasis of the conflictual and voluntaristic dimensions of social life by injecting into the Parsonian theory such social-integration/disintegration notions as conflict, class struggle and elite strategies. However, these notions were introduced in *ad hoc* fashion and do not fit well with such core building-blocks of the Parsonian *oeuvre* as the AGIL scheme. Since that onion-like, system-within-system construction subdivides each of its institutional subsystems – the economic (A), the political (G), the social (I) and the cultural (L) – into sub-subsystems (a, g, i, l) along the same systemic, institutional logic, no theoretical space is left for collective actors and their conflictual or co-operative relations. Whenever relatively autonomous collective actors appear in Parsons' work, it is *despite*, not because of, his conceptual framework. This means that to introduce successfully the notion of class conflict into Parsons' theory requires a restructuring of the AGIL scheme. More specifically, each of the four major institutional subsystems should be subdivided differently. Unless this is done we simply have juxtaposition rather than articulation of the social- and system-integration approaches.

While the oversystemic Parsonian theory does not offer conceptual tools for effectively articulating the social- and system-integration approaches, Marx's work, when taken in its entirety, offers better conceptual bridges between an actor-centred, internalist and a system-centred, externalist perspective. As Lockwood has already pointed out (see chapter 6), despite its economic reductionism, Marx's work exhibits a remarkable balance between social- and system-integration concepts. Systemic concepts such as the contradiction between the forces of production (consisting of not only material objects such as machines, but also the applied knowledge leading to their construction, as well as forms of work organization) and relations of production (property institutions, the way technologies are appropriated) lead quite smoothly to social-integration concepts. Such concepts refer to those who do and those who do not own or control technologies or the means of economic production. In their turn, structural cleavages of this kind may, in specific conditions, result in class conflict and/or social transformation. In Marx's case therefore, unlike Parsons', the transition from system to actor, from system to social integration/disintegration, is made via articulation rather than via juxtaposition.

To put this differently: whereas the Parsonian incompatibilities between the four institutional subsystems are conducive to 'role strains' and avoid *who*-questions on the collective-actor level, Marx's concept of contradictions between institutional complexes leads, on the social-integration level, to interesting questions about the varied ways in which macro-actors react or fail to react to systemic contradictions.

This fundamental difference between the two theorists is due to the fact that, being interested in different questions, they subdivide institutional subsystems differently. As far as economic institutions are concerned, Parsons further subdivides, according to the same systemic logic, the economic/adaptation subsystem (A) into four sub-subsystems (a, g, i, l) – this creating obstacles to an effective articulation between system integration and social integration. Marx, on the other hand, achieves effective articulation by mapping the economic subspaces in a way which leads to a focus on the *technological, appropriative* and *ideological* dimensions of economic production (t, a, i). As I will argue in the next chapter, it is possible to avoid Marx's economic reductionism while retaining his successful system–actor articulation, by applying the tripartite subdivision not only to the economy but to all institutional spheres. In other words, *the technological, the appropriative and the ideological should be considered as constitutive elements of all major institutional spheres.*

c. Avoiding reductionism: social hierarchies

Durkheim, in his attempt to avoid reductionism and to establish the specificity and relative autonomy of sociology as a distinct discipline, stressed that social facts must be explained primarily by other social facts rather than psychological or biological ones. This may be extended or slightly amended by saying that macro-facts must, in the first instance, be explained by other macro-facts. If for instance we examine the constitution, reproduction or transformation of such macro-institutional structures as state bureaucracies or national educational systems, the first focus should be on macro-actors (i.e. collective actors or very powerful individuals whose contribution to social construction is considerable), before moving on to meso- or micro-actors (i.e. actors who, in their individual capacity, contribute but slightly to the construction of the phenomena under investigation).

To explain, for example, the reproduction or transformation of the national university system, one should start by exploring the strategies and games of such macro-actors as representatives of the University, of the National Union of Students, of ministers and influential individuals disposing of considerable amounts of social or symbolic capital, etc.

In micro-sociology, the already discussed tendency to view actors and interactions as micro- and institutions as macro-phenomena often means the reduction of the latter to an aggregation of micro-acts or micro-situations. For instance, Collins (1981a, 1981b) has tried to replace methodological individualism by what he calls methodological situationalism. Macro-phenomena, in his view, consist of an aggregation of micro-situations or micro-encounters. The latter are considered to be discrete and commensurable units, and this makes it easy to pass from the micro- to the macro-level by simply aggregating a large number of them. In the same way that extreme methodological individualism reduces macro-phenomena to a 'heap' of isolated individuals, methodological situationalism reduces them to a heap of micro-encounters.

The above approach may have some validity when one considers 'aggregate wholes' such as a market where a great number of buyers and sellers interact under conditions of perfect competition. Even in such cases, however, the institutional framework within which micro-exchanges take place is not exclusively constituted or reproduced by micro-actors. Neither market constitution nor even its reproduction can be entirely explained by the fact that a great number of people, in a taken-for-granted manner, follow rules in their attempt to buy or sell goods or services. Market institutions are also being reproduced by the activities of such macro-actors as central bankers, government officials, agencies monitoring monopolistic/oligopolistic tendencies, NGOs whose goal is the protection of consumers, etc. In other words, the constitution, reproduction and transformation of institutional structures entails micro-, meso- and macro-situations/encounters. The non-hierarchization of interactions/encounters or even interactive networks[20] is as reductive as the non-hierarchization of actors.

Needless to say, methodological situationalism is even less helpful when we consider not aggregate wholes, but what Piaget (1950) has called 'configurational wholes'. Here, even if we examine non-hierarchical configurations such as social networks, we see the emergence, via different types of interaction, of macro-phenomena that cannot be reduced to their constituent units. According to Piaget (1950: 210), if aggregate wholes are formed by discrete interactions, configurational wholes 'do not represent the algebraic sum of these interactions but a whole structure analogous to the psychological or physical Gestalt' (my translation).[21]

The point becomes even more glaringly obvious when we look at hierarchical configurations like, for instance, a multinational corporation. Here it is quite clear that games played by powerful actors (i.e. macro-actors) at the top do not consist of an aggregate of games played by less powerful actors lower down the organizational hierarchy. To link macro-games (global level) with meso-games (national level) and micro-games (regional/local level) requires taking into account the formal, bureaucratic structure of the corporation, as well as the informal power relations between actors at each level as well as between those at different levels.

One way of conceptualizing micro–macro linkages in hierarchical configurations is to view the game outcomes or decisions taken at the top as factual or value premises in the decisional environment of those occupying subaltern bureaucratic positions.[22] Therefore, if in the case of non-hierarchical configurations emergence is the key concept which links micro- to macro-levels of analysis, in hierarchical configurational wholes we have both emergence from below and constitution/imposition

---

[20] Collins also talks about interactive chains and networks (2003), but does not distinguish between interactive chains/networks that are macro (i.e. whose functioning has a great impact on the constitution, reproduction and transformation of macro social wholes) and those that are micro (i.e. whose impact on such wholes is minimal). In other words, if macro-phenomena are not an aggregation of interactions, neither are they an aggregation of commensurable interactive chains or networks.

[21] For a discussion of Piaget's relational sociology, see Kitchener, 1985.

[22] For the concept of factual and value premises of an actor's decision-making environment in the context of hierarchical organizations, see the classic work of Simon, 1961. See also Mouzelis, 1975: 123–44.

from above. Micro-games at the bottom of the corporate hierarchy may lead to emergent phenomena that have to be taken into account by hierarchical superiors. At the same time, macro-decisions at the top set limits and create opportunities for those involved in games played lower down the organizational hierarchy (see Mouzelis, 1991a: 67–117).

Finally, it is worth mentioning that it is possible to link the macro- and micro-organizational levels with Giddens' distinction between dualism and duality of structure (see chapter 7, section 2a). Macro-actors at the top of the organizational hierarchy are usually supposed to distance themselves from existing rules and resources in order to assess an organization's overall performance and to plan its long-term strategy (dualism of structure). Those lower down the organizational hierarchy are supposed to follow the same rules in a taken-for-granted, quasi-automatic manner (duality of structure).[23] The clear-cut separation between planning and creating operating rules on the one hand, and strictly following or implementing them on the other can be seen in Taylor's scientific-management theory (Taylor, 1945).

In actual concrete situations, of course, all actors orient themselves to rules both in terms of duality (in a taken-for-granted manner) and in terms of dualism (taking distance). But the articulation of the two modes of orientation to rules varies according to the hierarchical position of the actors concerned. In hierarchically superordinate positions the emphasis is on subject–object dualism; in subordinate positions the emphasis is on duality. In both cases, however, actual subjects may or may not follow what their roles and positions require.

To conclude: in hierarchical configurational wholes, moving from micro- to macro-levels of analysis cannot be done via aggregation (of individual acts, interactions, encounters, etc.). Given power inequalities between the actors involved, there is, to paraphrase Marx, unequal access to the 'means of social construction'. In such cases the move from micro to macro requires the hierarchization of interaction networks, discourses, exchanges, encounters, etc.

---

[23] For a development of this point, see Mouzelis, 1991a: 99–117.

16 | *The inter-institutional dimension: beyond economism and culturalism*

Having discussed the type of action–structure and micro–macro linkages that are presupposed in a non-essentialist, open-ended, holistic conceptual framework in the two previous chapters, it remains to examine what presuppositions are necessary for examining the linkages between institutional spheres (economic, political, social and cultural) in a way that avoids aprioristic, not empirically founded positions about the dominance of one sphere over the others.

1 Economism

As pointed out in previous chapters, the strongest argument that can be made for Marx's holistic framework is that it avoids the conflation of objectivist and subjectivist approaches seen in Giddens' and Bourdieu's writings; it also avoids the imbalance between systemic and action approaches seen in Parsonian and Althusserian functionalism at one extreme, and in interpretative micro-sociological approaches at the other. Viewed as a whole,[1] Marx's work achieves a remarkable balance and successfully combines systemic-institutional and actor-oriented perspectives. It views social development in terms of both systemic contradictions of institutional parts (system integration/disintegration) and actors' struggles (social integration/disintegration).[2] It is important

---

[1] Contra Althusser (1969; Althusser and Balibar, 1973), I do not think that there is a radical break between Marx's early writings (where the approach is more actor-oriented) and the late, more 'scientific' ones (where there is greater emphasis on system and/or structuralist determinations). As I shall argue below, the conceptual tools (Generalities II) that Marx's work as a whole offers enable us to strike a theoretically congruent balance between internalist/actor-oriented and externalist/ system-oriented approaches to the study of social formations.

[2] For the initial formulation of this key point, see Lockwood, 1964. For an attempt to reformulate the distinction so as to avoid Lockwood's rather essentialist references to the 'material base' of society, see Mouzelis, 1974. For the problematic way in which Giddens and Habermas have used the initial distinction, see chapter 6.

to repeat once more that Marx not only accepts methodological dualism (i.e. the necessity, in Habermas' terms, of both an internalist and an externalist perspective), but changes from one to the other without any conceptual acrobatics – since the key concept of technology (the forces of production) plays a crucial role in moving in a theoretically coherent manner from systemic contradictions to actors' struggles. For Marx, the major contradiction in the capitalist mode of production is between the technological-institutional complex and that of the private ownership of the means of production. As these two institutional complexes become increasingly incompatible, as systemic contradictions grow, the chances for the development of class consciousness, class organization and class conflict increase. So here, institutional analysis is not merely juxtaposed with an actor analysis: instead of juxtaposition we have articulation of the two perspectives.[3]

In other words, Marx sees technology as an institutional complex in system-integration terms, i.e. in terms of its logical compatibility or incompatibility with other institutional complexes. On the other hand, technology on the level of social integration is also the means of 'social construction', something that actors struggle to control. Technology, therefore, pertains to both the objective (institutional complex) and the subjective (struggles over means). But unlike Giddens' concept of the duality of structure and Bourdieu's habitus, the subjective–objective distinction *is not transcended but maintained*. In Marx's analysis the dual character of the technology notion (its reference to both the objective and the subjective) does not result in a conflationist view of the social world. On the contrary, instead of transcending the distinction or abolishing it altogether (the post-structuralist position), it strengthens methodological dualism, linking in a theoretically and logically convincing manner externalist/systemic and internalist/actor-oriented perspectives.

While Marx was successful in integrating in a balanced, theoretically consistent fashion system and action approaches, his theory remained profoundly economistic. As is well known, when he shifted his attention from philosophical to historical materialism he translated the notion of ideas reflecting matter into more historical and social-organizational

---

[3] Once institutional incompatibilities develop, one is encouraged to raise *who*-questions, to ask how actors relate to growing systemic contradictions. Are they aware of them, and if not, why not? Which actors try to overcome the growing contradictions, and which attempt to maintain them?

terms: the forces and relations of economic production become the material base of a social formation and as such have primacy over the other institutional spheres (political, religious, ideological, etc.). Whether this primacy is interpreted in deterministic terms or less deterministic, more flexible terms, it constitutes the foundation of historical materialism.[4]

The primacy of the material base as a substantive theory (in Althusserian terminology, Generalities III) is meant to apply to all social formations past and present. Like all contextless, universal theories, however, it tends to be either trivial or wrong. It is trivial when it is defended by arguments such as that it is necessary for human beings to eat if they are to be able to do anything else; or that people, as a rule, prefer to accept rather than reject the material rewards provided by the continuous development of the forces of production (Cohen, 1978).

When, on the other hand, we move from reductive psychologistic to more sociological explanations (which may focus, for example, on class struggles as the main mechanism of transition from the dominance of one mode of production to that of another), this more interesting proposition is wrong – or, to put it differently, it is valid only under certain conditions which, given the universal character of the theory, are not specified. Weber, for one, has pointed out that struggles over the control of the means of domination or the means of violence are often more crucial to understanding social transformations.[5] Giddens (1981, 1985) too has developed a similar thesis, arguing that because social classes are not organized in complex, pre-capitalist societies, they play a lesser role in social change than do political or cultural collective actors.

If we now consider historical materialism less as a substantive theory and more as a conceptual framework (Gen. II), here too the theory is highly problematic. This is because Marxism does not provide conceptual tools specific to the analysis of the non-economic institutional spheres. Political and cultural phenomena are explored with the help of economic categories, such as class and/or the reproduction

---

[4] The crude, deterministic version views the material/economic base as strictly determining the superstructure. In the more flexible interpretation the material base operates as a limiting framework, restricting the number of possibilities on the superstructural level. See Mouzelis, 1990: 12–16, 45–50.

[5] See Weber, 1925/1978: 941–8. For the state as the major motor force in the advent of modernity, see Tilly, 1978, 1984.

requirements of capital. Thus the state is viewed either as an instrument of the dominant class, or as the institutional complex by means of which capital is reproduced or expands. This conceptualization (as already argued in chapter 13) rules out in aprioristic fashion situations (quite frequent in late development) where state elites are not the tools but the creators and/or masters of the bourgeoisie. It also excludes the possibility of the state preventing, by undermining rather than promoting, the reproduction of capital.[6]

Of course, non-deterministic, 'humanistic' Marxism argues that the political sphere can be relatively autonomous from the economic and material base. But if one takes the theory of relative autonomy seriously, one will have to create new conceptual tools to help explore the changing relationship between the economy and the polity in an empirically open-ended manner. If this is not done, the relative autonomy thesis remains an empty gesture, a strategy which can only lead to theoretical closure.

The Marxist theorist who has moved the farthest in the non-economistic direction is Louis Althusser. The French philosopher developed two major anti-economistic strategies. On the more substantive level (Gen. III) he accepts Weber's and Giddens' position that in certain types of social formation non-economic rather than economic institutions can be dominant. However, in a last-ditch attempt to save Marxism's sacrosanct first principle, Althusser makes a distinction between dominance and 'determination in the last instance': in social formations where the political or ideological sphere is dominant, the economy is still primary, since it determines which institutional sphere will become dominant. More specifically, it is the economy's need for the extraction of surplus from the direct producers that determine which institution will predominate. In capitalist social formations the extraction of surplus occurs automatically via market mechanisms; in which case the economic sphere is both dominant and determining-in-the-last-instance. In feudal social formations, however, where the extraction of surplus occurs through political means, it is the political sphere that is dominant and the economy that determines in the last instance. This means,

---

[6] This is the case for most Third World countries whose states, in stark contrast to the authoritarian but developmental states of Asian capitalism, constitute the major obstacle to economic growth (Mouzelis, 1994).

however, that the needs of the economy are transformed into causes, since it is the necessity to extract economic resources by violent or repressive means that renders the political sphere dominant (Althusser and Balibar, 1973: 95–106, 180–9). It means a move from economism to a system essentialism of the teleological-functionalist kind (see chapter 15, section 1a).

Althusser's second anti-economistic move is on the level of conceptual tools (Gen. II). Here he tries to create categories for the analysis of the non-economic spheres that are homologous to, but also analytically distinct from, economic categories. He argues that all institutional spheres (economic, political, ideological theoretical) entail a process of production. Therefore, economic as well as non-economic spheres encompass raw materials, tools and end-products. The famous Althusserian distinction between Gen. I (conceptual raw materials), Gen. II (conceptual tools) and Gen. III (substantive theories) makes the point that there is a process of theoretical production which is isomorphic with, but also analytically different from, the process of economic production (Althusser, 1969: 183–91). It is analytically different in the sense that the two productive processes can vary independently of each other. The same is true about the process of political and ideological production.

This conceptualization clearly transcends the economistic closure that results from the exclusive application of economic categories to the study of non-economic phenomena. It leads to a non-aprioristic, open-ended examination of the linkages between the economic, the political and the cultural/ideological spheres. However, here again Althusser, while avoiding economism, retains the type of structuralist determinism that views actors as mere 'carriers of structures'. In a manner more extreme than Parsons', Althusser's actors are the passive products of structural determinations.[7]

---

[7] For a comparison of Althusserian Marxism and Parsonian functionalism along these lines, see Mouzelis, 1995b: 130–6.

Bourdieu is another theorist who tries to overcome economism by creating specific tools for the non-economic sphere. While Althusser tries to do this by looking at different types of production, Bourdieu focuses on different types of capital (economic, political, social and symbolic). His actors struggle for the acquisition of *field-specific* capital. However, given his underemphasis of strategic interaction (see chapter 8), Bourdieu tends to adopt a type of functionalism that reduces the autonomy of collective actors.

2 Culturalism and the priority of the lifeworld: from Marx to Parsons and Habermas

Let us now turn our attention from Marxism to Parsonian functionalism. Parsons began by attempting to overcome economism, but ended up with an overemphasis on both culture and system.

a. Systemic culturalism

As noted earlier, Parsons' societal system is subdivided into four subsystems: the economic (adaptation, A), the political (goal achievement, G), the social (integration, I) and the pattern-maintenance (latency, L). The AGIL scheme in no way implies that any one of the four subsystems a priori dominates or is more important than the other three. Following Weber rather than Marx, Parsons argues that the 'primacy' issue is an empirical one. In some types of societal system or in some historical periods the economic subsystem can be or is dominant, whereas in others it is not.

In later writings, however, when Parsons formulates his general theory of action, he moves from his previous 'neutral' (i.e. empirically open) position to the a priori establishment of a cultural primacy based on cybernetic theory. Parsons' general scheme of action comprises four action subsystems – the cultural, the social, the personality and the behavioural. From this more abstract perspective Parsons hierarchizes his four action subsystems. He argues that the cultural subsystem of action, being high in information and low in energy, comes first in the 'hierarchy of cybernetic controls', whereas the behavioural subsystem, being low in information and high in energy, comes last as far as 'steering capacity' is concerned. This hierarchization of the four action subsystems does not entail strict determinism, but in terms of cybernetic control rather than conditioning, the cultural-action subsystem comes first and the behavioural one last.[8] This type of mild culturalism is

---

[8] At this stage, Parsons similarly hierarchizes a social system's four functional subsystems (AGIL) – regarding L and I as *controlling* subsystems, and G and A as *conditioning* ones. See, on this, Adriansens, 1980: 141–51.
    It should be mentioned here that Parsons often uses the terms 'culture' and 'cultural' in two ways:

   (i) as a set of abstract values constituting the *cultural* system (which is analytically distinct from the *social* and *personality* systems);

combined in Parsons' late work with a persistent attempt to derive action from system concepts. According to Habermas, this is where voluntarism disappears from Parsons' work:

Actors disappear as acting subjects; they are abstracted into units to which the decisions and thus the effects of action are attributed. In so far as actions are viewed in terms of their internal analytic structure and conceived as the outcome of a complex joint operation among the specific subsystems, actors are merely circumscribed by the places they can occupy – in each instance under different aspects – in the four subsystems. (Habermas, 1987: 163)

b. The theoretical primacy of the lifeworld

Habermas initially accepts Parsons' AGIL scheme, but rejects his culturalism as well as his oversystemic orientation. He tries to inject a dose of voluntarism into Parsonian structural functionalism in three basic moves.

The first move is the division of the AGIL scheme into the *system* (A, G) and the *lifeworld* (I, L). In simple, non-differentiated societies the distinction between system and lifeworld does not exist, as 'systemic mechanisms have not yet become detached from institutions effective for social integration' (Habermas, 1987: 163). This state of affairs changes as the all-inclusive kinship institutions weaken and as societal systems become more complex, more differentiated along AGIL lines. With the advent of modernity the clearly differentiated economic (A) and political (G) subsystems constitute the 'system', whereas the social (I) and the pattern/maintenance (L) subsystems constitute the 'lifeworld'. In the former social space, the co-ordination of action, given the decline of traditional forms, is achieved by the systemic media of money and power respectively. Here communicative understanding is not necessary, since monetization and bureaucratization reproduce the system more or less automatically – as it were, behind the backs of the individuals concerned. In the social space of the lifeworld, on the other hand, the co-ordination of action and interaction is achieved via the 'linguistified' media of influence and prestige or value commitment that

(ii) as a set of norms/roles/institutions which cope with a social system's twin functional requirements of *tension-management* and *pattern-maintenance* (the latency subsystem).

The context usually helps the reader to establish whether the terms 'culture'/ 'cultural' are used in the sense of (i) or (ii).

complement and reinforce the process of communicative understanding. Given these qualitative differences between system and lifeworld, methodologically speaking the system (A and G) should be explored by the adoption of an 'externalist', systemic perspective, and the lifeworld (I and L) by that of an 'internalist', actors' perspective.

Habermas' second theoretical move is to place the lifeworld rather than the system at the centre of his communicative theory of action. For Habermas, the lifeworld does not comprise only the Schutzian notions of intersubjectivity, stock of knowledge, typifications, etc., but a cultural, social and personality dimension as well. The Parsonian triad of the cultural–social–personality levels of analysis is incorporated into the lifeworld concept as *cultural knowledge and traditions, social solidarities* and *personal competences*. These three dimensions constitute the context in which communicative action takes place: 'Communicative action not only depends upon cultural knowledge, legitimate [social] orders and competences developed through socialization; it not only feeds off the resources of the lifeworld; it is it-self the medium through which the symbolic structures of the lifeworld are reproduced' (Habermas, 1987: 255).

The lifeworld does not, however, portray only symbolic structures; it also has 'material structures' which constitute its *material substratum.* This refers to 'the ecology of external nature and of the organisms of its members' (1987: 231). By this third theoretical move, which introduces the notion of material structures or a material substratum, Habermas claims to have overcome Parsons' oversystemic analysis. For the German theorist, action, in the form of the lifeworld, is not derived from systemic considerations (such as functional requirements or systemic strains). Contra Parsons, systemic or material structures are derived from 'internalist', actors' concepts; and it is material structures that constitute the *external environment* of the lifeworld. This fundamental distinction between material structures external, and symbolic structures internal, to the lifeworld allows him to move from action to system without abrupt changes in perspective. It allows him to turn the late Parsons upside down, and to establish the theoretical primacy of the lifeworld and the derivative nature of systemic concepts.[9]

---

[9] According to Habermas,

Parsons did, to be sure, start from the primacy of action theory, but because he did not carry that through in a radical fashion, the *methodologically derivative* status

c. Critique

As noted above, Habermas' fundamental strategy for correcting Parsons' oversystemic orientation consists of splitting the AGIL set into two, into the spheres of the system (A, G) and the lifeworld (I, L). The two are internally co-ordinated by different media (systemic and 'linguistified' respectively), and should be explored by different methodologies (an 'externalist', functionalist perspective is appropriate for the system, and an internalist, actor methodology for the lifeworld).

The attempt to link Parsons' AGIL scheme with the system–lifeworld distinction creates difficulties on both the substantive and the methodological levels. Concerning the former, it is not true that action and interaction in the polity or the economy are co-ordinated only via the systemic media of money and power. Consider, for instance, negotiations between trade unionists and employers on working conditions or wages; or between political elites on the formulation of any kind of new policy. The reproduction of economic and political institutions is never achieved, as Habermas argues, exclusively 'behind the backs' of economic and political actors. The mode of co-ordination of economic and political actions and interactions is an empirical matter. It cannot be assessed in a priori fashion. This being so, methodologically speaking the polity and the economy should be viewed not only from an externalist perspective but also from an internalist one. The same is, of course, true when we consider the social (I) and the cultural (L) institutional spheres. All four subsystems, as Lockwood has argued, can and must be explored in terms of both a social-integration/actor and a system-integration/institutional perspective (see, on this point, chapter 6).[10]

Habermas tried to 'voluntarize' Parsonian functionalism by simply renaming and/or rearranging its component parts: the cultural, social and personality subsystems of action became dimensions of the lifeworld, whereas the fourth, the behavioural action subsystem, became the external, material environment of the lifeworld.

Ascribing centre-stage position to the lifeworld is not, however, necessarily conducive to an actor–system balance. It does not show, for example, how political, economic or even social and cultural

of *basic systems-theoretical concepts remained in the dark.* After the failure of his attempt to make a conceptual transition from the unit act to the context of action, Parsons dispensed with introducing the *systems concept via the theory of action.* (Habermas, 1987: 234, emphasis added)

[10] A similar critique has been developed by McCarthy, 1985: 182.

contradictions will or will not result in collective actors' strategies and struggles. The fact that on the actor–system issue Habermas is influenced less by Marx than by Parsons leads him to a conceptualization which compounds instead of correcting Parsons' oversystemic orientation. It is not surprising, therefore, that his *Theory of Communicative Action* has very few references to *collective actors*. Regarding the issue of the colonization of the lifeworld by the system in modern, capitalist societies, for instance, we are left in the dark as to the collective agents who promote or resist colonization. In fact, apart from some brief references at the end of volume II to the new social movements, there is no systematic analysis of collective action, of how for instance the new social movements connect with the older, working-class organizations; or of how dominant groups in the political, economic, social and cultural spheres are linked with each other; or, on a more systemic level, of how relations of exploitation affect relations of domination/violence and relations of persuasion/influence. It is not, therefore, surprising that Habermas was criticized for viewing the system (i.e. the economy and polity) in an essentialist, reifying fashion (Bhaskar, 1989: 189).

Deriving systemic concepts from the lifeworld – however this may be reconceptualized – is by no means an adequate substitute for a serious analysis of how systemic contradictions between and within the economic, political, social and cultural spheres relate to collective actors and their ongoing struggles.

A different strategy for redressing the balance between action and system in Parsonian theory is to focus less on the lifeworld concept and more on *how one should reconceptualize the components of the four subsystems in a way that avoids the system-within-system, onion-like Parsonian approach*. This is to say that the central question is how to move in a theoretically congruent manner from institutional analysis to an analysis in terms of actors; or how to link institutional incompatibilities and contradictions with collective actors' strategies and struggles. For such a transition from system to action, Marx (minus his economism) is more relevant than Schutz.

3 Beyond economism and systemic culturalism

To stress the point once more, Marx's overall work portrays an admirable balance between the systemic/externalist and actor/internalist perspectives. It focuses both on systemic contradictions within and between institutional complexes, and on how collective actors react or fail to react to such contradictions. This actor–system balance is undermined, however, by Marx's economic reductionism. As has repeatedly been pointed out, the Marxist focus is on *economic* technologies and their control by the exploiting classes. Everything else is more or less automatically derived from institutional contradictions and actors' struggles on the level of the material-economic base. For even when the 'relative autonomy' of non-economic spheres is taken into account (as in so-called humanistic Marxism), the analysis of these spheres proceeds by the use of conceptual tools (Gen. II) derived from the economic – i.e. it proceeds in terms of class analysis or by reference to the reproductive requirements of capital (Mouzelis, 1990: 31ff).

The way to break out of the economistic straitjacket while retaining the successful social- and system-integration articulation is via the creation of new conceptual tools for the analysis of the non-economic spheres (political, social and cultural), tools that do not provide ready-made, prefabricated answers but *leave open to empirical investigation* the importance of economic institutions and actors.

Such an anti-economistic conceptual strategy entails the rejection of the profoundly essentialist base–superstructure dichotomy; it entails the conceptualization of the political (G), social (I) and cultural (L) spheres in terms that are *analytically distinct from, but comparable to or isomorphic with*, the economic (A) conceptual tools Marxism offers. As has been pointed out in the previous chapter, the non-economic spheres of the political, the social and the cultural could each be seen as entailing three dimensions:

(i) a specific *technological* dimension, so that, following Weber, one would speak of administrative-political, social and cultural technologies;

(ii) a specific *appropriational* dimension, i.e. institutionalized ways of controlling/owning such technologies which would lead to a reference not only to *relations of economic production* but also to *relations of domination/violence* in the political sphere, relations of *solidarity/cohesion* in the social sphere and relations of *persuasion/influence* in the cultural sphere;

(iii) an *ideological* dimension: specific ways of legitimizing and/or occluding appropriation arrangements.[11]

Such a conceptualization overcomes both systemic culturalism and economic reductionism. With regard to the former, instead of Parsons' subdivision of each of the four subsystems into four sub-subsystems (a, g, i, l), I would propose subdividing each institutional sphere (economic, political, social and cultural) into its technological (t), appropriational (a) and ideological (i) dimensions. These dimensions (unlike Parsons' a, g, i, l) do lead to actor-related *who*-questions. They enquire about cleavages and conflicts between those who do and those who do not control the economic, political, social and cultural technologies with the help of which modern social orders are constituted, reproduced and transformed.

With regard now to economism, the technological/appropriational/ideological *constitutive* dimensions of all four major institutional spheres can help us overcome or avoid any type of aprioristic 'primacy' of the economic (in terms of dominance, 'determination in the last instance', etc.). The issue of the causal importance of one sphere over another (as in the Weberian tradition) becomes a matter open to empirical investigation. This means that questions can now be asked, for example, about the possibility that those who control the means of domination/violence are more powerful than those who control the means of production – a situation very common in the capitalist periphery and semi-periphery (Mouzelis, 1994).

This means that the above conceptualization allows us to view economic, political, social and cultural technologies as leading to the possible formation of not only economically but also politically, socially and culturally antagonistic groups; as well as to specifically systemic contradictions between technologies and their mode of control within the political, social and cultural spheres – contradictions that do not necessarily 'reflect' economic ones. All this in turn allows the study of the relations between economic, political, social and cultural struggles and contradictions in a theoretically coherent and at the same time empirically open-ended manner.[12]

---

[11] For an extensive discussion of these three dimensions, see Mouzelis, 1990: 43–92.

[12] For an application of the t, a, i schema in an empirically oriented analysis of socio-political developments in twentieth-century Greece, see Mouzelis, 1990: 93–152.

In closing, it is worth mentioning that if, as social constructionists argue, social reality is symbolically constructed when one focuses on the construction of macro social structures (such as a nation-state, for instance), their concern with identity formation should be complemented with a concern for how economic, political, social and cultural technologies are formed, how they are appropriated and how modes of appropriation/control are legitimized.[13]

---

[13] For a non-essentialist and non-deterministic conceptualization of technologies and their relationship to social constructionism, see the debate between Hutchby (2001a, 2001b, 2003) and Rappert (2003).

Instead of Conclusion: Twelve rules for the construction of an open-ended holistic paradigm

In the volume's last part, in an attempt to overcome obstacles and to establish bridges between the more conventional, holistically oriented macro-sociology and the radical anti-essentialism of late/postmodern theorizing, I spelled out the preconditions for a non-essentialist holism in the social sciences. These preconditions can be summarized in terms of twelve rules which are necessary for the construction of an open-ended conceptual framework – open-ended along the actor–structure, the micro–macro and the inter-institutional dimensions.

The actor–structure dimension: anti-conflationist holism

(1) From a methodological/perspectival rather than a philosophical/ontological position, actors and structures must be viewed as analytically distinct entities. There should be neither conflation nor transcendence of the actor–structure, subjectivist–objectivist divide. Although structures do not constitute essences and although they are symbolically constructed, their causality is different from that of actors. *Structural causality* refers to enablements and constraints that actors face in specific social contexts, whereas actors' causality entails decision-making, agentic powers.

(2) Social wholes must be viewed both from a *social-integration* (internalist) and a *system-integration* (externalist) perspective – both as a figuration of actors establishing conflictual or co-operative relationships with each other, and as a system of role/institutional complexes portraying varying degrees of compatibility or incompatibility with each other.

(3) Structures, as sets of interrelated elements, constitute *internal as well as external environments of action* which set limits and create opportunities for situated actors. The former refer to internalized dispositions, whereas the latter refer to institutional, figurational, symbolic and

274

material configurations. Some of them operate on a *virtual, paradigmatic* level (ideal-dispositional, institutional and symbolic structures), whereas others operate on an *actual, syntagmatic* level (actual-dispositional, figurational and material structures).

(4) What links structural causality (constraints and enablements) to actors' causality (agentic powers) are processes of *intra- and interaction*. Actor A involved in a social game considers, via reflexive accounting, the enablements and constraints generated by her/his internal and external environments of action, and on the basis of such deliberations adopts a certain course of action which is under constant review in the light of actor B's reaction to A's strategy.

The micro–macro dimension: anti-essentialist holism

(5) In macro-sociology, essentialism is usually based on an actor–system imbalance. In *system essentialism*, actors are underemphasized and because of this, institutional structures are portrayed as essences separate from their producers. Given the passive portrayal or disappearance of actors, there is also a tendency either erroneously to ascribe agentic, decision-making characteristics to institutional structures; or to turn systemic-functional requirements into causes (teleological functionalism/'strong' essentialism).

In *actor essentialism*, the complex ways in which actors' identities and interests are symbolically constructed within actual institutional contexts are ignored. This leads to the creation of either fictitious actors with pre-constituted interests or fictitious characteristics of real actors.

(6) A fundamental precondition for avoiding essentialism is a balanced actor/internalist and system/externalist perspective. To avoid system essentialism one should always keep in mind that structures must be systematically linked to their producers. To avoid actor essentialism one should take seriously into account the fact that actors' identities and interests are not pre-constituted but symbolically constructed within specific institutional contexts.

(7) In micro-sociology it is reductionism rather than essentialism that generates obstacles to micro–macro linkages. This can take different forms: viewing macro-phenomena as aggregations of micro-situations; erroneously linking face-to-face interactions with the micro, and

institutional structures with the macro; ignoring social hierarchies and the fact that actors tend to contribute unequally to the construction of social reality. A fundamental rule for avoiding reductionism is to take into consideration the fact that *configurational wholes* (hierarchical or not) are qualitatively different from aggregate ones. Configurational wholes, because of *emergence from below and/or constitution from above*, cannot be reduced to the sum of their parts.

(8) In the case of *hierarchical configurations*, micro-games played at the bottom of social hierarchies lead to the emergence of institutional or figurational structures which more powerful or hierarchically super-ordinate subjects must take into account. On the other hand, decisions taken at the top constitute *factual or value premises* in the decision-making environment of less powerful actors or of those occupying subaltern positions.

The inter-institutional dimension: anti-economistic holism

(9) Marx, in analysing the economic sphere in capitalism, adopted a balanced social-/system-integration perspective. He viewed social processes both systemically and from an actor's perspective – both in terms of systemic contradictions between institutional complexes and in terms of potential conflict between the actors involved.

Moreover, contra Parsons, his conceptualization of the economy in terms of its *technological, appropriational and ideological* dimensions leads, logically, to the transition from a system to an actor analysis. Growing systemic contradictions between technological and property institutions are conducive to the raising of actor-related *who*-questions on the level of social integration: how aware are actors of the growing contradictions, and if they are aware, what do they do about them? However, when Marx and his followers go from the analysis of the economy to that of the non-economic spheres, their approach is invariably reductive. Even when the relative autonomy of the political or the cultural is stressed, non-economic spheres are always analysed in terms of economic categories (social classes and/or the reproductive requirements of capital). Having failed to create *conceptual tools specific to the non-economic spheres*, economic reductionism is built into the very categories they employ for analysing the political and cultural spheres.

(10) Parsons, following Weber, at first rejected economism but eventually moved to a type of *culturalism*. He argued that the cultural system, being high in information and low in energy, should be placed at the top of the 'cybernetic hierarchy'. Moreover, his attempt, in his middle and late work, to derive action from system has led to *system-/*social-integration *imbalance*; this in turn resulted in essentialist and/or teleological-functionalist explanations of social life.

(11) Habermas has tried to redress Parsons' oversystemic approach by developing his distinction between *system* (which comprises the Parsonian adaptation (A) and goal achievement (G) subsystems) and the *lifeworld* (which refers to the integration (I) and latency (L) subsystems). He turned Parsons' analysis upside down by deriving the system from the lifeworld concept. His reversal, however, is quite problematic. By linking the system (A and G) with an externalist perspective and the lifeworld (I and L) with an internalist one, he arrives at the erroneous conclusion that one cannot examine all four institutional spheres in both actor and systemic terms. This means that Habermas, like Parsons, remains unable to tackle the central problem of how growing systemic contradictions (economic, political, social and cultural) lead or do not lead to social conflict.

(12) A different strategy for redressing Parsons' *system*-actor imbalance is to maintain the AGIL schema but to subdivide each of the four institutional subsystems (the economic, political, social and cultural) in such a way that the analysis can move from system to actor in a logically coherent manner (i.e. via articulation rather than juxtaposition).

Borrowing from Marxism, each of Parsons' four institutional spheres can be subdivided in terms of its technological (t), appropriational (a) and ideological (i) dimensions. This then allows us to avoid both Parsons' oversystemic focus and Marxism's economism. As to the former, replacing the a, g, i, l subdivisions with the t, a, i ones helps us move without conceptual acrobatics from a systemic to an actor analysis. Concerning Marxist economism, the reference not only to economic but also to *political, social and cultural technologies, appropriation arrangements and ideological legitimations* permits the empirically open-ended examination of how those who own or control economic technologies (the means of production) relate to those who control political technologies (means of domination), social technologies (means of solidarity creation) and cultural technologies (means of persuasion). Moreover, in systemic terms, the t, a, i subdivision makes it possible to explore, in a non-aprioristic manner, how the reproduction requirements of the economy relate to the reproduction requirements of the non-economic spheres.

In closing, I would like to stress once more that the above rules constitute neither a substantive theory nor a fully worked out conceptual framework in the tradition of Parsons or Giddens. In a more modest manner they merely provide a set of guidelines for the empirical investigation of social wholes (groups, communities, formal organizations, nation-states, etc.) in a non-essentialist as well as non-reductive manner.

Appendix. In defence of 'grand' historical sociology

Goldthorpe's article 'The uses of history in sociology' (1991) raises very interesting problems on the status and future prospects of what Goldthorpe has pejoratively labelled 'grand' historical sociology – as this has been developed during the last three decades by historically oriented sociologists like Barrington Moore, Michael Mann, Theda Skocpol, John Hall and others. As I consider the rapid growth of this branch of sociology one of the most fruitful and promising developments in the discipline; and as my own work on the long-term historical developments of some Balkan and Latin American polities (Mouzelis, 1986) has been very much influenced by Moore's work, I would like to make a few brief points in its defence.[1]

1 The conflation of history and sociology

To begin with, I agree with Goldthorpe on the necessity of maintaining the distinction between history and sociology as two disciplines which, although closely interrelated, portray different logics and methodologies. From this point of view, I am against Abrams's (1982) well-known position as well as the more general postmodern tendency to ignore or demolish all boundaries between social-science disciplines and sub-disciplines. In fact, I think that Goldthorpe's criteria for distinguishing sociological from historical analysis (the monothetic/ideographic distinction and the types of empirical evidence that the two disciplines use) are useful for establishing differences of emphasis between history and sociology. I am not sure if, as Goldthorpe argues, Mann or Skocpol entirely agrees with Abrams's position; but since their major work is more substantive than methodological, their *theoretical* position on the

---

[1] This appendix was previously published as a paper in the *British Journal of Sociology*, vol. 45 (1994).

exact linkages between history and sociology is neither important nor relevant in the present context.

2 The comparison with Spencer

I think it is both unfair and misleading to compare the work of Moore, Mann and Skocpol with that of Spencer. Spencer, as well as Comte and other nineteenth-century evolutionist theorists, were trying to discover 'laws' of social development and in that sense the use of history in their writings was rather decorative. They were simply turning to historical works in order to pick up in an *ad hoc*, 'contextless' manner examples suitable for filling their complex theoretical boxes. In this process of picking arbitrary historical and anthropological material, there was hardly any attempt to relate the empirical data used with the broader socio-historical context within which they were embedded and which, to a large extent, gave them their meaning.

In contrast, present-day historical sociologists, *however broad their scope*, are much more sensitive to *context*. They are seeking neither rationalistically constructed laws nor statistically derived correlations between 'variables', which are supposed to be universally valid. Whether they look at nation-states, pre-industrial empires or ancient city-states, *their approach tends to be holistic without being teleological*.

To take Barrington Moore as an example: despite the grand scale of his analysis, his famous 'three routes to modernity' are explained not in terms of 'laws' but in terms of collective actors and their complex strategies – the intended or unintended consequences of which lead to different developmental outcomes. Given the emphasis on actors' strategies and games, or (to use Elias' apt terminology) on *figurations*, Moore clearly avoids the nineteenth-century evolutionist practice of treating historical material like goods in a market that one can pick up at will. Moore's non-teleological holism, in other terms, manages to strike a balance between *generality* and *context*, a balance which is absent both in purely descriptive, historiographical works and, at the other extreme, in the type of contextless, vacuous generalizations that have given sociology such a bad name.

In order to make the above point more clear, one has only to contrast Moore's context-sensitive use of history with the Spencerian/ Durkheimian/Parsonian-oriented modernization theorists, for instance, who, in a variety of ways, neglect context time- and space-wise. In the latter case, despite their constant reference to historical examples and despite their occasional direct use of primary sources, their approach is profoundly ahistorical. And this is so either in the sense that long-term historical developments are explained in terms of processes of structural-functional differentiation without any *systematic* reference to the actors who are at the root of such processes; or, even worse, in the sense that such developments are explained in terms of correlations of 'variables' which are supposed to be valid in a transhistorical, universal manner. A good example of the former tendency is Smelser's *Social Change in the Industrial Revolution* (1962) where the complex differentiation between kinship and economic institutions brought about by technological inventions is explained in terms of a seven-stage model conceived in purely systemic, functionalist terms.[2] As an example of the latter tendency, consider McLeland's attempt to establish a universal linkage between the need for achievement and economic growth. The author of *The Achieving Society* (1961), in a totally *ad hoc*, contextless manner draws his evidence from all types of society, past and present, without taking into account the cultural and socio-historical contexts within which the 'variables' that he tries to correlate are embedded and from which they derive their specific meaning and significance.

It is, in fact, in the above examples rather than in the cases of Moore (1967), Hall (1986, 1994) or Mann (1986, 1995) that the comparison with Spencer is appropriate; for it is here that the urge to establish universal, contextless generalizations leads, despite the occasional use of primary sources, to the ahistorical, decorative use of historical material and to generalizations which are either trivial or wrong.

3 On the tenuous linkages between evidence and interpretation

Goldthorpe finds that in 'grand historical sociology the links that are claimed, or supposed, between evidence and argument tend to be both *tenuous* and *arbitrary* to a quite unacceptable degree' (1991: 222). Let us look at the 'tenuous' charge first. For Goldthorpe the links are

---

[2] Smelser has subsequently admitted that the absence of *who*-questions and group conflicts as basic mechanisms of social differentiation was a major weakness of his early attempt to apply the Parsonian framework in the analysis of the British Industrial Revolution. See his contribution in Alexander and Colomy, 1990.

tenuous because the evidence used is based on secondary rather than primary sources. This means that grand historical sociologists base their interpretations not on 'relics' but on historians' interpretations of relics – or, even worse, on interpretations of historians' interpretations (1991: 223). As a consequence, the chain between primary evidence and interpretation become unacceptably long and tenuous.

Now there is no doubt that in so far as the scale of the comparative enterprise that historically oriented sociologists are typically undertaking precludes the use of primary data, this is obviously a disadvantage. But given that we live in an imperfect world and that all methodologies and approaches to history entail advantages and disadvantages, it is absurd to see this disadvantage as a reason for rejecting the type of macro-historical comparisons that, following Weber's steps, grand historical sociologists are attempting. And it is equally absurd not to realize that there are a variety of ways of minimizing the risks of not using primary sources.

Consider, for instance, the example that Goldthorpe himself provides: if, as Goldthorpe argues, Moore based his central thesis about the commercial orientation of the landed upper classes and their contributions to the English Civil War on 'shaky' secondary evidence, then it is the business of both historians and grand historical sociologists to point this out and raise new questions, which in turn can lead to a more careful examination of both secondary and primary sources. The end-result of such an exercise might be the qualification, radical restructuring or even rejection of Moore's initial hypothesis. And it is precisely through such a dialogic process, in the context of relatively open communications between scholars (some working more with primary and others more with secondary sources), that our knowledge about long-term historical transformations can advance.

From the above perspective, Goldthorpe's critique of Moore's interpretation of the English Civil War should be seen as a moment in the ongoing debate, rather than as an argument for abandoning the type of macro-historical, comparative work that Moore has done so much to promote among sociologists. After all, when Goldthorpe argues that at the time Moore was writing, 'the idea that the "rising", commercially oriented gentry were key actors in the parliamentary opposition to the king and his defeat in the civil war was, in fact, losing ground among English historians' (1991:223), one can easily turn the tables and use Goldthorpe against Goldthorpe. How has Goldthorpe found out that the thesis about the rising, commercially oriented gentry was losing ground? Did he look *directly* at the 'relics', at the primary sources, or did he base his judgement on secondary sources? If the latter is the case (and Goldthorpe provides no evidence to the contrary), then by following his logic one can argue that Goldthorpe's critique of Moore's hypothesis about the Civil War cannot be taken seriously.

4 On the arbitrary character of grand historical sociology's interpretations

For Goldthorpe, in the writings of grand historical sociologists the linkages between evidence and interpretation are not only tenuous but also arbitrary. When, as in the case of the English Civil War, historians disagree with each other, and when the disagreement is based on the fact that 'the relics that would be necessary to settle the disputed issues simply do not exist' (Goldthorpe, 1991: 223), then grand historical sociologists have no other choice but arbitrarily to select the secondary evidence that suits their overall theoretical interpretation.

However, one can argue that if they do that, they simply lack the necessary self-discipline and detachment that both historians and sociologists must strive to achieve – in which case it is the business of other historians and sociologists to criticize them accordingly. For if there are no available relics to settle a dispute, the solution is not to reject the whole theoretical project but simply to stress the inadequacy of the available evidence and the necessity, if possible, of improving it. In other words, grand historical sociologists do not have to be 'arbitrary'; they are not 'obliged' to choose the interpretation that suits their overall theory. If they are detached enough, nothing prevents them from admitting the inadequacy of relics to settle a specific issue and proceeding to build up or rearrange their macro-theories accordingly.

After all, historians who write grand synthetic works unavoidably base their synthesis on secondary materials and equally unavoidably face the same problems related to 'arbitrary' linkages between evidence and interpretation that grand historical sociologists face. Is Goldthorpe suggesting that one should give up not only the type of work that Moore is doing, but also the attempts by historians like Braudel (1966) for instance to provide an account of how whole societies or groups of societies are changing in the *longue durée*? And if we do this, what shall we put in their place? Should we simply turn our backs on the type of problems that both grand historical sociology and 'synthesizing/grand' history generate? Should we indulge in the type of methodological perfectionism that fetishizes 'relics' and stresses their importance to such an extent that one is unable to examine the type of problems that macro-historical comparisons generate? Should we also ignore the obvious fact that macro-historical interpretations, however 'tenuous and arbitrary', do generate new hypotheses which often lead to new interpretations of relics, or even to the discovery of new relics?

Goldthorpe gives no answers to the above questions. But he gives us some hints about his own view of the relationship between empirical evidence and theoretical argument. For instance, he criticizes grand historical sociology for engaging in second-order interpretations: 'in interpretation of interpretations of, perhaps, interpretations' (1991: 223). In doing so, he does not seem to realize that both 'relics' and the empirical data that a sociologist generates are themselves interpretations of interpretations. They are second-order interpretations referring to the first-order ones that individuals generate when they act and interact. Could it be that Comte's or Spencer's positivist/essentialist spirit is to be found more in Goldthorpe's critique than in the writings of those he criticizes?

References

Abrams, P. 1982. *Historical Sociology*. Bath: Open Books.

Adriansens, H. P. M. 1980. *Talcott Parsons and the Conceptual Dilemma*. London: Routledge & Kegan Paul.

Albert, M. 1995. *Capitalism against Capitalism*. London: Whurr.

Albrow, M. 1996. *The Global Age*. Cambridge: Polity.

Alexander, J. C. 1982. *Theoretical Logic in Sociology: Positivism, Presuppositions and Current Controversies*, vol. I. London: Routledge & Kegan Paul.

(ed.) 1985. *Neo-Functionalism*. London: Sage.

1995. *Fin de Siècle Social Theory: Relativism, Reduction, and the Problem of Reason*. London: Verso.

1997. 'The paradoxes of civil society', *International Sociology*, vol. 12, no. 2.

1998a. *Neo-Functionalism and After*. Oxford: Blackwell.

(ed.) 1998b. *Real Civil Societies*. London: Sage.

2003. *The Meanings of Social Life: A Cultural Sociology*. Oxford University Press.

Alexander, J. C. and P. Colomy (eds.) 1990. *Differentiation Theory and Social Change*. New York: Columbia University Press.

Alexander, J. C. and S. Seidman (eds.) 1990. *Culture and Society: Contemporary Debates*. Cambridge University Press.

Allport, G. W. 1962. 'Prejudice: a problem in psychological and social causation', in T. Parsons and E. A. Shils (eds.), *Toward a General Theory of Action*. New York: Harper & Row.

Althusser, L. 1968. 'Marxism is not a historicism', in Althusser and Balibar (1973).

1969. *For Marx*. London: Penguin.

1973. *Lire le Capital*. Paris: Maspero.

Althusser, L. and E. Balibar 1973. *Reading Capital*. London: New Left Books.

Anderson, B. 1991. *Imagined Communities*. London: Verso.

Anderson, P. 1974. *Lineages of the Absolutist State*. London: New Left Publications.

Appelbaum R. P. and L. Henderson (eds.) 1992. *States and Development in the Asian Pacific Rim*. London: Sage.

Archer, M. S. 1982. 'Morphogenics versus structuration: on combining struc-
    ture and agency', *British Journal of Sociology*, vol. 33, no. 4.
    1990. 'Human agency and social structure: a critique of Giddens', in
    J. Clark and C. Modgil (eds.), *Anthony Giddens: Consensus and
    Controversy*. Basingstoke: Falmer.
    2000. *Being Human: The Problem of Agency*. Cambridge University Press.
    2003. *Structure, Agency and the Internal Conversation*. Cambridge
    University Press.
Barber, B. 1985. 'Beyond Parsons' theory of the professions', in Alexander
    (ed.).
Barker, E. 1944. *The Development of Public Services in Western Europe,
    1660–1930*. Oxford University Press.
Barthes, R. 1999. *Contemporary Social Theory*. Oxford: Blackwell.
Baudrillard, J. 1976. *L'échange symbolique et la mort*. Paris: Gallimard.
    1979. *De la séduction*. Paris: Galiléo.
    1981. *Simulacres et simulation*. Paris: Galiléo.
    1983. *Les strategies fatales*. Paris: Grasset.
Bauman, Z. 1987. *Legislators and Interpreters: On Modernity, Postmodernity
    and Intellectuals*. Ithaca: Cornell University Press.
    1992. *Intimations of Postmodernity*. New York: Routledge.
Baxton, W. 1985. *Talcott Parsons and the Capitalist Nation-state*. University
    of Toronto Press.
Beck, U. 1992. *Risk Sociology: Towards a New Modernity*. London: Sage.
Beck, U. and E. Beck-Gernsheim 1996. 'Individualization and "precarious free-
    doms": perspectives and controversies of a subject–object oriented sociol-
    ogy', in P. Heelas, S. Lash and P. Morris (eds.), *Detraditionalization*.
    Oxford: Blackwell.
Beck, U., A. Giddens and S. Lash (eds.) 1994. *Reflexive Modernization: Politics,
    Tradition and Aesthetics in the Modern Social Order*. Cambridge: Polity.
Becker, H. S. 1974. 'Labelling theory reconsidered', in Rock and McIntosh
    (eds.).
Bellah, R. N. 1957. *Tokugawa Religion: The Values of Pre-Industrial Japan*.
    Glencoe, IL: Free Press.
Bello, W. and S. Rosenfield 1992. *Dragons in Distress*. London: Penguin.
Bendix, R. 1969. *Nation-Building and Citizenship*. New York: Action
    Books.
    1978. *Kings or People*. Berkeley: University of California Press.
Benhabib, S. 1992. *Situating the Self*. New York: Routledge.
Benton, T. 1984. *The Rise and Fall of Structural Marxism*. London: Verso.
Berger, S. and R. Dore 1996. *National Diversity and Global Capitalism*.
    Ithaca: Cornell University Press.
Bhaskar, R. 1978. *A Realist Theory of Science*. Brighton: Harvester.

1989. *Reclaiming Reality: A Critical Introduction to Contemporary Philosophy*. London: Verso.

Blau, P. 1987. 'Micro processes and macrostructures', in K. S. Cook (ed.), *Social Exchange Theory*. London: Sage.

Blumer, H. 1969. *Symbolic Interactionism*. Englewood Cliffs, NJ: Prentice Hall.

Boudon, R. 1987. *The Micro–Macro Link*. Berkeley: University of California Press.

Bourdieu, P. 1977. *Outline of a Theory of Action*. Cambridge University Press.

1990. *The Logic of Practice*, Cambridge: Polity.

Bourdieu, P. and L. Wacquant 1992. *An Invitation to Reflexive Sociology*. Cambridge: Polity.

Braithwaite, R. B. 1964. *Scientific Explanation*. Cambridge University Press.

Braudel, F. 1966. *La Méditerranée et le monde méditerranéen a l'époque de Philippe II*. Paris: Armand Colin.

Brunhoff, S. 1978. *État et capital*. Presses Universitaires de Grenoble.

Burkitt, I. 1999. *Bodies of Thought*. London: Sage.

Butt, T. and D. Langdridge 2003. 'The construction of self', *Sociology*, vol. 37, no. 3.

Carter, B. 2002. 'People power: Harré and the myth of social structure', *European Journal of Social Theory*, vol. 5, no. 1.

Castoriadis, C. 1999. 'The individual and representation', in A. Elliott (ed.), *Contemporary Social Theory*. Oxford: Blackwell.

Chambliss, W. J. and M. Mankoff 1976. *Whose Law? What Order?* New York: Wiley.

Chase-Dunn, C. 1989. *Global Formation: Structures of the World Economy*. Oxford: Blackwell.

Cicourel, A. 1976. *The Social Organization of Juvenile Justice*. London: Heinemann.

Cobban, A. 1967. 'The "middle class" in France 1815–1848', *French Historical Studies*, vol. 5, Spring.

Cohen, A. K. 1955. *Delinquent Boys*. Glencoe, IL: Free Press.

1966. *Deviance and Control*. Englewood Cliffs, NJ: Prentice Hall.

Cohen, G. A. 1978. *Karl Marx's Theory of History: A Defence*. Oxford: Clarendon.

Cohen, J. L. and A. Arato. 1992. *Civil Society and Political Theory*. Boston: Beacon.

Coleman, J. S. 1990. *Foundations of Social Theory*. Cambridge, MA: Harvard University Press.

Collins, R. 1981a. 'Micro-translation as a theory-building strategy', in K. Knorr-Cetina and V. Cicourel (eds.), *Advances in Social Theory and*

Methodology: Towards an Integration of Micro- and Macro-Sociology. London: Routledge & Kegan Paul.

1981b. 'On the micro foundations of macro-sociology', *American Journal of Sociology*, vol. 86.

2003. 'A Network–Location theory of culture', *American Sociological Review*, vol. 21, no. 1.

Craib, I. 1995. 'Some comments on the sociology of emotions', *Sociology*, vol. 29, no. 1.

1998. *Experiencing Identity*. London: Sage.

Crothers, C. 1996. *Social Structure*. London: Routledge.

Crozier, M. 1963. *Le phénomène bureaucratique*. Paris: Seuil.

Dahrendorf, R. 1959. *Class and Class Conflict in Industrial Society*. London: Routledge & Kegan Paul.

Derrida, J. 1978. *Writing and Difference*. University of Chicago Press.

1981. *Positions*. University of Chicago Press.

Dews, P. 1987. *Logics of Disintegration: Post-Structuralist Thought and the Claims of Critical Theory*. London: Verso.

Deyo, F. C. (ed.) 1987. *The Political Economy of the New Asian Industrialism*. Ithaca: Cornell University Press.

Diamond, L. and M. Plattner (eds.) 1996. *The Global Resurgence of Democracy*. Baltimore: Johns Hopkins University Press.

Diani, M. and D. McAdam (eds.) 2003. *Social Movements and Networks: Relational Approaches to Collective Action*. Oxford University Press.

Dobb, M. 1968. *Studies in the Development of Capitalism*. New York: International Publishers.

Dore, R. 1961. 'Function and cause', *American Sociological Review*, vol. 26.

Dragonas, T. 2004. 'Negotiating identities: the Muslim minority in Western Thrace', *New Perspectives in Turkey*, no. 30, Spring.

Dreyfus, H. L. and P. Rabinow 1982. *Michel Foucault: Beyond Structuralism and Hermeneutics*. Chicago: University of Chicago Press.

Dunning, E. and C. Rojek (eds.) 1992. *Sport and Leisure in the Civilizing Process: Critique and Counter-critique*. London: Macmillan.

Dunning, E. and K. Sheard 1979. *Barbarians, Gentlemen and Players*. Oxford: Martin Robertson.

Durkheim, E. 1964. *The Division of Labour in Society*. New York: Free Press.

Eisenstadt, S. N. 1963. *The Political Systems of Empires*. New York: Free Press.

1990a. 'Differentiation theory, elite structure and cultural visions', in Alexander and Colomy (eds.).

1990b. 'Modes of structural differentiation, elite structure, and cultural visions', in Alexander and Colomy (eds.).

Elias, N. 1978. *What is Sociology?* London: Hutchinson.

1978/1982. *The Civilizing Process*, 2 vols. Oxford: Blackwell.

1987a. *Involvement and Detachment*. Oxford: Blackwell.

1987b. 'On human beings and their emotions: a process-sociological essay', *Theory, Culture and Society*, vol. 4, nos. 2–3.

1991. *The Sociology of Individuals*. Oxford: Blackwell.

Eliou, P. 2002. 'A conference for historiography' (in Greek), *Ta Istorika*, no. 37.

Elliott, A. 2001. *Concepts of the Self*. Cambridge: Polity.

Elliott, G. 1987. *Althusser: The Detour of Theory*. London: Verso.

Elster, J. 1985. *Making Sense of Marx*, Cambridge University Press.

1986. *An Introduction to Karl Marx*, Cambridge University Press.

1989. *Nuts and Bolts for the Social Sciences*. Cambridge University Press.

Elton, G. 1953. *The Tudor Revolution in Government: Administrative Changes in the Reign of Henry VIII*. Cambridge University Press.

Etzioni, A. 1996. *The New Golden Rule*. New York: Basic Books.

Exertzoglou, H. 2002. 'History and historiography' (in Greek), *Kiriakatiki Avgi*, 15 December.

Foucault, M. 1972. *The Archaeology of Knowledge*. New York: Random House.

1975. *Discipline and Punishment: The Birth of the Prison*. Harmondsworth: Penguin.

1978. *The History of Sexuality: An Introduction*. Harmondsworth: Penguin.

1979. 'My body, this paper, this fire', *Oxford Literary Review*, vol. 4, no. 1.

1980. 'Truth and power', in Gordon (ed.).

1984. *The Use of Pleasure*. Harmondsworth: Penguin.

1986. *The Care of the Self*. Harmondsworth: Penguin.

Fuchs, S. 1988. 'The constitution of emergent interaction orders: a comment on Rawls', *Sociological Theory*, vol. 6.

1989. 'Second thoughts on emergent interaction orders', *Sociological Theory*, vol. 7.

Furet, F. 1978. *Penser la Révolution Française*. Paris: Gallimard.

Garfinkel, H. 1967. *Studies in Ethnomethodology*. Cambridge: Polity.

Gasman, D. 1971. *The Scientific Origins of National Socialism*. New York: Elsevier.

Geertz, C. 1964. 'Ideology as a cultural system', in D. Apter (ed.), *Ideology and Discontent*. New York: Free Press.

1973. *The Interpretation of Cultures*. New York: Basic Books.

Gellner, E. 1969. *Thought and Change*. London: Weidenfeld & Nicolson.

1992. *Postmodernism, Reason and Religion*. London: Routledge.

1994. *Conditions of Liberty*. London: Hamish Hamilton.

1996. *Nations and Nationalism*. Oxford: Blackwell.

Geras, N. 1987. 'Post-Marxism?', *New Left Review*, no. 163.

Gerschenkron, A. 1982. *Economic Backwardness in Historical Perspective*. London: Praeger.

Gerth, H. H. and C. W. Mills (eds.) 1961. *From Max Weber: Essays in Sociology*. London: Routledge & Kegan Paul.

Giddens, A. 1979. *Central Problems in Social Theory*. London: Macmillan.

   1981. *A Contemporary Critique of Historical Materialism*, vol. I: *Power, Property and the State*. London: Macmillan.

   1983. *The Nation-state and Violence*. Cambridge: Polity.

   1984. *The Constitution of Society*. Cambridge: Polity.

   1985. *A Contemporary Critique of Historical Materialism*. London: Macmillan.

   1990. *The Consequences of Modernity*. Cambridge: Polity.

   1991. *Modernity and Self-identity: Self and Society in the Late Modern Age*. Cambridge: Polity.

   1993. *New Rules of Sociological Method*, 2nd edn. London: Hutchinson.

Ginsberg, M. 1956. *Essays in Sociology and Social Philosophy*, vol. II: *Reason and Unreason in Society*. London: Heinemann.

Goffman, E. 1959. *The Presentation of Self in Everyday Life*. Harmondsworth: Penguin.

   1961. *Asylums*. Garden City, NY: Anchor.

   1983. 'The interaction order', *American Sociological Review*, vol. 48.

Goldthorpe, J. 1967. 'Social stratification in industrial society', in R. Bendix and S. M. Lipset (eds.), *Class, Status and Power*. London: Routledge & Kegan Paul.

   1991. 'The uses of history in sociology', *British Journal of Sociology*, vol. 42, no. 2.

Gordon, C. (ed.) 1980. *Power and Knowledge*. Brighton: Harvester.

Gouldner, A. 1971. *The Coming Crisis of Western Sociology*. London: Heinemann.

   1976. *The Dialectic of Ideology and Technology*. London: Macmillan.

Habermas, J. 1984. *The Theory of Communicative Action*, vol. I: *Reason and the Rationalization of Society*. London: Heinemann.

   1987. *The Theory of Communicative Action*, vol. 2: *Lifeworld and System: A Critique of Functional Reason*. London: Heinemann.

Hagen, E. E. 1962. *On the Theory of Social Change*. Homewood, IL: Dorsey.

Haggard, S. 1990. *Pathways from the Periphery*. Ithaca: Cornell University Press.

Hall, A. P. and R. C. R. Taylor 1994. 'Political science and the four institutionalisms', presented to the Annual Meeting of the American Political Science Association, New York, September.

1996. 'Political science and the three new institutionalisms', *Political Studies*, vol. 44, no. 6.

1998. 'The potential of historical institutionalism: a response to Hay and Wincott', *Political Studies*, vol. 46.

Hall, J. 1986. *Powers and Liberties: The Causes and Consequences of the Rise of the West*. London: Penguin.

1994. *Coercion and Consent: Studies on the Modern State*. Cambridge: Polity.

Hall, J. and I. Jarvie (eds.) 1995. *The Social Philosophy of Ernest Gellner (Poznan Studies 48)*. Amsterdam: Rodopi.

Hall, S. and B. Grieben (eds.) 1992. *Formations of Modernity*. Cambridge: Polity.

Harker, R., C. Mahar and C. Wilkes (eds.) 1990. *An Introduction to the Work of Pierre Bourdieu*. London: Macmillan.

Harré, R. 1993. *Social Being*. London: Blackwell.

2002. 'Social reality and the myth of social structure', *European Journal of Social Theory*, vol. 5, no. 1.

Hay, C. and D. Wincott 1998. 'Structure, agency and historical institutionalism', *Political Studies*, vol. 46.

Hekman, S. 1983. *Weber, the Ideal Type and Contemporary Social Theory*. University of Notre Dame Press.

Hilton, R. (ed.) 1976. *The Transition from Feudalism to Capitalism*. London: New Left Books.

Hindess, B. and P. Hirst 1975. *Pre-Capitalist Economic Formations*. London: Routledge & Kegan Paul.

Hirschman, A. 1970. *A Bias for Hope*. New Haven: Yale University Press.

Hirst, P. Q. 1972. 'Marx and Engels on law, crime, and morality', *Economy and Society*, vol. 1.

Hirst, P. Q. and G. Thompson 1996. *Globalization in Question*. Cambridge: Polity.

Hobsbawm, E. 1968. *Industry and Empire*. London: Penguin.

Hollingsworth, J. R., K. H. Muller and E. J. Hollingsworth 2002. *Advancing Socioeconomics: An Institutionalist Perspective*. Lanham, MD: Rowman & Littlefield.

Hoogvelt, A. M. M. 1978. *The Sociology of Developing Societies*. London: Macmillan.

Howarth, D. 2000. *Discourse*. Buckingham: Open University Press.

Howarth, D., A. J. Norval and Y. Stavrakakis (eds.) 2000. *Discourse Theory and Political Analysis: Identities, Hegemonies and Social Change*. Manchester University Press.

Howarth, D. and Y. Stavrakakis 2000. 'Introducing discourse theory and political analysis', in Howarth, Norval and Stavrakakis (eds.)

Hutchby, I. 2001a. 'Technologies, texts, affordances', *Sociology*, vol. 35.
  2001b. *Conversation and Technology: From the Telephone to the Internet.*
  Cambridge: Polity.
  2003. 'Affordances and the analysis of technologically mediated interaction: a response to Brian Rappert', *Sociology*, vol. 37, no 3.
Hutton, W. 1995. *The State We're In*. London: Cape.
Iasch, C. 1995. *The Revolt of the Elites and the Betrayal of Democracy*. New York: Norton.
Jackson, S. 1993. 'Even sociologists fall in love: an exploration in the sociology of emotions', *Sociology*, vol. 27, no. 2.
Jacobs, R. 1998. 'The racial discourse of civil society', in Alexander (ed.)
Jenkins, R. 1991. *Pierre Bourdieu*. London: Routledge.
  2000. 'Pierre Bourdieu and the reproduction of determinism', in D. Robbins (ed.), *Pierre Bourdieu*, vol. II. London: Sage.
Joas, H. 1996. *The Creativity of Action*. Cambridge: Polity.
Julius, D. 1990. *Global Companies and Public Policy*. London: Royal Institute of International Affairs.
Kemper, T. (ed.) 1990. *Research Agendas in the Sociology of Emotions.* Albany: State University of New York Press.
Kerr, C., J. T. Dunlop, F. H. Harbison and C. A. Mayers 1962. *Industrialism and Industrial Man*. London: Heinemann.
King, A. 1999. 'Against structure: a critique of morphogenetic social theory', *Sociological Review*, vol. 47, no. 2.
Kitchener, R. F. 1985. 'Holistic structuralism, elementarism and Piaget's Theory of Relationism', *Human Development*, vol. 28.
Kristeva, J. 1999. 'Revolution in poetic language', in A. Elliott (ed.), *Contemporary Social Theory*. Oxford: Blackwell.
Labica, G. 1971. 'Quatre observations sur le concept de mode de production et de formation économique de la société', *La Pensée*, Sept.–Oct.
Lacan, J. 1977. *Ecrits: A Selection*. London: Tavistock.
Laclau, E. 1990. *New Reflections on the Revolution of our Time*. London: Verso.
Laclau, E. and C. Mouffe 1985. *Hegemony and Social Strategy: Towards a Radical Democratic Politics*. London: Verso.
Lechner, F. J. 1964. 'Fundamentalism and sociocultural revitalization', in Zollschan and Hirsch (eds.).
Lehman, E. (ed.) 2000. *Autonomy and Order: A Communitarian Anthology.* Oxford: Rowman & Littlefield.
Lévi-Strauss, C. 1968. *L'origine des manières de table*. Paris: Plon.
  1973. *Anthropologie structurale*. Paris: Plon.
Lockwood, D. 1964. 'Social integration and system integration', in Zollschan and Hirsch (eds.).

1992. *Solidarity and Schism: The Problem of 'Disorder' in Durkheimian and Marxist Sociologies*. Oxford University Press.

Lopez, J. 2003. *Society and its Metaphors: Language, Social Theory and Social Structure*. London: Continuum.

Luhmann, N. 1982. *The Differentiation of Society*. New York: Columbia University Press.

1998. *Observations on Modernity*. Stanford University Press.

Lyotard, J. F. 1974. *La condition postmoderne*. Paris: Minuit.

Maines, D. R. 2001. *The Faultline of Consciousness: A View of Interactionism in Sociology*. Hawthorne, NY: Aldine de Gruyler.

Mann, M. 1986. *The Sources of Social Power*. Cambridge University Press.

1995. 'The emergence of modern European nationalism', in Hall and Jarvie (eds.).

Marshall, T. H. 1964. *Class, Citizenship and Social Development*. Garden City, NY: Doubleday.

Marx, K. 1859/1964. *Pre-Capitalist Economic Formations*. London: Lawrence & Wishart.

1859/1970. *A Contribution to the Critique of Political Economy*. New York: International Publishers.

Maza, S. 2003. *The Myth of the French Bourgeoisie: An Essay in Social Imaginary 1750–1850*. Cambridge, MA: Harvard University Press.

McCarthy, T. 1985. 'Reflections on rationalisation in "The Theory of Communicative Action"', in R. J. Bernstein (ed.), *Habermas and Modernity*. Cambridge: Polity.

McIver, R. M. 1942. *Social Causation*. New York: Harper.

McLeland, D. T. 1961. *The Achieving Society*. Princeton University Press.

McLennan, G. 1995. 'After postmodernism – back to sociological theory?', *Sociology*, vol. 29, no. 1.

2003. 'Sociology's complexity', *Sociology*, vol. 37, no. 3.

McNay, L. 1994. *Foucault: A Critical Introduction*. Cambridge: Polity.

1999. 'Gender, habitus and the field: Pierre Bourdieu and the limits of reflexivity', *Theory, Culture and Society*, vol. 16, no.1.

McNeil, W. H. 1963. *The Rise of the West*. University of Chicago Press.

1995. 'A swan song of British liberalism?', in Hall and Jarvie (eds.).

Mead, G. H. 1934. *Mind, Self and Society*, ed. C. Morris. University of Chicago Press.

Merton, R. K. 1963. *Social Theory and Social Structure*. Glencoe, IL: Social Press.

Michels, R. 1949. *Political Parties: A Sociological Study of the Oligarchic Tendencies of Modern Democracy*. Glencoe, IL: Free Press.

Miliband, R. 1969. *The State in Capitalist Society*. London: Weidenfeld & Nicolson.

Mills, C. W. 1959. *The Sociological Imagination*. Oxford University Press.

Mingers, J. 2002. 'Can social systems be autopoetic? Assessing Luhmann's social theory', *Sociological Review*, vol. 50, no. 2.

Moore, B. 1967. *The Social Origins of Dictatorship and Democracy: Lord and Peasant in the Making of the Modern World*. London: Allen Lane.

Mouzelis, N. 1969. 'Silverman on organizations', *Sociology*, vol. 5, no. 1.

    1971. 'Peasants, modernization and development', *Development and Change*, vol. 4, no. 3.

    1974. 'System and social integration: a reconsideration of a fundamental distinction', *British Journal of Sociology*, vol. 24, no. 4.

    1975. *Organization and Bureaucracy: An Analysis of Modern Theories*. London: Routledge & Kegan Paul.

    1978. *Modern Greece: Facets of Underdevelopment*. London: Macmillan.

    1980. 'Types of reductionism in Marxist theory', *Telos*, no. 45 (Fall).

    1986. *Politics in the Semi-periphery: Early Parliamentarianism and Late Industrialization in the Balkans and Latin America*. London: Macmillan.

    1988a. 'Marxism versus post-Marxism', *New Left Review*, no. 167, Jan.–Feb.

    1988b. 'Marxism and the sociology of development: reflexions on the present crisis', *Sociology*, vol. 22, no. 1.

    1989. 'Restructuring structuration theory', *Sociological Review*, vol. 37.

    1990. *Post-Marxist Alternatives: The Construction of Social Orders*. London: Macmillan.

    1991a. *Back to Sociological Theory: The Construction of Social Orders*. London: Macmillan.

    1991b. 'The interaction order and the micro–macro distinction', *Sociological Theory*, vol. 7.

    1992. 'The future of the LSE: an alternative view', *LSE Economic and Political Sciences Magazine*, Autumn/Winter.

    1993a. 'Evolution and democracy: Talcott Parsons and the collapse of the Eastern European regimes', *Theory, Culture and Society*, vol. 10.

    1993b. 'On figurational sociology', *Theory, Culture and Society*, vol. 10.

    1993c. 'Comparing the Durkheimian and the Marxist traditions', *Sociological Review*, vol. 41, no. 3.

    1994. 'The state in late development: comparative and historical perspectives', in D. Booth (ed.), *Rethinking Social Development: Theory, Research and Practice*. London: Longman.

    1995a. 'Rethinking the left: social-democratic tasks and prospects', Working Paper, Dept. of Sociology, London School of Economics.

    1995b. *Sociological Theory: What Went Wrong? Diagnoses and Remedies*. London: Routledge.

1995c. 'Greece in the 21st century: institutions and political culture', in D. Constas and T. G. Stavrou (eds.), *Greece Prepares for the 21st Century*. Baltimore: Johns Hopkins University Press.

1996. 'After postmodernism: a reply to Gregor McLennan', *Sociology*, vol. 30, no. 1.

1998. 'Multi-cultural Europe: conceptualizing complexity on the socio-cultural and educational levels', in M. Pereyra and A. Kazamias (eds.), *Education and the Structuring of European Space*. Athens: Seirios.

1999a. 'Exploring post-traditional orders: individual reflexivity, pure relations and duality of structure', in O'Brien, Penna and Hay (eds.).

1999b. 'Post-Parsonian theory', *Sociological Forum*, vol. 14, no. 4.

1999c. 'Differentiation and marginalization in late modernity', in I. Gough and G. Olofson (eds.), *Essays on Exclusion and Integration*. London: Macmillan.

Nadel, S. F. 1962. *The Theory of Social Structure*. London: Routledge.

Nash, R. 2003. 'Social explanation and socialization: on Bourdieu and the structure, disposition, practice scheme', *Sociological Review*, vol. 51, no. 1.

Nettl, P. 1967. *Political Mobilisation*. London: Faber.

Norris, C. 1993. *The Truth about Postmodernism*. Oxford: Blackwell.

O'Brien, M., S. Penna and C. Hay (eds.) 1999. *Theorising Modernity: Reflexivity, Environment and Identity in Giddens' Social Theory*. London: Longman.

Olson, M. 1965. *The Logic of Collective Action*. Cambridge, MA: Harvard University Press.

Ostrow, J. 2000. 'Culture as a fundamental dimension of experience: a discussion of Pierre Bourdieu's theory of human habitus', in D. Robbins (ed.), *Pierre Bourdieu*, vol. I. London: Sage.

Parker, J. 2000. *Structuration*. Buckingham: Open University Press.

Parsons, T. 1937. *The Structure of Social Action*. New York: Free Press.

1951. *The Social System*. London: Routledge.

1964a. 'Evolutionary universals in society', *American Sociological Review*, vol. 29, June.

1964b. 'Communism and the West: the sociology of conflict', in A. Etzioni and E. Etzioni (eds.), *Social Change: Sources, Patterns and Consequences*. New York: Basic Books.

1966. *Societies: Evolutionary and Comparative Perspectives*. Englewood Cliffs, NJ: Prentice Hall.

1971. *The System of Modern Societies*. Englewood Cliffs, NJ: Prentice Hall.

1977. *The Evolution of Societies*. Englewood Cliffs, NJ: Prentice Hall.

Parsons, T. and G. Platt 1973. *The American University*. Cambridge, MA: Harvard University Press.

Parsons, T. and N. J. Smelser. 1956. *Economy and Society*. London: Routledge & Kegan Paul.

Piaget, J. 1950. *Introduction à l'épistémologie génétique*, vol. III. Paris: Presses Universitaires de France.

Popkin, S. L. 1979. *The Rational Peasant: The Political Economy of Rural Society in Vietnam*. Berkeley: University of California Press.

Poulantzas, N. 1968. *Pouvoir politique et classes sociales*. Paris: Maspero.
   1978. *L'état, le pouvoir, le socialisme*. Paris: Presses Universitaires de France.

Przeworski, A. 1986. *Capitalism and Social Democracy*. Cambridge University Press.

Radcliffe-Brown, A. R. 1940. 'On social structure', *Journal of the Royal Anthropological Institute*, vol. 70.

Rappert, B. 2003. 'Technologies, texts and possibilities', *Sociology*, vol. 37, no. 3.

Rawls, J. 1987. 'The idea of an overlapping consensus', *Oxford Journal for Legal Studies*, vol. 7.
   1988. 'The priority of right and ideas of the good', *Philosophy and Public Affairs*, vol. 17, no. 4.

Reckwitz, A. 2002. 'Toward a theory of social practices: a development in culturalist theorizing', *European Journal of Social Theory*, vol. 5, no. 2.

Riggs, F. W. 1964. *Administration in Developing Countries: The Theory of Prismatic Society*. Boston: Houghton Mifflin.

Rigney, D. 2001. *The Metaphorical Society: An Invitation to Social Theory*. Lanham, MD: Rowman & Littlefield.

Robertson, R. 1992. *Globalization: Social Theory and Global Culture*. London: Sage.

Rocher, G. 1974. *Talcott Parsons and American Sociology*. London: Nelson.

Rock, P. and M. McIntosh (eds.) 1974. *Deviance and Social Control*. London: Tavistock.

Roemer, J. 1986. *Analytical Marxism*. Cambridge University Press.
   1988. *Free to Lose: An Introduction to Marxist Economic Philosophy*. Cambridge, MA: Harvard University Press.

Roethlisberger, F. T. and W. J. Dickson 1939. *Management and the Worker*. Cambridge, MA: Harvard University Press.

Rogers, E. M. 1969. *Modernization Among Peasants: The Impact of Communication*. New York: Holt, Rinehart and Winston.

Rostow, W. W. 1961. *The Stages of Economic Growth*. Cambridge University Press.
   1962. *The Process of Economic Growth*. New York: Norton.

Sahlins, M. D. and E. R. Service (eds.) 1960. *Evolution and Culture*. Ann Arbor: University of Michigan Press.

Said, E. 1978. 'The problem of textuality: two exemplary critiques', *Critical Inquiry*, vol. 4, no. 4.

Sapir, A. 2004. *An Agenda for a Growing Europe*. Oxford University Press.

2005. 'Globalizing and the reform of European social models', presented to an ECOFIN informal meeting, Manchester, 9 September.

Saussure, F. 1915. *Cours de linguistique générale*. Paris: Payot.

Savage, M., A. Warde and F. Devine 2005. 'Capital, assets and resources: some critical issues', *British Journal of Sociology*, vol. 56, no. 1.

Sayer, A. 1997. 'Essentialism, social constructionism and beyond', *Sociological Review*, vol. 45, no. 3.

Shils, E. 1997. *The Virtue of Civility: Selected Essays on Liberalism, Tradition and Civil Society*. Indianapolis, IN: Liberty Fund.

Sibeon, R. 2004. *Rethinking Social Theory*. London: Sage.

Simon, H. 1961. *Administrative Behavior*. New York: Macmillan.

Skocpol, T. (ed.) 1984. *Vision and Method in Historical Sociology*. Cambridge University Press.

Smelser, N. 1962. *Social Change in the Industrial Revolution: An Application of Theory to the Lancashire Cotton Industry 1770–1840*. London: Routledge & Kegan Paul.

1985. 'Evaluating the model of structural differentiation in relation to educational change in the nineteenth century', in Alexander (ed.).

1990. 'Can individualism yield a sociology?', *Contemporary Sociology*, vol. 19, no. 6.

Smith, D. 1983. *Barrington Moore Jr: A Critical Appraisal*. Armouk, NY: Sharpe.

Spencer, H. 1972. *On Social Evolution: Selected Writings*, ed. J. D. Y. Peel. University of Chicago Press.

Spohn, W. 2001. 'Eisenstadt on civilizations and multiple modernity', *European Journal of Social Theory*, vol. 4, no. 4.

Stouffer, S. A. 1962. 'An empirical study of technical problems in the analysis of role obligation', in T. Parsons and E. A. Shils (eds.), *Toward a General Theory of Action*. New York: Harper & Row.

Strydom, P. 2002. 'Is the social scientific concept of structure a myth? A critical response to Harré', *European Journal of Social Theory*, vol. 5, no. 1.

Swedberg, R. 2003. *Principles of Economic Sociology*. Princeton University Press.

Sweetman, P. 2003. 'Twenty-first century dis-ease? Habitual reflexivity or the reflexive habitus?', *Sociological Review*, vol. 51, no. 4.

Taylor, F. 1945. *The Principles of Scientific Management*. New York: Harper.

Thelen, K. and S. Steinmo (eds.) 1992. *Structuring Politics: Historical Institutionalism in Comparative Perspective*. Cambridge University Press.

Theotokas, N. 2002. 'Postmodernism and history' (in Greek), *Politis*, no. 106.

Thompson, E. 1963. *The Making of the English Working Class*. London: Allen Lane.

Tilly, C. 1978. *From Mobilisation to Revolution*. Reading, MA: Addison-Wesley.

   1984. *Big Structures, Large Processes, Huge Comparisons*. New York: Russell Sage.

   1990. *Coercion, Capital and European States*. Oxford: Blackwell.

Turner, J. H. 1990. *A Theory of Social Interaction*. Cambridge: Polity.

Urry, J. 2000a. 'Mobile sociology', *British Journal of Sociology*, vol. 51, no. 1.

   2000b. *Beyond Societies: Mobilities for the Twenty-first Century*. London: Routledge.

Wade, R. 1990. *Governing the Market*. Ithaca: Cornell University Press.

Wade, R. and F. Veneroso. 1998. 'The Asian crisis: the high debt mode versus the Wall Street Treasury–IMF complex', *New Left Review*, no. 228.

Wallerstein, I. 1974. *The Modern World System*, vol. I. New York: Academic Press.

Weber, M. 1925/1978. *Economy and Society*, ed. G. Roth and G. Witich. Berkeley: University of California Press.

Wendt, A. 1999. *Social Theory and International Relations*. Cambridge University Press.

White, G. and R. Wade (eds.) 1985. *Developmental States in East Asia*. Brighton: Institute of Development Studies.

Wight, C. 2006. *Agents, Structures and International Relations: Politics as Ontology*. Cambridge University Press.

Williams, P. and I. Chrisman (eds.) 1993. *Colonial Discourse and Post-Colonial Theory*. New York: Harvester.

Wolf, E. C. 1971. *Peasant Wars of the Twentieth Century*. London: Faber.

Woodiwiss, A. 1992. *Law, Labour and Society in Japan: From Repression to Reluctant Recognition*. New York: Routledge.

   1998. *Globalisation, Human Rights and Labour Law in Pacific Asia*. Cambridge University Press.

Zollschan, G. K. and W. Hirsch (eds.) 1964. *Explorations in Social Change*. London: Routledge.

Index

Abrams, P. 279
accounting, reflexive 134–5, 141
The Achieving Society (McLeland) 281
action
  and agency 70
  co-ordinating mechanisms 101
  collective, theories of 89–90
  and culture 72
  environments of 235
  theories of: Alexander 67–8, 71,
    77–8, 81–2, 128–9, 208, 226, 232;
    criticized by Joas 87–9; Habermas
    267–8, 269–70, 277; Joas 86–7,
    89–90, 90–1, 92, 94, 208–9;
    Parsons 86, 91–2
action–structure divide in social sciences
  3–4, 274–5
  overcoming of 90, 92–3
actor essentialism 242, 275
  ascription of characteristics to groups
    245–9
  transformation of quasi-groups into
    groups 242–5
actors
  analysis of, and institutional
    analysis 262
  autonomy of 249, 252; and moral
    order 164–7, 168
  Bourdieu on 136–7
  causality of 192, 274
  collective 13, 77, 269–70
  instrumental control of bodies of 88
  internal and external constraints and
    enablements of 208
  passiveness of: in Althusser's theories
    265; in Parsonian functionalism
    13–14, 39, 50, 70–1, 267
  and social structures 35, 232–6
  strategies of 36–7

and time and space dimension 227–8
adaptive upgrading
  and modernity 152–4
  Parsons on 50–1
  in Western societies 53
agency 3, 232
  Alexander on 68, 70, 226
  Archer on 226, 232
  and development of rights 44–5
  and institutional structure, rejection
    of 246
  and structure 205, 209–10, 211,
    212–13, 226–7
  in textualism 28
Alexander, Jeffrey 32–3, 65
  on civil society 73–7, 78
  on culture 68–9, 72, 78, 81, 82, 85
  on the Holocaust 80–1, 84–5
  on sociology of culture 78–9
  structural hermeneutics of 79
  theories of: action 67–8, 71, 77–8,
    81–2, 128–9, 208, 226, 232; post-
    Parsonian 66–7, 70, 77
Althusser, Louis 10, 22, 139
  anti-economistic strategies of 264–5
Anderson, Benedict 9
anthropological structuralism 22
  hidden codes in 22–3
anti-developmental states 64
anti-essentialist orientations
  discourse analysis 247–9
  and holistic conceptual frameworks
    4, 5, 223–4, 275–6
  of micro-sociology 249–50, 252
anti-representation thesis
  (postmodernism) 178–9, 180
  and Greek historiography debate
    180–1
apophatic reflexivity 135–6

Arato, A. 73
Archaeology of Knowledge (Foucault)
    185–6
Archer, Margaret 118
    on agency 226, 232
    critical realism of 192
    criticism of Giddens 199
    on reflexivity 206–7
    on social causation 206, 211–12;
        criticism of 210–11, 212
    on social structures 199–201;
        criticism of 201–3, 210
articulatory practices 31
Asia, modernization in 53, 62–4,
    152, 153
Athens, battle of (1944) 180–1, 184–5
attitudes, Habermas on 116
autonomy
    of actors 249, 252; and moral order
        164–7, 168
    relative, thesis of 264
    of social structures 227–8
    of symbolic structures 229

balance of power, between labour and
    capital 254–5
balanced inclusion, in modern societies
    151–2
Barthes, R. 23
Baudrillard, J. 38
Beck, Ulrich 135, 166
Being Human (Archer) 206
Bhaskar, Roy 21, 226
Blau, Peter 251
bodies, instrumental control of 88
bodily movements, and habitus
    concept 230
boundaries between disciplines
    Marxism advocating abolition of 38–9
    postmodernists advocating abolition
        of 38–9
    sociology and history 279–80
Bourdieu, Pierre 37, 3, 4, 36–8
    attempts to overcome economism 265
    on classes 139
    conception of subjects of 136–7
    on habitus concept 119–21, 123–4,
        131–2, 139, 231; and reflexivity
        132, 133–6, 138; as set of
        dispositions 193, 194–5, 208, 230

on strategies 137–8
on subjectivism and objectivism 108
theory-of-practice scheme of 131,
    140–1
transcendence strategy of overcoming
    subjectivist–objectivist divide
    107–8, 138
bourgeois revolutions 243
bourgeoisie, role in French Revolution
    243–4
bridges
    between micro- and macro-
        sociologies *see* micro–macro bridges
    between structuralism and structural
        sociology 23–4
    between theoretical paradigms in
        social sciences 40, 33–4, 108,
        127–30, 224
Butt, Trevor 134

capital
    balance with labour in Western
        Europe 254–5
    states preventing reproduction of 264
capitalism
    Asian 53, 62–4, 152, 153
    development of 170
    social-democratic 152
capitalist societies, convergence with
    socialist societies 59, 60–1
Carter, Bob 191
change
    evolutionary, Parsons' scheme of
        49–51
    intra-societal mechanisms of 93
    social 99
China, modernity in 159
citizenship
    Marshall's analysis of 43–5
    Parsons on development of 46
civil rights, development of 51
civil society
    Alexander on 73–7, 78
    Parsons on 73
    and solidarity 74–5, 76
classes 244
    Bourdieu on 139
    Giddens on 263
    inequalities between, and citizenship
        rights 44

struggles between 139
classical sociology 9–10
closure in holistic conceptual
 frameworks
 Marxism 222
 Parsonian functionalism 222–3
cognitive relativism 4, 146
 avoidance of 181–2, 183, 188,
 189–90
 of postmodernism 176, 180, 184
Cohen, J. L. 73
collective action theories 89–90
collective actors 13, 77, 269–70; *see also*
 groups
Collins, R. 258–9
communicative theory of action
 (Habermas) 267–8, 277
 criticism of 269–70
communism
 collapse of 55
 Parsons on 55, 59–60, 61
communitarian theories, criticism
 of 164
comparative sociology 112
Comte, Auguste 169–70
conceptual frameworks 217, 221; *see
 also* holistic conceptual
 frameworks; theoretical
 paradigms
conceptual tools, of sociology 5
configurational wholes 275–6
constitution theories 90
 and Parsonian functionalism 93
constructionism *see* social
 constructionism
context-sensitive theories 219–21
contextless theories 217–19
convergence thesis 59, 60–1
core values 13, 238–9
 of late modernity 171, 172–4
creativity
 emphasized by postmodernism 89
 Joas on 94
The Creativity of Action (Joas) 86, 89,
 90–1, 94, 208–9
criminology 184, 187–8
critical realism
 debate with social constructionism 4,
 191, 213
 on social causation 192

Crozier, M. 133–4
cultural modernity 155
cultural narratives 84–5
cultural relativism 146–7
 attempts to overcome 166, 167
 postmodern 167
cultural sociology 32–4, 85
 and sociology of culture 78–9
cultural structures *see* symbolic structures
culturalism
 attempts to overcome 267–8, 269–70,
 272, 277–8
 of Parsons 266–7, 277
culture
 Alexander on 68–9, 72, 78, 81,
 82, 85
 Geertz on 69–70
 interpenetration of 169–71
 Marxism on 69
 of organizations 83–4
 Parsons on 68–9, 79–80,
 229, 266–7
 and social structures 81–2
 sociology of, and cultural sociology
 78–9

Dahrendorf, R. 64
decentring of subjects 24–5, 27, 33, 39
 and recentring 23–4, 33
dedifferentiation 150
deep structures *see* hidden codes
democracy
 and modernization 57, 62–3, 152–3
 Parsons on 55, 58–9, 62
 transition to, in Eastern Europe 57
democratization 170
 Joas on 90
Derrida, Jacques 29
developing countries 264
 'late-late' 157, 172
development, sociology of 114–15
differentiation
 and adaptive upgrading 153
 and democracy 57
 formal and substantive 150–1
 institutional 148–50
 and modernity 148–9
 Parsons on 45, 49–50, 56
discourse analysis 31
 anti-essentialism of 247–9

discourses
  conceptualization of 28
  first- and second-order 101
  subjectless 24–7
discursive and non-discursive practices
  conflated in textualism 28–32
  Foucault on 185–7
dispositional structures 230–2
dispositions
  habitus concept as set of 193, 194–5,
    208, 230
  reflexive 135
  in social games 193–5, 212
distributional structures 113
  and social-relational structures 115
  virtual and actual 229
dualism
  methodological 226–7, 261–2
  ontological 205, 226–7
  perspectival 203–5, 212
duality 116–17
  and dualism 35–6, 118, 182
duality-of-structure scheme (Giddens)
  35–6, 38, 107, 115–19, 182,
    197–8
  and micro–macro linkages 260
  and reproduction 122–3
Durkheim, E. 9–10
  on social structures 228

Eastern Europe
  collapse of communism in 61–2
  transition to democracy in 57
economic interests 30–1
economic modernity 155
economic subsystem, development
  of 45–6
economism
  of Marxism 10, 263–4, 270–1, 276;
    attempts to overcome 264–5, 271–2
  Parsons' rejection of 14
economy, and political sphere 264–5
education, development of social right
  to 46–9
Elias, Norbert 112
Eliou, P. 181
emotions, and habitus concept 230
empiricism, postmodern rejection of 176
England, industrial revolution in 45–6,
  51, 281

environments of action, internal and
  external 235
equivalent narratives 176
essentialism 237–8
  actor 242, 275; ascription of
    characteristics to groups 245–9;
    transformation of quasi-groups
    into groups 242–5
  and holistic conceptual frameworks 90
  of Marxism 11, 245–6
  and organizational goals 249
  of Parsons 238
  rejection of: by discourse analysis
    247–9; by micro-sociologists
    249–50, 252
  system 242, 275; of Parsonian
    functionalism 238–40; of
    teleological functionalism 240–1
ethical relativism 4, 146
ethnomethodology 15, 231
Etzioni, Amitai
  attempts to overcome relativism 166
  'golden rule' concept of 164–6, 167,
    168, 173
  on values of moral order 165
Eurocentrism, and modernity 145–7,
  161, 171
evolutionary change scheme,
  of Parsons 49–51
evolutionary perspectives 64
  of Habermas 102
  of Parsons 3, 57–8, 149
evolutionary universals 146, 156
  values as 172, 173–4
Exertzoglou, H. 180
external constraints and enablements,
  of actors 208
externality, of social structures 203–5,
  211, 212

face-to-face interactions, micro-
  sociology on 104
figurational structures 83, 111–13, 132–3
  and institutional structures 114–15,
    133–4, 138, 228
  see also relational structures
first-order discourses 101
first-order symbolic constructs (I-sc) 182
  distinct from second-order symbolic
    constructs (II-sc) 187, 189

formal differentiation 150–1
Foucault, Michel 24–7, 28
  on construction of subject matter
    184, 185
  on discursive and non-discursive level
    185–7
  functionalism of 26, 240–1
  ideology rejected by 177
  power/knowledge notion of 186–7
French Revolution
  Parsons on 46, 51
  role of bourgeoisie in 243–4
functionalism
  of Bourdieu 139
  criticism of 89–90
  essentialism of 240–1
  of Foucault 26, 240–1
  neo- 65–7
  normative 89, 111
  Parsonian 2, 3, 12–15, 39, 56;
    attempts to overcome culturalism
    267–8, 269–70; closure in 222–3;
    and constitution theories 93;
    essentialism of 238–40; Lockwood
    on 98; social structure in 111, 129
  teleological explanations in 240–1

games *see* social games
Geertz, Clifford 69–70
Gellner, Ernest 154, 168
Gerschenkron, A. 62
Giddens, Anthony 3, 94
  criticism of 199
  duality-of-structure scheme of 35–6,
    38, 107, 115–19, 182, 197–8; and
    micro–macro linkages 260; and
    reproduction 122–3
  on modernity 145
  on reflexive modernization 135
  on social causation 192, 197, 198–9
  on social classes 263
  on social-/system-integration
    distinction 104–6
globalization 170
  and modernity 159–61
  and nation-states 11–12, 64, 159–60
  neoliberal 1, 55
Goffman, E. 250
'golden-rule' concept (Etzioni) 164–6, 168
  criticism of 167, 173

Goldthorpe, J. 279
  criticism of 'grand' historical
    sociology 281–4
  on sociology and history 279–80
Gordon, C. 240
Gramsci, A. 69
grand narratives *see* holistic conceptual
    frameworks
Greek historiography, modern–
    postmodern debate in 180–1
groups 244
  ascription of characteristics to 245–9
  quasi- 242, 244; transformation into
    groups 242–5
  see also collective actors

Habermas, J. 94
  on attitudes 116
  communicative theory of action of
    267–8, 277; criticism of 269–70
  criticism of Parsons 267, 268–9
  on late capitalism 152
  perspectivism of 103
  on social-/system-integration
    distinction 101–3, 105
habitus concept 4, 36–8
  Bourdieu on 119–21, 123–4, 131–2,
    139, 231
  and emotions and bodily
    movements 230
  and reflexivity 132, 133–6, 138
  and reproduction 123–4, 139
  as set of dispositions 193, 194–5,
    208, 230
  and social structures 231–2
  and strategic interaction 132
  and structuralism 230–1
Hall, Stewart 19–20, 145–6
Harré, Rom 191–2
  on social causation 192, 197, 212
  on social structures 193
hermeneutics, combined with
    structuralist analysis 79
hidden codes 113–14, 120, 136
  in anthropological structuralism
    22–3
  and habitus concept 230–1
hierarchies
  social 29; and micro–macro linkages
    259–60, 276

hierarchized space dimension, 204–5, 212
historical disciplines, construction of subject matter in 184–5
historical institutionalism 20
historical materialism 263
  criticism of 219, 262–3
historical sociology 4
  'grand' 279; criticism of 281–4
historical time, externality of social structures in terms of 204
historiography, Greek, modern–postmodern debate in 180–1
history
  and sociology 279–80
  use of: by modernization theorists 280–1; by Moore 280
History of Sexuality (Foucault) 27
holistic conceptual frameworks 217, 225
  anti-conflationist 226, 274–5
  anti-economistic 276–8
  anti-essentialist 4, 5, 223–4, 275–6
  closure in: Marxism 222; Parsonian functionalism 222–3
  context-sensitive theories 219–21
  contextless theories 217–19
  and essentialism 90
  Marxism 10–11, 261–2, 276
  methodological dualism in 226–7
  and micro–macro bridges 237, 275–6
  open 225–6
  postmodern criticism of 217, 221, 223
Holocaust, Alexander on the 80–1, 84–5
Howarth, D. 31, 248

ideal types, in rational-choice theory 17–19
identities
  formation of, postmodernism on 33
  social 30–1
ideology, postmodernist rejection of 177
inclusion, balanced and unbalanced 149–50, 151–2
individual autonomy *see* actors, autonomy of
individual rights, in Western societies 3
individualization 166
Industrial Revolution (England)
  Parsons on 45–6, 51
  Smelser on 281

industrial sociology 177–8
inequalities
  Parsons on 48–9
  in United States 48
institutional analysis, and actor analysis 262
institutional complexes, and system integration 100
institutional differentiation 148–50
institutional structures 83, 111
  and agency, rejection of 246
  and essentialism 247–9
  and figurational structures 114–15, 133–4, 138, 228
  micro- and macro-levels of 251–2
  in social games 203
institutionalism
  historical 20
  in rational-choice theory 19–21
institutions
  incompatibilities between 99
  malleability of 99–100
integration
  Parsons on 50, 51–4, 149
  social 97, 100, 101, 104
  system 97, 100, 101, 104
  system of nation-states 63–4, 170
  see also social-/system-integration distinction
interaction
  face-to-face 104
  mediating mechanism between agency and structure 208–9
  micro- and macro-levels of 250–3
  in Parsonian theories 87–8
  strategic 19–20; and habitus concept 132
interactive dimension
  of social games 195–6
  and social structures 232–4
interactive structures *see* figurational structures
internal constraints and enablements, of actors 208
internal conversation, reflexivity of 206–7, 212
internalization of objective structures 231

interpretative micro-sociology *see*
micro-sociology
intra-active dimension, and social
structures 232–4
intra-habitus contradictions 134
intra-societal mechanisms, of change 93
Iran 157

Jacobs, Ronald 75
Japan, modernity in 158–9
Joas, Hans
attempts to overcome action–structure
divide in social sciences 92–3
on creativity 94
criticism of conventional action
theory 87–9
on democratization 90
on holistic theories and
essentialism 90
theory of action of 86–7, 89–90,
90–1, 92, 94, 208–9

King, Anthony 205
knowledge, and power 186–7, 188,
189–90

Laclau, E. 28, 30–2, 246, 247–9
Langdridge, Darren 134
'late-late' developing countries 157
modernity in 157, 172
late modernity 1–2, 161
core values of 171, 172–4
and reflexivity 135–6
see also postmodernism
latency sub-system 47
legal equality 43
Lévi-Strauss, C. 22, 23, 120, 136–7
on social structures 113–14
linguistic reductionism 29
localism, resurgence of 160–1
Lockwood, David 3–4, 10
on Marxism 256
on Parsonian functionalism 98
perspectivism of 103
on social change 99
on social structures 228
on social-/system-integration
distinction 97–100, 105, 254–5
London School of Economics (LSE), as a
social system 121–7

Luhmann, N. 27
Lyotard, J. F. 38

macro-concepts, rejected by micro-
sociologists 252
macro-levels of interaction 250–1, 252–3
macro-phenomena
analysis of 259; by micro-sociologists
258–9
macro-sociology
bridges with micro-sociology *see*
micro–macro bridges
essentialism in 275
metaphors used in 244–5
micro-sociologists' criticism of 16
Mann, M. 153
marriage rules, reproduction of 35–6
Marshall, T. H. 43–5, 54, 55–6
Marx, Karl 10
on social structures 228
on technology 262
Marxism
and articulation of social- and system-
integration approaches 256–7
on boundaries between disciplines
38–9
on culture 69
economism of 10, 263–4, 270–1, 276;
attempts to overcome 264–5, 271–2
essentialism of 11, 245–6
historical materialism 219, 262–3
holistic framework of 10–11, 222,
261–2, 276
on social structure 129–30
structuralist 22
Weber on 263
material/ideal distinction 100–1
Maza, Sarah 244
McLeland, D. T. 281
McNeil, William 172
The Meanings of Social Life (Alexander)
78–9, 81
means–end schema, of Parsons 203
Merton, R. K. 241
metaphors, use of 244–5
methodological dualism 226–7, 261–2
methodological situationalism 258–9
micro-level
of institutional structures 251–2
of interaction 250–1

micro–macro bridges
  avoidance of reductionism 259–60,
    275–6
  balanced social- and system-
    integration analysis 253–4
  effective articulation of social- and
    system-integration perspectives
    255–7
  and holistic conceptual frameworks
    237, 275–6
  of Parsonian functionalism 14–15
micro-sociology 15–17, 39, 111–12, 129
  analysis of macro-phenomena
    258–9
  anti-essentialism of 249–50, 252
  on autonomy of actors 249, 252
  bridges with macro-sociology *see*
    micro–macro bridges
  criticism of macro-sociology 16
  on face-to-face interactions 104
  macro-concepts rejected by 252
  reductionism in 275–6
Mills, C. W. 64
modernity 4, 154
  and adaptive upgrading 152–4
  balanced inclusion in 151–2
  cultural 155
  economic 155
  and Eurocentrism 145–7, 161, 171
  Giddens on 145
  and globalization 159–61
  Habermas on 102
  and institutional differentiation
    148–9
  late 1–2, 161; core values of 171,
    172–4; and reflexivity 135–6
  peasantry's role in shaping of 201–2
  political 154–5, 219
  postmodernism on 146–7
  social 155
  social-structural approaches
    to 147–8, 161–2
  and solidarity 76
  in United States 48
  and value generalization 151–2
  variants of 156–9, 162
  Western 156, 157, 162–3, 171–2
modernization
  from above 61–2
  in Asia 53, 62–4, 152, 153

  and democracy 57, 62–3, 152–3
  non-Western 172
  reflexive 135
  theorists, ahistorical approaches
    of 280–1
Moore, Barrington 201–2, 219
  criticism of 282–3
  historical sociology of 280
moral order
  and autonomy of actors 164–7, 168
  values of 165
morphogenesis (Archer) 199–200,
    211–12
  criticism of 201–3
Mouffe, C. 28, 30, 246, 247–9

Nadel, S. F. 114
narratives
  cultural 84–5
  equivalent 176
  grand *see* holistic conceptual
    frameworks
nation-states
  emergence of 9
  and globalization 11–12, 64, 159–60
  resource-mobilization capacity of 148
national community 46, 155
natural performative attitudes 116
neo-evolutionary perspectives,
    of Parsons 57–8
neo-functionalism 65–7
  and articulation of social- and system-
    integration approaches 256
Neo-Functionalism and After
    (Alexander) 66–7
neoliberal globalization 1, 55
  and nation-state system 64
network-analysis research 112
networks, of social relations 110
The New Golden Rule (Etzioni) 164,
    166–7
non-essentialist holistic conceptual
    frameworks 223–4
non-Eurocentric approaches, to
    modernity 147, 161
non-Western modernization 172
normative functionalism 89, 111
normative/non-normative distinction
    98–9
Norval, A. J. 31

objectivism 108
objectivist–subjectivist divide in social sciences *see* subjectivist–objectivist divide in social sciences
objectivity
  alternative definitions of 176–8, 189
  rejected by postmodernism 175–6, 188–9
oligarchic parliamentarianism 114–15
ontological dualism 205, 226–7
organizations
  culture of 83–4
  goals of, and essentialism 249

paradigmatic levels, of relationships 109–10, 205, 228
paradigmatic strategying 117, 122, 124–5, 128
paradigms *see* conceptual frameworks; theoretical paradigms
parliamentarianism, oligarchic 114–15
Parsonian functionalism 2, 3, 12–15, 39, 56
  attempts to overcome culturalism 267–8, 269–70
  closure in 222–3
  and constitution theories 93
  essentialism of 238–40
  Lockwood on 98
  social structure in 111, 129
Parsons, Talcott 2, 12
  on civil society 73
  on communist societies 55, 59–60, 61
  criticism of 64, 70–1, 79–80, 93, 268–9
  culturalism of 266–7, 277
  on culture 68–9, 79–80, 229, 266–7
  on democracy 55, 58–9, 62; in United States 58–9
  means–end schema of 203
  on social differentiation 45, 56; development of citizenship rights 46; development of economic subsystem 45–6; development of social right to education 46–9; integration processes 51–4, 149; scheme of evolutionary change 49–51
  successors of 65–7

theories of 3, 13–14, 32, 54; action 86, 91–2; essentialism in 238; evolutionary perspectives 3, 57–8, 149
particularistic solidarity, and modernity 76
peasantry 201–2
perspectival dualism 203–5, 212
perspectivism
  of Habermas 103
  of Lockwood 103
Piaget, J. 259
political modernity 154–5, 219
political rights
  development of 44, 51
  as evolutionary universals 172
political sphere, and economy 264–5
post-colonial studies 147
postmodern societies 1
postmodernism 1
  boundaries between disciplines rejected by 38–9
  cognitive relativism of 176, 180, 184
  creativity emphasized by 89
  and cultural relativism 167
  empiricism rejected by 176
  holistic conceptual frameworks criticized by 217, 221, 223
  on identity formation 33
  ideology rejected by 177
  on internality of subject matter 183–4
  on modernity 146–7
  objectivity idea rejected by 175–6, 188–9
  on social theories as part of social reality 178–9, 189
post-structuralism 2, 24–7, 39–40, 107
  teleological explanations in 240–1
Poulantzas, N. 139
power
  balance of, between labour and capital 254–5
  Foucauldian concept of 25
  and knowledge 186–7, 188, 189–90
  relations 83
praxiology 21
pre-industrial states 148
production processes, Althusser on 265

proletariat, revolutionary goals of 245–6
psychoanalysis 136

quasi-groups 242, 244
    transformation into groups 242–5

Radcliffe-Brown, A. R. 110
rational-choice theory 89
    ideal-typical nature of 17–19
    institutionalism in 19–21
Real Civil Societies (Alexander) 66–7,
    73, 76
realism
    on agency and structure 205
    critical: debate with social
        constructionism 4, 191, 213; on
        social causation 192
recentring
    and decentring, of subjects 23–4, 33
    of subjects 33
reductionism
    avoidance of 257–8, 275–6
    linguistic 29
reflexive accounting 134–5, 141
reflexive modernization 135
reflexivity 4, 117–18
    Archer on 206–7
    Bourdieu on 132, 133–6, 138
    through internal conversation
        206–7, 212
    in revised theory-of-practice
        scheme 141
relational structures
    and distributional structures 115
    in social games 196
    see also figurational structures
relationships
    interactive 111–13
    networks of 110
    paradigmatic and syntagmatic levels
        of 109–10, 205, 228
relative autonomy thesis 264
relativism
    cognitive 4, 146; avoidance of 181–2,
        183, 188, 189–90; of postmodernism
        180, 184
    cultural 146–7; attempts to overcome
        166, 167; postmodern 167
    ethical 4, 146
religions, world 169–70

religious fundamentalism, and
    modernity 157–8
reproduction
    of capital 264
    in duality-of-structure scheme 122–3
    and habitus concept 123–4, 139
    of marriage rules 35–6
revolutionary goals, of proletariat
    245–6
revolutions
    bourgeois 243
    educational, in United States 46–9
    French: Parsons on 46, 51; role of
        bourgeoisie in 243–4
    industrial, in England 45–6, 51, 281
    scientific (seventeenth century) 154
rights
    development of: Marshall on 43–5,
        54, 55–6; Parsons on 51, 54, 56
    individual 3
    political 44, 51, 172
    social 44
routine reflexivity 134–5
rugby, dispositional dimension of 193–5
rules 194
    of marriage, reproduction of 35–6
    and social structure 110

Saussure, F. 179–80
Savage, Mike 139
Scandinavian countries, and neoliberal
    globalization 55
scientific revolution (seventeenth
    century) 154
second-order discourses 101
    cultural narratives as 84–5
second-order symbolic constructs (II-sc)
    182, 183
    distinct from first-order symbolic
        constructs (I-sc) 187, 189
Shils, E. 76
Sibeon, R. 118
signs, notion of arbitrariness
    of (Saussure) 179–80
Silverman, David 249
situationalism, methodological 258–9
Smelser, N. 281
social causation 192, 195, 205, 213
    Archer on 206, 211–12; criticism of
        210–11, 212

Giddens on 192, 197, 198–9
Harré on 192, 197, 212
social change, Lockwood on 99
*Social Change in the Industrial
    Revolution* (Smelser) 281
social constructionism 273
    debate with critical realism 4,
        191, 213
social differentiation *see* differentiation
social environment 67–8
social games 37, 120–1
    and causal powers of actors and
        structures 234–6
    dimensions of 133, 196–7, 203–4;
        dispositional 193–5, 212;
        interactive 195–6
    relational structures in 196
    and strategies 138
social hierarchies 29
    and micro–macro linkages
        259–60, 276
social identities, notion of 30–1
social integration 97, 100, 101, 104
    and system-integration perspectives
        253–4, 255–7
    in Western Europe 254–5
    see also social-/system-integration
        distinction
social reality
    and social theory 178–9, 180, 189;
        and Greek historiography debate
        180–1
    virtual and actual distinction 205
social relations, networks of 110
social rights, development of 44
social sciences
    action–structure divide in 3–4, 274–5;
        overcoming of 90, 92–3
    disciplines in 279–80
    subjectivist–objectivist divide in 3–4,
        108; in Marxism 261–2;
        overcoming of 38, 40, 128–9: by
        Bourdieu 107–8, 138, by Giddens
        104–5, 115–19
    theoretical paradigms in: bridges
        between 33–4, 40, 108, 127–30,
        224; proliferation of 34–5, 107,
        224; transcendence strategies
        107–8, 115–19, 128–9,
        138, 224

social sphere 77
social structures
    and actors 35, 232–6
    and agency 205, 209–10, 211,
        212–13, 226–7
    Archer on 199–201; criticism
        of 201–3, 210
    autonomy of 227–8
    causal efficacy of 192
    and culture 81–2
    Durkheim on 228
    externality of 203–5, 211, 212
    and habitus concept 231–2
    Harré on 193
    Lévi-Strauss on 113–14
    Lockwood on 228
    Marx on 228
    in Marxism 129–30
    in micro-sociology 129
    and modernity 147–8, 161–2
    in Parsonian functionalism
        111, 129
    reality of 191–2
    and rules 110
    typology of 108–15, 130
    see also figurational structures;
        institutional structures
social system
    Giddens on 118–19
    London School of Economics (LSE) as
        example 121–7
    Parsons on 238
social theory 1, 66
    and social reality 178–9, 180, 189;
        and Greek historiography debate
        180–1
social-/system-integration distinction
    97, 253–4, 255–7
    Giddens on 104–6
    Habermas on 101–3, 105
    Lockwood on 97–100, 105, 254–5
social-democratic capitalism 152
social-relational structures *see* relational
    structures
socialist societies, convergence with
    capitalist societies 59, 60–1
socialization
    through education 47–8
    reflexive dispositions acquired
        through 135

societies
  adaptive capacities of 57–8
  convergence of capitalist and socialist
    59, 60–1
  developmental stages of 58
  modern, balanced inclusion in
    151–2
  postmodern 1
  Western: adaptive upgrading in 53;
    individual rights in 3; Parsons on
    58–9
  see also states
sociology
  classical 9–10
  comparative 112
  conceptual tools of 5
  cultural 32–4, 85; and sociology
    of culture 78–9
  of development 114–15
  historical 4, 279; criticism of 281–4
  and history 279–80
  industrial 177–8
  see also macro-sociology; micro-
    sociology
solidarity
  and civil society 74–5, 76
  and modernity 76
Soviet Union
  collapse of 64
  modernity in 157
space dimension, actors and social
  structures in 212, 227–8
Spencer, H. 9–10
states
  anti-developmental 64
  pre-industrial 148
  preventing reproduction
    of capital 264
  see also nation-states; societies
statism, decline of 160
statistical linkages 113
Stavrakakis, Y. 31
strategic interaction 19–20
  and habitus concept 132
strategies
  of actors 36–7
  Bourdieu on 121, 137–8
  transcendence, of theoretical
    paradigms 107–8, 115–19, 128–9,
    138, 224

strategying 126
  paradigmatic 117, 122,
    124–5, 128
  syntagmatic 120–1, 124,
    125–6, 128
stratification system in United States 48
strong essentialism
  of Parsonian functionalism 239–40
  of teleological functionalism
    240–1
structuralism 21–2, 39
  anthropological 22–3
  bridges with structural sociology
    23–4
  combined with hermeneutics 79
  and habitus concept 230–1
  Marxist 22
  teleological explanations in 240–1
structuration theory *see* duality-of-
    structure scheme
*Structure, Agency and the Internal
    Conversation* (Archer) 206
The Structure of Social Action
    (Parsons) 86
structure–disposition–practice (SDP)
    scheme *see* theory-of-practice
    scheme (Bourdieu)
structures
  causality of 274
  conceptualization of 3, 35
  see also social structures
subjectivism, Bourdieu on 108
subjectivist–objectivist divide in social
    sciences 3–4, 108
  in Marxism 261–2
  overcoming of 38, 40, 128–9: by
    Bourdieu 107–8, 138; by Giddens
    104–5, 115–19
subjectless discourses 24–7
subjectless meanings 27
subjects
  Bourdieu's conception of 136–7
  decentring of 24–5, 27, 33, 39; and
    recentring 23–4, 33
  recentring of 33
substantive differentiation 150–1
Sweetman, P. 195
symbolic constructs, of first and
    second order (I-sc and II-sc) 182,
    183, 187, 189

symbolic interactionism 175
symbolic structures 27–8, 32, 229–30
  autonomy of 229
syntagmatic levels, of relationships
  109–10, 205, 228
syntagmatic strategying 120–1, 124,
  125–6, 128
system essentialism 242, 275
  of Parsonian functionalism 238–40
  of teleological functionalism 240–1
system integration 97, 100, 101, 104
  and social-integration perspectives
    253–4, 255–7
  in Western Europe 254–5
  see also social-/system-integration
    distinction
systemic concepts, micro-sociologists'
  rejection of 16–17
systemic contradictions 255
systemic incompatibilities 99
systems, conceptualization of 3

Taylor, F. 19–20
technology, Marx on 262
teleological explanations
  of Foucault 26, 240–1
  in functionalism 240–1
  in structuralism and
    post-structuralism 240–1
textualism 27–8, 39–40
  conflation of discursive and
    non-discursive practices 28–32
theoretical paradigms
  bridges between 33–4, 40, 108,
    127–30, 224
  proliferation of 34–5, 107, 224
  transcendence strategies 107–8,
    115–19, 128–9, 138, 224
  see also conceptual frameworks
theory-of-practice scheme (Bourdieu)
  131, 140–1
Theotokas, N. 181
Third World centrism 146–7
time dimension
  actors and social structures
    in 227–8
  of externality of social
    structures 204
total relativism 168–9

transcendence strategies of theoretical
  paradigms 107–8, 128–9, 224
  of Bourdieu 138
  of Giddens 115–19
Turner, J. H. 218–19

unbalanced inclusion 149–50
United States
  democracy in, Parsons on 58–9
  educational revolution in 46–9
  modernity in 48
  and neoliberal globalization 55
universal values 168
universalistic solidarity, and civil
  society 74–5
'The uses of history in sociology'
  (Goldthorpe) 279

value generalization
  and modernity 151–2
  Parsons on 47, 50
value neutrality 175
values
  core 13, 238–9; of late modernity
    171, 172–4
  of moral order 165
  spreading of 168–9
  universal 168
voting rights *see* political rights

Wallerstein, Immanuel 170
weak essentialism, of Parsonian
  functionalism 238–9
Weber, M. 10
  on Marxism 263
  on value neutrality 175
Western Europe, capital–labour
  balance in 254–5
Western modernity 156, 157, 162–3,
  171–2
Western societies
  adaptive upgrading in 53
  individual rights in 3
  Parsons on 58–9
Wight, C. 226–7
Williams, Kenneth 134
Wilson, Eliot 210–11
Wolf, E. C. 30, 31
world religions 169–70